W9-CEJ-070

Spoiled Rotten America

Spoiled Rotten
AMERICA
★ Outrages of Everyday Life ★

LARRY MILLER

REGAN

An Imprint of HarperCollinsPublishers

HarperCollins books may be purchased for educational, business, or sales promotional use. For information please write: Special Markets Department, HarperCollins Publishers Inc., 10 East 53rd Street, New York, NY 10022.

FIRST EDITION

Designed by Kris Tobiassen

Library of Congress Cataloging-in-Publication Data

Miller, Larry, 1953–
   Spoiled rotten America / Larry Miller.—1st ed.
      p.   cm.
ISBN-13: 978-0-06-081908-8
ISBN-10: 0-06-081908-1
   1. United States—Social life and customs—1971—Anecdotes.   2. United States—Social life and customs—1971—Humor.   3. National characteristics, American—Anecdotes. 4. National characteristics, American—Humor.   5. Social values—United States— Anecdotes.   6. Social values—United States—Humor.   7. Interpersonal relations—United States—Anecdotes.   8. Interpersonal relations—United States—Humor.   9. Miller, Larry, 1953—Anecdotes.   Title.

E169.Z83M55   2006
306.0973'09045—dc22   2006042915

06 07 08 09 10 DIX/RRD 10 9 8 7 6 5 4 3 2 1

TO MY WIFE

(That's it, and I had to. Seriously. We were out to dinner a few months ago, and she asked how the book was coming, and I told her it was good, and she asked about the dedication, and I said, Well, the acknowledgments are going to be in the back, at the end. And she said, No, the dedication. You have to have a dedication. And I said, Oh, okay, and she said, It should be to me. I didn't say anything right away, and she said, Really, it should. Well, we don't get out much, and it was a Thursday night, and I was just starting my second drink and thinking about how later on, back home, we might—you know. So I said, Okay. And we did. So I kind of had to. I can't speak for other writers, but that's how you get one from me.)

CONTENTS

INTRODUCTION

I DON'T KNOW ABOUT YOU, BUT I SPEND HALF MY LIFE looking at people through Norman Rockwell lenses: loving them, seeing their decency and generosity, smiling at the foibles of their children, feeling their sweetness and cheerful good manners in every small encounter of the day; watching the gentle rustle of a tree in the low, western sun and knowing, really knowing, the perfect joy of it; and so, so grateful for the mysterious good fortune to be born here, now, together.

The other half of the time, I look around me and think, "How sweet it would be to kill them all."

Do you know that feeling? Do you know what I mean? Of course you do. We all do.

Most people swing back and forth between light and dark like a silver-backed gorilla with nothing but time. Sometimes people act out their good instincts. This is called charity. Sometimes they act out their bad instincts. This is called strangling. And sometimes they shuffle quietly from home to work and back again, simply puzzled by it all. This is called The Rest of Us.

Remember that old game where you pull the petals off a flower while saying, "She loves me . . . She loves me not . . . She loves me . . . She loves me not"? (You know, the one where we seek to confirm our affections by taking the most beautiful thing we can find and then mutilating it?) I'm thinking of patenting an updated version: "She loves me . . . She can't believe we ever went out . . . She loves me . . . She's stunned by how the passage of time doesn't make my stories any funnier . . . She loves me . . . She wants to bludgeon me whenever I'm chewing cereal . . ."

Sunny Jim, that's me. You, too?

I don't know how long ago water glasses were invented, but I'll bet it wasn't long before one of the designer's cavemates held it up and said, "Say, Og, what do you think? Is the glass half empty or half full?" The nearest alpha probably responded with a narrow look and a sudden, two-handed arc from one of those Geogassic bats they all carried. Thus began our obsession with duality.

"Are you an optimist or a pessimist?" we ask each other constantly, which would be the dumbest question in history if it weren't so busy being trite. I reject it, because I'm neither and both. Don't we understand? Macro isn't bigger than micro; macro *is* micro.

After all, what's more noteworthy? A hundred thousand North Koreans turning placards in unison at a stadium, or one bite of a really good hamburger? (I know which one I'd rather have, and I'll bet you a signed glossy of The Dear Leader that the North Koreans would agree.)

That's what this book is about—the hamburger and the stadium, the large and the small, the innocent and the cynical, division and unity. The joyous sylph dancing 'round the glade, while the plump bureaucrat glances up just in time to see Western Civilization spiraling down like a gumball at the Guggenheim.

The American pendulum only swings to extremes. The news is on all day, but we know less and less; there's music in every mall, but we don't hear it; everyone has a phone but nothing to say. The chubbiest of us have the strictest diets, because we can't learn to modulate and moderate. It's all or nothing. One bite of a cookie, and suddenly you're on a plane to Vegas with a hooker. Extremes. Contrasts. Opposites. She loves me, she loves me not.

For centuries, the book world has been divided into fiction and nonfiction. I'd like to propose a third category: *friction*. And, boy, am I the guy for that job.

You see, to the Cranky Nitpickers of America—a club I'd join in a second if I weren't already its president—it's long been understood that the world is going to Hell in a handbasket. Concerning which, there are three things to remember:

First, every generation in history has said the same thing since, oh, forever.

Second . . . What in the world is a "handbasket," anyway? Is it significant that it rhymes with a-tisket, a-tasket? And why is hopping one to Hell any worse than getting there the old-fashioned way? I mean, at that point, I wouldn't think it mattered.

Does anyone arrive in The Infernal Regions and buttonhole Satan on the subject? "Now look, bub, I'm sure this is all going to get pretty unpleasant, and probably stay that way longer than I'd like. I'm also guessing you don't have a very active complaint department down here. Yes, yes, I see that poker you're hiding, and I'll bet I know where it's going, but before we start this wingding there's something I need to get off my chest: That trip over here in the handbasket was no day at the beach, let me tell you. Here, look at that. See those mesh marks? They're probably going to scar. We're like peaches in my family. And while we're on the subject, a Lubriderm concession at the gift shop wouldn't go amiss, either. Anything with aloe. Well, I'm an idea man. Say, isn't that Stalin?"

Third, and most important: Every other generation in history was wrong. Ours really *is* going to Hell, handbasket and all. Luckily, the boatman on that gondola is as feckless as we are, and we're not there yet. Soon, though. Soon enough.

The world is about to see (a) a thousand years of horror, (b) a giant battle of good and evil, or (c) a lot more of the same.

What better time for a collection of seventeen comic essays?

In any event, here they are. That's the goal of this book, and that's what it's about. To be funny. I think it is, and I hope you do, too.

Which, come to think of it, must make me an optimist.

She loves me . . . She loves me not . . .

She loves me.

What other way is there to live?

—*Larry Miller*

ONE

ROYAL FLUSH

MY WIFE JUST GOT A NEW DISHWASHER FOR US. SHE didn't tell me, she just got it. I discovered this the other day when I came home from work and saw it being installed, but it was difficult to learn any more just then, since she was in the living room with her friend Ilana, planning a party at our house that weekend for twenty-seven or so Little League parents. I didn't know about this, either.

"Oh, you'll love it," she said, with a wink and a wave of her hand, and turned back to Ilana, who was animatedly saying something like, "I think the pasta station should go in the playroom."

And I remember thinking, "You know, there may be some things I disagree with about Arab society, but, on the whole, you've got to admire the way they treat their women."

The thing about the new dishwasher was, I'd just gotten used to loading the old one. "It wasn't cleaning well anymore," she said after Ilana left. "Yes, it was," I said. "No, it wasn't," she said.

We could have batted this shuttlecock back and forth for a few more hours, easy, but ultimately it would've led me to turning curt and saying, "How would you know?" (Another night sleeping with one eye open.) Instead, I looked down at the shiny new appliance and muttered, "But I just figured the old one out."

My eagle eye and spaniel nose tell me that the principles of correct dishwasher use are one of those tiny-but-huge subjects debated by all households; and in this case I mean everyone. Man, woman, gay, straight, American, Norwegian—put any two adults together in a house, and they'll very quickly develop different, and fiercely rigid, views of how best to load the dishwasher.

You could pair an English supermodel with a Cambodian rice farmer, or two Sherpas who grew up on the side of Mount Everest and never even heard of electricity, and within four days you'd hear one telling the other, "No, idiot, the salad plates go *behind* the cereal bowls." Sounds like a new reality show, doesn't it? "She only speaks Hungarian, and he's never even seen a rocks glass, but watch the sparks fly when it's time to clear the table!" (That one's probably in development at NBC.)

I consider myself a dishwasher virtuoso even with my one great flaw, to wit: I rinse. I know you don't *need* to rinse before you load, but I do. Even toast crumbs. I just have to.

Still, I think I save more water than any reasonably sane American.

I never leave the faucet running while I'm scrubbing a pan, and only turn it on again when it's time to rinse, and then still only halfway.

I listen like a hawk (or just a maniac) when the kids go to brush their teeth, and run shouting down the hall the second I sense they've got the water on too high or too long, or that they're spraying each other, or—worst of all for a parent—that they're just giggling and enjoying life too much.

When it's time for me to shower, I'm like a marine boot being monitored by Lee Ermey with a stopwatch. Even when I'm a little fuzzy-headed in the morning, I allow myself just a brief cascade down the head and neck . . . unless of course someone's in there with me. (Oh, stop your cackling. This does so happen to me, though not every day, and almost always in a fancy hotel for one of those Mommy and Daddy nights away.)

In fact, I used to shower with the kids, too, when they were little.

At least until my sister told me not to.

This was when they were two and five, and after two and five years (respectively) spent getting an achy back and soaked shoes while leaning in to wash their hair, one evening at bath time the clouds parted, the angels sang, and I climbed in with them.

Well, I thought I had invented the wheel. It was so easy, I was staggered by the brilliance of the thing. Each "shower" at that age only takes fifteen or twenty seconds anyway. I don't know about you, but I just wash their hands and faces, lather up their hair, and let the residual shampoo do the rest on its way toward the drain. So we'd all get in together, and *zing-clop-boom*, we were done. Beautiful. Hell, that's still far more scrubbing than any fifty people north of the Pyrenees get in a year.

I was so thrilled with my brainstorm that one night I was talking to my sister back East and told her about it. And she said, "Are you wearing anything?" And I said, "What kind of a question is that?" And she said, "Not now, idiot, when you're in the shower with them."

And I said, "Do I wear anything in the shower? What are you talking about? It's a shower."

And she said, "Not if you're in there with them. They're naked, right? What about you? I hope you at least have gym shorts on."

And I said, "Gym shorts? Sheryl, it's a shower. Just a few seconds and we're done."

And she said, "Larry, you're in there naked with them?"

And I said, "Well, *technically*, yes. For a few seconds."

"Well, you shouldn't be. Ever."

This was a new one on me. I told my wife about it with a

chuckle when she got home, and she put down the mail and said, "Oooh, I'm so mad at your sister."

"Why?" I asked.

"Because there's nothing wrong with it, but you're so stupid, now you'll probably never do it again." And I said—chuckling again, but still a little annoyed at being called stupid—"Honey, please, I agree. There's nothing wrong with it. It makes the whole bathtime thing easier. I'm glad I came up with it."

But I never did it again.

This is a big part of my relationship with my sister. We love each other, but she's very fact- and survey-based, and most of the time I don't even know what year it is. She must have read somewhere in the latest issue of *American Paranoia* that little kids shouldn't be subjected to the sight of their big, hairy fathers in the shower. After all, she wasn't the one who went with my dad to the public steam baths twice a week, a place filled with naked old men who'd never been told that towels could be used for more than drying. And it never hurt me any, although to this day I can't eat plums.

She had a million of them. "Do you leave your coffeemaker plugged in at night?" she asked me a few months later. "Sure," I said, "but only when I take it in the shower with me." She just kept talking as if I hadn't said anything, which in a sense I hadn't. "Well, I just read where coffeemakers sometimes explode for no reason at all and set the house on fire. You should always unplug it."

Later that night, I passed the coffeemaker as I was turning off lights on my way to bed. I shook my head and moved on. But then, halfway down the hall, I stopped, groaned, winced, sighed, and muttered, "Oh, come on . . ." Finally, resigned and slumped, I turned around and walked back to the kitchen to unplug it.

Naturally, I've unplugged it every night since. Every other appliance in the place—toaster, grinder, phone-charger, lamps, fans, computers, printers, fax, answering machine, everything—all remain pronged to their sockets of death, but that coffeemaker will never bring us down.

If my sister ever calls with news about how whiskey is distilled, I'm going to hang up in her face.

THERE'S ONE WATER-SAVING DEVICE I DON'T UNDER-stand, primarily because I don't think it saves any water.

We replaced our downstairs toilet a year ago. It came with the house, which is forty years old, and seemed to me to work just fine. But when it came time to retile the bathroom anyway (another decision I wasn't in on, but I'll bet Ilana was), The Divine Mrs. M. said, "It's good we're doing this, because I ordered a water-saving toilet." I had no idea what she was talking about—so unusual in a marriage—and closed my Elmore Leonard collection to ask why.

"I would've thought you'd know," she said triumphantly. "The old toilet is a six-gallon flush. That wastes water. The new one is a three-point-five-gallon flush. That's a big difference." True, as far as it goes, but there was an even bigger difference, one we were both about to learn: What they don't tell you in the brochure (and can you blame them?) is that sometimes a three-point-five-gallon flush doesn't quite, ahem, flush. That is to say, fully flush. That is to say, fully flush what's in there.

Look, I don't mean to be indelicate, but there are two reasons I know of to flush a toilet. The first is, so to speak, not necessarily imperative. But I believe all of you will agree in classifying the second reason as very important-to-vital, unless you're the mayor of Calcutta and love giving walking tours. Some things that come out of us, like ideas and inventions, should be kept around for a while. Others should not.

I'm not talking about *my* others, by the way. I keep my cranky journals of opinion in a half-bath on the other side of the laundry room, if you take my meaning (and I think you do), and am as shy as a cat about using any other place my wife might walk into at the wrong time. (I took a less secretive and more exuberant tack one night earlier in our tenure, a few months after we'd started dating, and it is not a moment I care to repeat.) The children and I, though, have constant and colorful chats about this final step of nourishment, as kids and fathers will, and it is they around whom the new convenience was soon to pose a sticky, if not thorny, situation.

You see, we have boys, and much as I try to discourage it, they have friends. They all play downstairs, and in case you didn't know it, an eight-year-old boy's body can percolate some astonishing evacuations.

The point is, while I'm certain a brand-new, water-saving, three-point-five-gallon flush can easily handle anything produced by a tiara-topped, pink-slippered, wand-wielding, carrot stick–eating, eight-year-old princess, I am here to tell you it simply does not for a mud-covered boy.

Oh, sometimes it does, but not all the time. Not nearly, and when it doesn't, you have to flush again, and I'm sure a lot of you former math majors and Quiz Kids out there can see with just a few mental moves that two, three-point-five-gallon flushes add up to seven gallons, or, when viewed through a different prism . . .

Exactly one gallon more than the toilet you had before.

Well, that's progress.

PLUMBING FIXTURES, FOR ME, HAVE COME TO REPRE-sent the Decline of the West—and somewhat ironically, too, since the East is not widely known for its plumbing fixtures to begin with. (And by the East I don't mean New Jersey, although, come to think of it, maybe I do.)

We've been in our house since we got married thirteen years ago—a California record, I think, in both matrimony and real estate—and got a new water heater when we moved in. A year later, during a quake, the water heater tipped a little (as did I); the next day we called the plumber, who said the problem was that the last plumber hadn't metal-banded the unit to the wall. That made good sense to me, and after gently reminding him that *he* was the last plumber—to which he reacted no more than an oil painting of him would have—he said, "Well, that's the problem. Got to fasten it to the wall."

I asked if he could do it, which I guess makes me a moron, and he said sure and shrugged, which I guess makes him a genius.

So he put it in, and about a year later the same unit sprung a pretty big leak, though it stayed fastened to the wall the whole time, as immovable as a Spartan at Thermopylae. This was a great source of pride for all involved, and it warmed me greatly as I stood there for three hours brooming out the four inches (and rising) of water on the floor, feeling very much like the last guy working a hand pump in the engine room of the *Titanic*.

This time I called a different plumber, and he came by the next day and said, "Where's your pan?" Heroically resisting the temptation to say, "Where it ought to be. Where's yours?" I instead said, "What?" And he said, "For the leak. The last guy didn't know what he was doing. A water heater needs a catch-pan underneath that holds the runoff while you shut off the valve and check the main." He might as well have been speaking Chechen for most of that sentence, but I quickly said, "Can you do it?" and he said—just as quickly—"Sure."

A year after that, the thing backed up. It stayed fastened beautifully to the wall, and the pan was dry, but the pipe leading into it from the street burst and flooded the basement. The new plumber (unless they were all the same guy with different masks) took a look and said—I kid you not—"The last guy didn't know what he was doing." He did, naturally, and installed a shutoff on the line in case it ever happened again.

It did. But the next new guy, after saying "The last guy didn't know what he was doing"—which we both finished in unison—noticed that the line from the street didn't have a valve with a pressure gauge to bleed it off before it burst. I think that's what he said, anyway. Whatever it was, he had one and put it on.

Of course, something else exploded like a grenade twelve months later, and as the next guy was looking things over I preemptively said, "Let me just begin by saying, I don't think the last guy knew what he was doing." And he actually said, "Oh, I don't know, it looks like pretty good work to me. It's just that the lead pipe from the frammis is too big for the Hollis joint . . ." I was laughing so hard I didn't hear the rest, and just told him to put in anything he had on the truck.

This went on and on, once a year, every year.

Came the seventh year, and the seventh leak, and the seventh plumber. (I'm trying my best to avoid saying *The Seventh Seal*, although it's probably worth mentioning that I have a weekly game of Chinese Checkers with Death.)

This fellow, of course, brought more new discoveries and attachments, but when he started to say something about the part of the line out to the street that was owned by the city, I stopped him. "Let me ask you something," I said. (He was in his early sixties and seemed like a decent and bright guy.) "Why didn't any of the other plumbers know this stuff?"

He smiled and rubbed his chin for a few seconds. "I'll be honest," he said. "Most of the new fellas don't get a lot of training or experience. They just send them out and hope for the best."

I was so pleased with this straightforward answer that I offered him a soda and a sandwich. He just smiled and passed, and did the work, and it hasn't broken since.

Other things have, though, lots of them; and the kindly woodsman retired, and the parade of pleasant boneheads resumed.

Before long, it was our bathroom sink that started breaking. Every few months, the handles on the faucet and the drain connectors snapped apart, and the sink was unusable, and I really don't know why. I'm no Lou Ferrigno, and I wasn't slapping them on and off in the morning like a howler monkey. I'm actually a very gentle turner of knobs and opener of things, as hundreds of women in the eighties can tell you. (Not *their* eighties, *the* eighties. I'm exaggerating, in any case, but not a lot. Okay, a lot.) The problem was that the designer fixtures we kept picking as replacements from the brochure had all the tensile strength of a swizzle stick. Ah, but you see, that's why they kept snapping: They were made to break.

Finally I told one guy, "Look, let's forget the designer stuff, okay? Do me a favor and find two handles from a junkyard, one that says 'H,' and one that says 'C.' Never mind how they look. I don't even care if they match. For the drain get me a piece of hard, round, black rubber, an old-fashioned stopper with a ring and a chain on it, the kind from a hundred years ago that's never broken and never will. If you can't find the chain, that's fine. I'll reach in and yank it out myself. In fact, you know what? Just get a picture of Teddy Roosevelt's bathroom, and make it look like that. If Roosevelt is too modern, get me a tin bowl, a straight razor, and an oiled stone from The Crimea. I usually pee out back when I've been drinking, anyway, so it won't be a big stretch for me."

Then there was the time we needed another new toilet downstairs, and this time it had nothing to do with saving water. The bathroom was smelling. Not every day, but bad when it did. My wife and I figured it was either sewer gas from the line, or the house was built on an incompletely relocated cemetery.

The plumber, whose shirt was so new he looked like a character on a sitcom, installed the toilet, but a few days later the smell came back and spread to the hall. Another guy came and told me it wasn't sealed around the bottom. Okay. But the smell continued, and soon it had taken over the office. Then the garage. The next guy came with a long electric snake with a camera on the end of it, and fed it through. My wife was standing behind him, watching the whole thing, when he hit something. The house literally shuddered. "What was that?" she said.

"What was what?" he said.

"The house shook when you hit something."

"The house didn't shake, but if it did, I didn't hit anything."

"Look, sir," she said, "I'm not angry, okay? But I think you hit something."

And he said, "I'm not angry, either, but no, I didn't."

We live with the smell now, like a relative. It's worse when it's hot, but not so bad if we close the door. We're not exotic people, but it's kind of like having a summer home in Ho Chi Minh City. If it ever reaches the bar, though, I'm getting a musket and a powder horn and marching off down the road.

IT'S NOT THAT I HAVE ANYTHING AGAINST PLUMBERS. My grandfather was a plumber, and my Uncle Harry, too. "If they put in a joint," my mother used to say, "it'll be there for a thousand years." It's not that. It's everything we make and everything we do. It's all of us.

My wife and I had those custom-made closets installed in our bedroom a year ago, the ones that organize everything, with the separate shelves for sweaters and shoes and shirts. I came home at the end of the day and saw the guy finishing it. The young saleswoman who'd sold it to us was there to meet me and collect her check for the balance.

We said hello, and I looked at the empty new racks and compartments and smiled. "Looks pretty good." She smiled in return. I reached for one of my suits on the bed to try it out, and she said, "Can I get that check? I still have a couple more jobs to check." "Sure," I said, "one second," and reached for the suit again. Then she said (a little quickly, I thought), "If you're interested I could take a look at the kids' rooms. We have special deals for kids." "Well, thanks anyway," I said, "but I think they're okay, it's just T-shirts and sneakers for them," and reached for the suit again, and hung it up as she started to say a credit card would be fine, too.

That's when I saw the jacket dragging on the floor. My suit was crumpled at the bottom, where it hit the floor, and not just a little. Three or four inches. The closet bar they'd just installed was too low. I looked at it for a second, not understanding, and then turned to her and said, "Uh, it's on the floor."

She kept smiling but didn't speak, so I looked behind me, as if someone else nearby could explain what was happening. Perhaps I hadn't spoken out loud? Yes, that had to be it. Probably best to try again: "Uh, pardon me, but the suit rack? It's on the floor. I mean the suit. The suit is hanging on the floor. I think the bar is too low."

Folks, she looked me right in the eye with the same warm smile and said, "No, it's not."

Do you know, she was so honest and sincere about it—I was so thrown—I actually jerked my head back and looked over at it again before turning back to her and saying, "Uh, yeah, I think it is. I mean, it *is*. My suit is on the floor."

Unbelievably (and I mean that precisely: unbelievably), she actually said, one more time, with the same smile, "No, it's not."

It was so sweet, so grounded, so warm, I blanched again. Was she right after all? She must be, because no one would just say it like that, no one *could* just say it like that, if it weren't true. I felt like that dark-side-of-the-force soldier Alec Guinness did the mind trick on in *Star Wars*, where he looks at him steadily and says, "There's nothing for you here. Move on." And the soldier turns to his partner after a beat and stammers, "There's nothing for us here. Let's move on."

I looked at this nice, young, polite woman with the warm smile and thought, "Well, clearly I'm mistaken. I must have lost my mind and hallucinated the whole thing. The greatest liars in history (and I've met most of them here in Hollywood) simply couldn't look someone in the eye like that and so completely contravene a premise that wasn't already riddled with falsehood." There's nothing for you here. Move on.

But of course I wasn't wrong. I looked at the closet one more time, and there was the suit on the floor. And I turned back and said, "I'm sorry, but—" (Why do we always apologize at moments like that?) "—I'm sorry, but if you'd just look . . . You can see . . . If you'd just . . ." The installer, who hadn't moved this entire time, was on his knees in a Geisha position, absently rubbing a mark on his pants.

She still didn't even look at the closet. Her eyes never left mine, her smile never wavered, and now with the same cheerful, calm voice, she said, "We can fix it." That's when I saw the tiniest movement of something in her eyes (or behind them). That's when it hit me, and I almost gasped.

She knew. Of course she knew. She'd known before I got there. She had tried it out, and saw that it was wrong. She knew, and so did he, and so did everyone but me. They had made a mistake, and the closet was unusable.

But they just wanted to get out of there.

I wasn't even mad. Just . . . sad. So sad that they felt they had to pull this, and without thinking I said, "Why would you want to live this way?"

Now her smile vanished and was replaced by a hard look, the look of the thing behind her eyes, and she glanced at the installer, and then at her watch. "Look, sir, I really do have to get to another house, so if you have a complaint I'll have Gabe come back tomorrow. Will that be all right?" (If I have a *complaint*?)

If I were wiser, or something better than I am, if our culture were different somehow, I would have said something like, "Please listen to me. Don't live this way. You have to care about your work. Not for me, for yourself. You must care about me, too, but it starts with caring about yourself and what you do. It doesn't matter whether you take out garbage or spleens, you have to care. It's better to care. You're too young not to care."

But I'm not wiser or something better than I am. So I just said, "Yes, tomorrow is fine. Thank you." (I thanked her, too, another thing we all do at times like that.) "Yes, please have Gabe come back—are you Gabe? Can you do it tomorrow? Can he do it tomorrow? Good. Okay. Thank you."

She picked up her bag and sample case, sourly checked her watch again, worked herself into something of a smile without looking at me, and said, "Okay, great, we're on for tomorrow then!" and walked out.

And then I did say something, quietly. "It's not right to do this."

That got through on some level, and she whipped back around. "What?" she said. "I said he's coming back. Okay?" The pout of a put-upon child.

Whatever moment had been there was gone, and we just looked at each other for a beat, and then she walked out, fast. And you just know, as she squealed out of the driveway with one hand and lit a cigarette with the other, she said one word aloud, softly but sharply, and it has two syllables, and the second one is "hole."

Back in our bedroom I looked over at Gabe, who still hadn't moved. I guess he wanted to get that spot out of his pants.

IT'S US, FOLKS. IT'S US, TOO. I LIKE TO THINK I DO MY work well, and so do you, but it's our fault, too, because we've let this happen for too long in too many others, and all we say to them is, "I'm sorry. Please. Thank you." We let our schools and businesses and children swirl ceaselessly down, down, down, and the rot spreads until someone stops it, and that someone can only be us. Corruption doesn't attack, it strolls in whistling, and we bow and curtsy as it passes by, not opposing it. And I'm talking about the guys at the top, too, the ones who steal and think it's fine, and who don't seem to know anything's wrong even after they're sentenced. I don't care whether it takes a village, or parents, or a friend, or a teacher, but more of us, some of us, one of us—all of us—have to stand up and quietly say, "It's not right."

BY THE WAY, I'VE FINALLY GOTTEN THE HANG OF THAT new dishwasher. Juice glasses in the center, coffee cups on the side, dinner plates here, soup plates there. I like it, too. It's a good model. I like it a lot.

Of course, that means it's time to get a new one.

TWO

SUNDAY,
BLOODY SUNDAY

EVERY SUNDAY STARTS THE SAME FOR ME AND MY FAMILY. The kids get up at six, I get up with them, and my wife sleeps in.

In this respect, Sunday is very much like Saturday. The kids get up, I get up, and my wife sleeps in.

Likewise, Saturday is similar to Friday, which is eerily reminiscent of Thursday, which is a carbon copy of—well, you get the idea. (By the way, I recently used the phrase "carbon copy" in conversation at the dinner table, and one of my kids said, "What's a carbon copy?" I excused myself with a smile, dabbed my lips with the napkin, and withdrew to the study to open up my wrists.)

As you know, the only women these days who merrily pop out of bed and hum through their chores are in those movies about the fifties where the husband suddenly discovers he's gay. This is fine with me, but it's not a price I'm willing to pay for a hot cup of Joe in bed. So to speak. Not yet, anyway.

And I certainly don't want to paint with too broad a brush here—Lord knows, that's not my way—but if my tenure as a parent amounts to roughly three thousand days, and if someone set out to learn the total number of those days on which my wife rose first, set the table, made the breakfast, fed the dog, brought in the paper, made the coffee, poured the juice—or, frankly, did any of these things—that number would come to roughly, oh, I don't know, let's say, about . . . zero.

I don't recall when this deal point was negotiated, or at what moment it officially became the unchangeable way of our lives. Like Mount McKinley, or Elton John, it's always just been there. It's her privilege to dispute this, of course, and I'm sure she will, to which I would like to offer what I think is pretty good advice: Write your own book, toots.

Now, part of the reason The Divine Mrs. M. sleeps like a lioness that's been tagged is simplicity itself: She can. The woman still conks out and stays conked like a nineteen-year-old. I can't. Even with the aid of sleeping pills (which, thank goodness, I don't have to take more than every single night), five hours of eye-fluttering is a giant victory for me, and as rare as a funny boss. If I ever slept like a nineteen-year-old (and I did) it was only when I was nineteen.

Just before I pad out of the bedroom each morning and gently close the door to leave her in repose, I always look back at that sweet face breathing deeply, blow a kiss, and only briefly consider putting the kids' CD player an inch from her head and blasting my *Royal Marines Band Most Popular All-Time Sousa Marches* album. But that would be cruel, wouldn't it?

Sunday mornings can be a wee bit harder than the others, though, if Daddy has had anything to drink the night before, anything at all, up to, but not necessarily surpassing, six or seven giant tumblers of whiskey. This is a very stupid thing to do. It hasn't stopped me, but it's a very stupid thing to do.

I get up, beg the Almighty's forgiveness for the night before, swear it will not happen again (never forgetting to acknowledge that I made the same prayer the week before), install the kids downstairs in front of a cartoon, and go through the traditional twenty-minute search for the Advil, which is (a) never where it should be, and (b) always where I left it the previous Sunday. Ah, well, if you can't play with pain, you can't play.

Next, I set the newspaper out on the table in three neurotically perfect columns, section by section, and smile fondly at my handiwork, since that is all I will ever get to read of it. (Come Monday, my first chore is scooping the whole pile up, undisturbed, and dumping it in the blue recycling bin.) There used to be a national commercial for the *New York Times* Sunday edition that always left me staring in disbelief, where an impossibly handsome couple in their forties rapturously goes on about how Sundays just wouldn't be the same if they couldn't read their beloved paper cover to cover over coffee and Cinnabuns, or some goofy thing. "I like the Travel section," chirps the wife. "Arts and Entertainment is for me," adds the hip husband with the full head of hair. They obviously have no children, since even goldfish would be an imposition on the me-time necessary to absorb all the news that's fit to print. I loathe them.

Then come the pancakes, or panny-cakes as the kids and I call them—the kids because they're cute, and me because I'm cute, too. Panny-cakes is our Sunday ritual, and I'm a pretty good panny-cake maker, if I do say so myself. I take all the fixin's (including whatever berries and bananas are lying around) and throw them all into one of those old, thick, mom-bowls, the kind that weigh fifty-three pounds empty.

Now comes the fun part. Conventional restaurants make conventional pancakes, six or eight inches in diameter, or silver dollar pancakes, a silver dollar in diameter, or Mickey Mouse pancakes, a Mickey Mouse in diameter, because we just don't cater enough to our children. Not me. I pour the entire batter, at once and with glee, into a pan the size of an Escalade's tire, and let the thesaurus-thick goop cook on one side until my flawless instincts tell me it's ready to be turned. The kids come up to witness this, mostly because it's as likely to come off without a hitch as Evel Knievel jumping the Snake River, and the dog comes with them. (You know how animals can always sense an approaching disaster.) Flipping a panny-cake this big is not easy; you need a Rod Laver forearm just to lift the thing, while rapidly easing the breathing mass free with a spatula in the other. Then, using my legs like a Russian weight lifter, up and over it goes, turning slowly in the air like a disc at Mount Palomar. I've gotten very good at this. Great, in fact, and eight times out of ten it lands perfectly back in the pan (though with an unwholesome plop), and I return it to the stove for the rest of its mission. The kids cheer, and so do I. The dog, at least outwardly, remains impassive.

Of course, two times out of ten I miss, and half of it lands on the dog's head, which sounds like a pub in England, but isn't; it's the dog's head, not The Dog's Head. In any event, it doesn't upset him overmuch, since it's what he was praying for, anyway. The kids still cheer, and so do I. So does the dog. So would you.

After breakfast we clean up, which is to say the kids go back downstairs and I clean up. Mind you, they don't spend the whole morning watching television. Not in our house, by Cracky. Children should be able to amuse themselves with just their imaginations, and I'm proud, quite proud, to tell you that mine come up with ideas that occupy them beautifully, which allows Daddy the Deep Thinker time to sit at the kitchen table and work. It can't come as a shock that the games they invent would surely, if she ever saw them, make their mother shriek. This occurred recently, and she did. Shriek, that is.

We'd just had a couple of rooms painted. (Or should I say

repainted? Or is there no difference, like *flammable* and *inflammable?*)
Anyway, we'd just had them done. (*Redone?* Oh, the heck with it.)
Something was painted by someone, that much I know, because
there was a bill. I didn't even know the project was necessary, but I
soon realized why it was vital: My wife wanted to. I was told nothing
about it since, like matters of high national security, decorating deci-
sions in our home are carried out on a strictly need-to-know basis.
She asks my opinion concerning the decor about as often as Beyoncé
asks Dennis Franz how to shake it.

One part that was painted to a fare-thee-well was the long, far
wall of our living room, which she'd had them do in some sort of
orangey, Northern Italian splotch-plaster. I'm sure those aren't the
words they use in the brochure, but that's what it looked like to me.
Anyway, it's smooth and shiny, and she loved it.

So the first Sunday morning after the wall was done—no kidding, the first—I idiotically told the kids to leave the downstairs den,
where they were happily playing with razor wire or something, and
hang out in the living room while I wrote in the kitchen. I still don't
know why I did this, since it's the exact opposite of letting sleeping
dogs lie, and is known in the parenting trade as stupid. We who are
about to die salute you.

Now, whether you're male or female (or Martian), everyone
knows that men get very focused on whatever they're doing, and
don't notice things. No matter what the guy's doing—watching a
game, thinking about girls from high school, writing a column,
thinking about girls from college, whittling, craning your neck out
the window to stare at thy neighbor's wife . . . Where was I? Oh, yes,
men can get very focused. On this particular Sunday my fancy took
me back to Ellen Herbstman, whom I adored in tenth grade, but
was too petrified to ask out. I do much better with her these days in
my daydreams, and thus only vaguely remember the kids saying

[23]

something like, "Daddy, is it okay if we. . . ?" I must've grunted an assent, but can't recall.

Next thing I knew—which is what most people say after committing a murder—I had a distant sense of a thwocking sound, steadily, about every five seconds, punctuated by lots of giggling. It obviously didn't mean much to me, as I never looked up, and it went on for three or four minutes, which can be a very long time, you know, especially if it's being used to hit golf balls full strength at a newly painted living room wall.

Thwock . . . thwock . . . thwock . . . I had moved from Ellen Herbstman onto Carol Schector (so to speak), and when that ended—very successfully, from my point of view—I finally blinked out of my fugue state, glancing up just in time to see my heirs, thirty feet away, acting out the opening number from *Nice Hat: The Sammy Snead Story*.

You know how sometimes you don't react to something right away, but slowly put it together in pieces? It was probably only three quarters of a second in real time, but I actually remember looking at them with a smile and thinking, "God, how fast they grow up. Say, those lessons are really helping. Good follow-through." Then, eyes bugging out and mouth dropping open, I finally stood and spoke. "Hey. Hey. HEY." I raced over and said the same idiotic thing we all say at a time like that: "What are you doing?"

Now, to fully understand what happened next, you need to know that on the other side of the new Italian wall is our bedroom. Adding the resonance and volume provided by Sheetrock and studs, this boyish prank must have sounded to my sleeping wife like the first few minutes of Gettysburg.

So at the exact moment I was saying, "What are you doing?" to the children, the bedroom door flew open, and out ran their gasping, terrified, barefoot mother.

She looked at me, and I looked at her. Then she looked at the kids, and they looked at her. Then I looked at the kids, and they looked at me. This went on for a while, since there's really very little to say at a time like that.

Picture it: The woman has just been nuzzled from her reverie by what she must imagine is either an earthquake or an assault by hardline ex-Soviets. She careens down the hallway (stubbing toes left and right), slips the last foot and a half on a stray ball that left the fairway, and skids around the corner to find that her living room floor looks very much like the first thirty yards of a driving range. And the perpetrators are holding golf clubs.

Except that they weren't the ones holding the clubs: I was.

Just before she appeared, you see, I grabbed them out of their hands (an iron and a field wood, if you're curious) and slung them over my shoulder like Bob Hope at a USO show, ready to fix the boys with a fierce, if red, eye and growl out a sermon to rival Wesley. But when my wife came caroming off the hall closet and onto the ladies' tee, she saw me holding the clubs, and we acted out that scene in *North by Northwest* where Cary Grant takes the knife out of the guy's back just in time for everyone to turn around and think he did it. More good news: This is also the moment Number One Son looked puzzled and said, "But Dad, you said we could. Remember?" Mmm, mmm, good.

Can't get any worse, you say? Ah, but you'd be wrong. After all, what's an ice cream soda without the cherry on top? As if we'd rehearsed it, The Divine Mrs. M. and I turned to look at the target wall at the exact moment, both instantly perceiving every spot where the thick (and still slightly soft) Neapolitan plaster had accepted each volley to the depth of almost half an inch, creating dozens of perfectly dimpled molds. All that was missing was the word "Titleist" in reverse. The wounds weren't grouped, either; they went down the length of the wall, since I believe the little one is developing a slice.

She found her voice then, all right. (Perhaps you heard her? It was a clear Sunday in early spring, noon Eastern, eleven Central, ten Mountain, nine Pacific.)

The next few minutes you can probably guess. There was some screaming, though not a lot, considering. We nurturingly pointed out to the boys that perhaps this was something that didn't need to happen again. They graciously agreed, and then she turned to me and said/yelled, "And you just sat there while they did it?"

There was a lot I might have said; there always is. But what came out was, "Well, now, honey, I was . . . writing." No one was astonished when this proved inadequate, so I followed it up with the even cleverer "Why don't you go back to sleep?" Now she looked at me in a way that certainly included the word "daggers," and instead of shutting up I added, "Unless you're hungry. There's plenty of panny-cake left."

Realizing that the only possible outcome of more talk would be someone's wrongful death, she turned to leave and immediately toed another ball the groundskeeper had missed. It rolled the length of the tiled hallway, slowly, without varying a hair in its path, very loud in the otherwise silent house. When it finally pocked lightly against the far molding and came to rest, she sighed, shook her head, glanced once more at the wall, once more at me, and resumed her exit.

OF COURSE, THIS WAS JUST ONE SUNDAY, AND NOT EVERY weekend includes the wow-finish of my superintending the complete ruin of a part of the house she particularly adores. Some do, maybe a lot—after all, who could forget another past Sunday's boys-

and-dog-only, post-panny-cake trek to a local garage sale for the massive, ancient, ten-dollar croquet set that one of us, and I'm not saying which one, managed to wallop so hard in our yard on only the second shot that the heavy, green, wooden missile sailed up an invisible *Dukes of Hazzard* ramp and clean through the recently installed, beveled, smoked, circular bathroom window—but that's all water under the bridge. (Not a large window, by the way, and just before my wife stormed out of the balcony screen door with curled cartoon lines of anger coming off her head to look down upon what she, on some level, already knew had happened, one of the boys mumbled, "Wow, nice shot," and I had to agree with him. There was nothing to do but wave up at her with painted smiles, so that's what we did. This time she went back to sleep.) No, none of this matters. It's not what makes every Sunday the same.

What matters is that I cook breakfast, lunch, and dinner, do the dishes, get the guys ready for baseball, make a list and shop, and bring her meals in bed. And that's not all.

I take her car and the dog to be washed, and jump like a seal at anything I think needs to be straightened or done, anything that might surprise her and make her feel good. I do everything that could be included under "it all." Some awful wife I have, huh?

Of course not. I think she's the best mom since mine, and the best wife since Rebecca (the Bible's, not the movie's). I do all these things for a simple reason: I love to. Many's the Saturday night when she's told me, "Stay in bed tomorrow, I'll take care of the kids," and I say, "Okay," and I mean it, but then tomorrow comes, and I let her sleep, and get up anyway.

And many's the Sunday evening she's said, "Relax, honey, I'll clear the table," and I say, "Okay" again, and I mean it again, but then I grab a couple of plates and do it anyway. I may grumble, but I love it all. Taking care of my family in the little ways is a great joy to me, the most wonderful work in the world, and I wouldn't change a thing, not for all the tea in China. (Especially not for that. There are things I want from China, like Taiwan and all of our nuclear secrets back, but tea isn't one of them.)

Maybe men used to sit like kings at the kitchen table as their wives swirled about with a pan of eggs and a pot of coffee, and maybe some men still do, but I wouldn't know how to be served any more than I'd know how to let a butler lay out my clothes. (Can you imagine that? "Would you like me to draw your bath, sir?" "No, I'd like you to leave.")

I'm not crazy, either. That is, I'm not obsessive-compulsive, or anything else where you eventually meet beefy fellows in white coats. I don't straighten towels, I don't line everything up facing forward—forget what I told you earlier about the newspaper—and I don't need to be in charge of anything. I'm not neat; in fact, I'm probably a slob. And she's a great cook, whereas I'm just okay.

There's just something so satisfying about feeding your loved ones in your own little corner of the universe. The world is full of sorrow and suffering—in case you hadn't noticed—and I can't control it, but unpacking groceries, laying out silverware, making omelettes, shampooing kids, and letting someone who can sleep peacefully, sleep peacefully, are things I can control. And for as long as I live—hopefully, even when my kids come visiting with kids of their own—I'll get up on Sunday and make panny-cakes.

BY THE WAY, IT'S BEEN OVER A YEAR, AND THE GOLF ball marks are still in the wall. Seriously. We got lazy and forgot about it, and then figured we'd wait till the next time, and . . . you know how it is. We point the holes out to anyone who notices—they have to be the ones to ask—and I think "puzzled" and "hesitant" adequately describe their reactions. Anyway, my wife actually laughs about it now as much as I do. Well, not quite as much. And never in front of the kids.

You know what? If I ever get into Heaven someday, it might just look a lot like my house on a Sunday morning. I sure couldn't do any better.

Besides, I'll bet God always knows where the Advil is.

THREE

THE YOGURT
OF WRATH

I WORKED IN THE DINING HALL WHEN I WAS AT SCHOOL, and it's the best job I ever had.

Well, not really, but you know what I mean. It was the best "Hey, maybe I'll try this for a while" job I ever had, which means for four years it provided all the pocket money a soft-spoiled, sexually ignorant, upper-middle-class dink needed for extra liquor and cigarettes (never books) when he and the other upper-middle-class dinks in his fraternity ran low at their fancy-pants, all-male private college. Little hard on myself? No, just clarifying.

A particularly annoying brand of fertilizer that politicians love to spread is when they try to sell you the I-split-rails-and-dad-worked-in-the-plant-just-like-you image. I always want to say, "You ever miss a meal? You ever not had pants? You ever steal bread for the kids? Then you've never been poor, real poor, dirt poor, so shut up. Neither have I, but neither have you, and if you didn't have the exact car you wanted in law school, I'll bet you have it now."

One of my favorite moments in *Driving Miss Daisy* is when

Morgan Freeman wonders aloud to his cranky charge why she's so shy about being a rich lady. Jessica Tandy jumps back at him angrily and says, "I am not rich, and I won't be called it. I grew up on Forsythe Street, and many's the time that we did without, and had grits and gravy for our dinner."

"Yeah," the puzzled Freeman says in return. "But you doin' all right now."

I could tell you this or that story about what my parents had or didn't have, or where they started and how they finished, or what their parents went through before them, and you could probably tell me the same, but the only thing that matters is that they never went without. I grew up in a terrific, regular house in a Little League, paper-route neighborhood, and we never lacked anything. We were rich beyond measure in health and love (which are the only important things in the world anyway, unless you're stupid). All my schooling was paid for, I was set foursquare on the road in life, and I ought to be horsewhipped if I ever complain.

Recently, I saw the biography of a supermodel. (Now there's a sentence you don't get to say every day.) My friend, the great writer Barry Marder, loves to tease the A&E show *Biography*. "There's no rhyme or reason to it," he says. "Monday, Hitler. Tuesday, Mussolini. Wednesday, Roy Clark. Two are mass murderers, and the other is the grinnin', pickin' star of *Hee-Haw*." As Barry points out, the creators of *Biography* probably never counted on getting renewed for so many seasons—after all, they've long since run through all the good people, like Jonas Salk and Amelia Earhart. "Next Monday, Jack from the Pep Boys."

Anyway, the model I saw on the episode is someone we all know; I don't need to tell you her name. She seemed to be a smart, likable person, and I was actually riveted by the show, in large part because they showed her large parts—shots, that is, taken years ago when she did a highly publicized spread, er, pictorial in *Playboy*. I remember they called it tasteful when it came out, and this was okay with me. They could've called it maidenly for all I cared; these things either work or they don't, and this one worked just fine. As a matter of fact, that's why I stayed for the entire biography, hooked like a lab rat hitting the adrenaline lever. So much so I even sat through three cooking shows and the reliably unendurable Jane Austen movie that followed, hoping against hope they'd show the scanty segment again, or at least a promo for it. (They didn't.) Well, Lord, you made us the way you made us.

The point is that during the far less useful (non-naked) part of the program, they presented this woman as having spent summers doing stoop labor in the field with swarms of migrants. *Whoa*, pretty dramatic, right? But it turns out the whole thing was just one summer her uncle brought her down to stay on his farm, and she spent a few hours for a couple of days picking fruit. That was about as *Grapes of Wrath*ish as it got—a job as a fruit picker, but only if you put the word "job" in quotes. Now, it's not the woman's fault they made her sound like one of the Joads, but here's a good rule: If you ever worked in a field or a factory or a slaughterhouse, congratulations, but you don't get to bring it up with reverence as a character-building keystone in your life, unless you only worked there because you had to. I cleaned public toilets one summer, but when it was over I went back to school. The guys I was working with didn't.

That's why I always add the phrase "upper-middle-class" when mentioning something like working in a dining hall: I don't want to sound like I'm trying to pass myself off as Abe Lincoln. Anyone who can spend his teenage money on beer instead of putting food on the table at home should call himself upper-middle-class, even if both his parents were plumbers.

. . .

WHICH RETURNS ME TO THE DINING HALL AND THAT
job. I learned a lesson there one shift long ago that never left me, and
that's why it's the best job I've ever had. Like most great lessons, it
wasn't apparent to me at the time; in fact, I thought the whole thing
was just a useless and annoying episode. Once I realized it was I who
was useless and annoying, I saw it for what it was, and have been
grateful ever since.

One day, while prepping lunch downstairs, I was told to dish out
a giant tub of blueberry yogurt into small bowls, and slide each one
forward onto the dessert shelves, where the peckish scholars could
grab them. They were going to move fast, as does all food for colts,
so before the doors opened I carried three tubs of the stuff from the
walk-in fridge and set them down next to me. Then I stacked hundreds of bowls at hand on the counter. Fine so far, and I was very
pleased with myself, but that's where the cleverness ended: How to
ladle it out? Hmm.

I looked around and opened all the drawers until I hit a deep one
full of those huge, yard-long metal spoons, the ones usually reserved
for recipes with the word "cauldron." I picked one up, hefted it a few
times, and tried it out in the air like Errol Flynn before a duel. ("Do
you know any prayers, my friend?" "I'll say one for you!") I looked
around for approval, didn't see any, didn't need any, shrugged, kicked
the drawer shut, and started filling bowls. How smart am I! Assign
me a chore, send me off, and consider it done.

Not so fast. Turns out the *Land of the Giants* spoon wasn't very
efficient. The top was longer and wider than the diameter of the
bowls, so you couldn't just slap the stuff in. It was so huge you had to
ease it in slowly, and even with choking up, and my elbow jutting
out, each drop had to be shaken off in little jerks, and one load didn't

even come close to filling it up; it took another, and another, and another. (Is it my imagination, or are we suddenly talking about something very different? Don't worry, I'll get us out of it.) In other words, the process I had so brilliantly designed was slow, difficult, sloppy, and awkward. Other than that, I guess I was a genius.

What did I do then, and why is this even important? It's just a bunch of yogurt from the seventies, right? But it's not just that, not at all, and that's where the lesson begins. In a sense, every problem in history—large, small, cultural, industrial, military, religious, scholastic, parental, political—is like that huge spoon.

What does virtually everyone in the world do when confronted with a failed idea? Rethink the problem, or plod on? Of course— plod on. It's the rare person, young or old, who is humble enough and wise enough to step back, take a look, and pick another approach. So what did I do when I saw how inefficient that giant utensil was—rethink or plod? Yup, plod. A second idea never even flickered across my screen. I found that spoon, by gum, and I was sticking with it. Besides, the job was progressing smoothly—though at roughly the same rate canyons are formed by rivers—so why get one's undies in an uproar? Or worse, a bunch?

Well, here's one possible reason: Eleven seconds after the cafeteria doors opened, every serving was gone, and my method of restocking ran neck-and-neck with the Portage Glacier. I might as well have waited for the milk on the next counter to turn into yogurt on its own. The worst part was, I knew my system had failed and that it would continue to fail, and I didn't care. I just stood there until one of the kids said, "Hey, Lar, where's the yogurt today?" I looked up dully, showed him the spoon by way of saying, "Here," and resumed the process that had already brought me so much acclaim. (And this, ladies and gentlemen, was one of the finest schools in the country.)

That's when May came over. She was a full-time worker there in the kitchen, in her sixties, and much loved by one of the fraternities, a sort of mealtime mom who always had a kind word for them or a tease about a new girlfriend. She had a small speech problem, a kind of slowness, I think, but her smile was as real as smiles get, and her eyes were framed by laugh lines, and they were a very bright, twinkling blue.

Not for me, though. I wasn't in the fraternity she liked, and she displayed an admirable, if crusty, loyalty to them alone. You'd think there would have been room for us to develop even a small bond, since I was in that kitchen every day, but May and I passed each other thousands of times and never spoke. I tried, early on, but the more time went by, the harder it got, until I just stopped. She was the Sweetheart of Sigma Chi, and nothing was going to change that.

No, the first words May and I ever exchanged were on account of that spoon, and they were inauspicious.

After the kid asked me why there was no yogurt, and I resumed my twenty-five-seconds-a-bowl method, May passed by and saw what I was doing. "Hey," she said, "That's not the way you do it." Then she came over, grabbed a coffee cup off the rack on the way, and held it out to me. We looked each other in the eye, another first for our relationship. Then, when it became obvious I wasn't receiving whatever she was sending, she stepped forward and wordlessly dipped the coffee cup into the tub, grabbing a dessert bowl at the same time. Then she shot the exact right amount of yogurt into it, set it on the shelf (already dipping the cup again), and did five more in a row like an FBI marksman on the range. This took a total of, maybe, three seconds. (Those were the days before plastic gloves, but she didn't even get a drop on her hand.) Then she shook the cup off and held it out to me again.

Before I tell you what I did then, I'll tell you what I've done every day since: accept advice; change; learn. In my work, at home, in my views of the world, on a grand or prosaic scale, if something isn't working I jam on the brakes, hop out, and look under the hood. And if someone is there with the right answer, I smile, say thank you, and do it immediately, always giving credit wherever it's due. Sometimes I'm right, but sometimes I'm not, and I like it just as much when I'm wrong, because constantly trying new ideas means you're not afraid to get corrected. Sometimes I'm the one who says, "Nope. That didn't work," and sometimes it's the guy next to me. On a movie set, for instance, I don't care if it's the director or the kid with the sandwich tray, I listen to every suggestion, and they all know it, too. I don't do this because I'm trying to be affable. I'm not. I do it because I'm trying to be as good as I can be, and make something as good as it can be, and that's what I want to do every second of my life.

When Marlon Brando died, we were talking about him in my acting class (the wonderful Milton Katselas), and someone raised his hand and said, "Well, here's hoping we'll all be as great as Brando." But I immediately said, "No. Here's hoping we all have the clarity and work habits to be as great as we're supposed to be."

Back to the yogurt. May's method wasn't just a good one, it was kind of perfect, but I was too young and stupid to know that—or, more accurately, to allow myself to know it. So what did I do when she held that cup out? I stiffened and snorted and said, "Come on, May, what's the difference?" I was too far gone even to turn around and leave it at that. I stood there with a sullen "And what are you going to do about it?" look. Now she reddened slightly, placed the cup in the sink and walked away, again saying, softer this time, "That's not the way you do it."

Now why did I behave that way? Adolescent snottiness at anyone trying to teach me something? Insecurity? Brittleness? Residual pique because she hadn't smiled at me for three years? Smugness? The stupidity of youth? All of these?

I've never behaved like that since—never—but there was something else that happened there that day, something far more important. The practical part was easy: Don't get stuck in a bad idea. No, there was a far bigger lesson that day. A sin, actually, and I've never forgotten it, either, and never done it again.

I'd been rude to someone. Just a little, maybe, but I had, and it was compounded by the fact that I was a young man and she was an older woman. The world grows coarser every day, and the most basic good manners often seem as quaint as a knight tying a lady's scarf around his lance. We should all be more polite, but few things are worse than a teenage boy showing disrespect to a lady in her sixties, and at the core of it all, that's what I had done.

MY MOM WORKED HARD HER WHOLE LIFE, AND SO DID my dad, and she always wanted a mink coat, and he finally got her one, and they went out that night. And the first thing that happened was a guy came running up to her in the street and screamed right in her face that she was a murderer for wearing it. And when my dad stepped up, the kid pushed him back, hard, and stormed off. She would have been just about May's age at the time. I suppose you can guess how old the young guy was.

Concepts of virtue have changed so much in the last thirty years I'll bet you a dollar most of the people reading this think the kid was right, that my mom was the sinner, that wearing fur is so bad, and any behavior that stops it is valid.

Well, he stopped her, that's for sure. She never wore it again. But I think the evil was his, and it was gigantic. Wearing fur is just an issue, like SUVs, and you're welcome to make your choices and legislate anything you want, if you've got the stamina to push it through. Yelling at an older woman, though, and scaring her half to death out of some misplaced, loopy passion is never okay. That was the only sin committed that night.

Someday on the other side I'll have a chance to apologize to May, but I know she'll laugh and say, "You been carryin' that around all these years? Lord. You were just a little stupid, is all, and I ain't much of a talker. Only shift you ever missed was that Tuesday you and your friends had that morning tequila party, and you came to work so shined up Mr. Harvey had to give you the bum's rush. Oh, I'll bet you do 'member. Ayuh."

Thanks all the same, May. Might have been just another day to you, but it was an important lesson to me. Two, actually, and I've made a point of passing them on to my kids as well. Like most things, they'll probably have to learn it for themselves, but that's all right. I did. Ayuh.

I think the other side of life will be a good place to settle lots of things, don't you? In fact, I believe I'll look up that kid who yelled at my mom. Naturally, I expect to be past all earthly, vengeful thoughts, but we'll see. Maybe they have little courts, or meetings, or rooms where all the new angels work these things out. Oh, I'm sure he's already apologized to my folks, and they've forgiven him. Maybe he's even been waiting there to say something affectionate to me, too. Yeah, we'll all be bathed in light and floating around hugging each other.

If not, though, I'm going to be wearing that son of a bitch for a coat myself, by God. Only for a few thousand years, you understand. Give him a chance to explain just one more time why he was such a rotten jerk and screamed at my mother. Ayuh.

I mean, that would actually be helping him, wouldn't it?

FOUR

MY SLACKS AT SAKS

THE STORY YOU'RE ABOUT TO HEAR IS TRUE. THE PANTS have been changed to protect the innocent.

My wife has always wanted to change the way I dress. Maybe all women do this with their men, maybe no women do it, or maybe it's somewhere in the middle. Whatever the case, there are three points I can state with certainty: My wife wants to change the way I dress; she has not won; she will never give up.

She seemed to like the way I dressed just fine when we met, up to and including our wedding and honeymoon. It was shortly after I carried her over the threshold (during that event, in fact) that she spotted something hanging in the hallway—still in my arms, mind you—and said, "Why do you still wear that?" Since I was breathing a little hard at the time (shortage of strength, not surplus of bulk), I could only muster a wheezy, "I . . . don't . . . know." She immediately countered with, "Oh, well, it's got to go." Now, she'd seen the same hallway and jacket many times, but had never said anything. Too busy kissing me, I suppose. Ostensibly.

But let's back up, way up, to my single days as a rake and a boule-vardier. For the average, relatively sane young man, it's difficult to go too awfully wrong in matters of dress unless you're a Trekkie, but then I did say relatively sane.

Like most swains of my ilk in the eighties, my fashion sense began and ended with two words: Brooks Brothers. It's not that I liked the stuff so much, but patronizing Brooks was, first, a question of tradition: My father took me there, just as his father had taken him. Many cultures around the world have similar rituals, of course, though not necessarily involving clothes. It's not hard, for instance, to imagine a proud father somewhere in the Near East taking his young son one day to buy the lad his first long, wide knife to cut off heads. See? We're really more alike than different.

The other important plus to Brooks Brothers is that a guy can walk into any of them around the U.S., pull the first twelve things off the first twelve shelves, walk out, and look about the same as the week before, which is, after all, the goal: sameness. Call it skull-crushing uniformity if you want, but I think the large majority of men feel most at ease when they look the same as the guy sitting next to them on the train. It's rigidity as a positive, masculine metaphor: "The mountains and the stars don't change. Why should I?"

A quick story. Years ago, soon after I moved to Los Angeles, I'd just gotten my first booking as a comic on a talk show, when I realized this meant I would need something other than a loud sweater-vest to wear. So I went to Brooks, which was still in a beautiful old building downtown. (There really is such a thing as beautiful old downtown Los Angeles. Nobody goes, but it's there.) I was leafing cluelessly through a rack when I heard an unmistakable voice across the room, a warm, creaky sound you would have recognized as quickly as I did.

"Gray flannels. Long as you got 'em," the voice croaked, and my mouth opened as I turned, and, sure enough, there was Jimmy

Stewart and his wife, Gloria, smiling at a salesman whose eyes were as wide as mine. They got the pants, and a blue blazer to go with it, and I thought, "Well, if it's good enough for him . . ." So I got the same outfit, gray flannels and a blue blazer, with a white button-down and a rep tie. Kind of a classic, which was just as well, because I wore that getup on every TV show I did for so long even my mother eventually said, "Okay, you made your point. Get something else."

It got even easier with Brooks Brothers (or "The Brothers," as my father used to call them) when they began using catalogues. I'd call and give the credit card number, and when my name popped up, they'd greet me politely and say, "What would you like this time, sir?" And I'd say, "You know what? Just send me the first two pages and the last two pages again." This approach was fast and blunt, which suited me to a T (whatever that means); it became sharply less effective after they began adding sundresses in the back for women, although it still took several shipments before I noticed.

I remember as a kid in the sixties reading in my dad's *Esquire* (a pretty racy magazine in those days) that the definition of a well-dressed man was someone who "could walk into a cocktail party, mix for the entire evening, leave, and no one would be able to remember what he wore." This forgetfulness may have been made easier by some of the things that were passed around at cocktail parties in the sixties—though not fully, because what made Sean Connery, for instance, such a powerful male icon had nothing to do with the clothes he wore (which were always the same: suits, tuxes, dinner jackets), but with how he carried himself in them.

Now, I'm not an idiot, and I know things have changed. Well, I am an idiot, but I still know things have changed. Many, probably most, young men like to be peacocks today, and I'm pretty sure *Esquire* has changed its definition of a well-dressed man, if it still even has one. Now it probably goes something like, "Someone who can stride straight through a crowded club surrounded by fireworks, a smokescreen, and a phalanx of bodyguards, and illuminated only by flashing seizure-strobes, and still have the copulating folks in the balcony recall to a police artist months later every stitch he wore, down to the 'I ♥ CHE' embroidered on his socks."

This goes along with a new definition of masculinity, which is fine with me. It's a brave new world, and they don't need me in it. More important, I don't need me in it. The toughest athletes, biggest recording artists, and manliest movie stars can be very flashy dressers, and often sport surgical enhancements, makeup, and hair colors unavailable to them at birth, or even in this solar system. That's fine, too. I'd just like to add that it's difficult to imagine Humphrey Bogart with blond tips.

THROUGH TWELVE YEARS OF MARRIAGE, THE DIVINE Mrs. M. has seen fit to use every gift-giving occasion to buy me clothes. At several of these per year (depending on whether or not I remember one's coming up and ask her to stop), that comes to roughly forty shirts, sweaters, ties, belts, socks, et cetera. I'm indifferent to the particulars, since, like most men, I don't get excited about a gift unless I can hear it slosh.

But I'm a good enough actor to tear open whatever it is with a high-pitched giggle, gasp, hold it up, kiss my wife, and dash like a girl with a crush into the bedroom to put it on. That night, of course, when I take it off and ram it into the closet, that's the last anyone will ever see of it. Occasionally, she'll say something like, "Oh, Janis and Michael are coming over. Why don't you put on that pink silk shirt with the pockets on both sides and the flap that covers the buttons?" I do this happily, or at least I do it. Janis will coo, but

Michael rarely says anything, since the chances are very good he's wearing one, too.

I love my wife, and the infinitesimal drops of anxious rage I feel at these narrowly cut, too thin, strangely collared, merrily patterned gifts never amount to much. Like many things in marriage it becomes an orchestrated dance, a pavane, a Virginia reel, and everyone knows the steps: Somebody bows, somebody curtseys, and then you hold hands in the middle and twirl, glaring hatefully at each other through frozen smiles the whole time.

But these particular steps, on this particular minuet—buy clothes, open clothes, be thrilled with clothes, never wear clothes— were in a good place, certainly from my point of view, where no one got hurt, and everyone hit his mark.

Or so I thought. Then one day Du Barry sprung her intrigue, and the astonished courtiers held their breaths. *Ecoutez bien:* What I am about to tell you began five years ago, which is significant, because it still has not ended. *Cinq ans! Zut alors!*

In October 2000 (the Year of the Praying Mantis) she abandoned her only slightly upscale haunts here in the San Fernando Valley and glided reverently over the Hill of Sighs to Saks Fifth Avenue in Beverly Hills for the purpose of buying me some extra-special threads for my birthday—extra-special not only in cost, but in her quiet determination that this time I was actually going to wear them. I still mightn't have cared too much, but this time it wasn't just one piece, it was a whole outfit: shirt, tie, socks, slacks, vest, and a sport coat, all from Giorgio Armani. I've had a slogan for that fellow in my back pocket for years, but somehow I don't think he'll ever use it: "Giorgio Armani. Where your money . . . is Ar-mani."

This time, when I unwrapped my presents over the SpongeBob table cloth and the cake-smeared faces, my professionally fixed smile cracked a hair, since an outfit like this takes six separate boxes, and you can multiply each one by three hundred dollars. This was all perfectly clear since stores like Saks are no shyer about putting their names on their bags than Burger King. By the way, those light blue Tiffany boxes, with their well-known hypnotic powers, have to be the heavyweight champion of all time in packaging. I don't know if there's a male equivalent except cleavage, and that's only for teenagers, not worldly, sensible men like us, eh?

Any Tiffany salesperson who's been there more than a year can tell you how, around five o'clock on Christmas Eve, battalions of Church's cap-toe wingtips dash in and offer to buy the boxes, when the store is sold out. "Name your price. She just needs to see the box. Just give me a box and a bag, and I'll throw in an ashtray and wrap it myself." I've long believed that Tiffany robin's-egg blue is the color we should paint women's prisons.

Balefully eyeing my six Saks sacks (sorry, I couldn't resist), and seeing no way out in the short run, I put the whole getup on in the bedroom—which led to a good deal of giggling from everyone (including my wife) when I reappeared, since it was all way too small. This was not merely a question of size but of shape as well since, near as I can tell, European designers cut their clothes assuming the only people who will ever wear them are built like Heather Graham and Christian Bale. I'm built like neither, last time I checked, and with the jacket buttoned looked very much like Fred Mertz in his World War I uniform. (Talk about doughboys . . .)

"Don't worry," said my wife. (I wasn't, but never mind that now.) "They'll exchange the whole thing. Just take it back to Saks, and get one that fits you perfectly. But I love the colors on you! And style is just what you need, something contemporary, even a little hip. That Giorgio Armani is a genius. He makes colognes, as well. Maybe we can wean you off that silly aftershave, too, that Old Spice you've been using forever."

Several responses fought for the chum, but one kept swimming back up like the fortune on an eight ball, and I knew it was the only one that mattered. Her words began to blur and echo as I narrowed my inner eye and thought: This is not good.

I have nothing against Beverly Hills itself, you understand. It's not necessarily my kind of place, but I respect success and eccentricity. I've been there a great many times, and happily, too, although only to do important things, like act or drink. Never to look for clothes, no, never, nor even to exchange them, nor even to carry them. Now, worse, I was apparently going to have to enter one of their stores. And it was this I found to be . . . this that was really . . .

Well, this was unacceptable.

Technically, of course, it was perfectly acceptable; I was going to do it, and that was that. Ah, but no one had said *when,* had he? Or she? Or they? (Pick the pronoun with which you feel most politically comfortable.) This was October 2000, remember, and I slyly hung the whole mess in the back of my closet behind the varsity jacket and the seersucker from New Orleans, neither of which I ever expected to be a big enough fool to wear again. I could buy a few months, at least, with this gambit, and then wait and see what the new year brought. Yes, out of sight, out of mind, that was the ticket. Heh, heh, heh. Old Spice, eh? Silly, eh? We'll see who the silly one is.

THE NEW YEAR BROKE BRIGHT AND CLEAR AND HOPEFUL on a crisp eighty-three-degree day in Los Angeles, and with it came a job that, as I had suspected, would push The Case of the Stupid Clothes onto a burner so far back it was actually in someone else's front.

It was a dandy job, too. Back in New York, Henry Winkler and John Ritter (a wonderful man whom I miss very much) were starring in Neil Simon's new play *The Dinner Party* on Broadway, and they were ready to leave. Jon Lovitz was asked to take over Henry's part, and when the author asked if he had anyone in mind for Ritter, Lovitz suggested me. Neil said great, and all the Millers went off to a wonderful chunk of life as New Yorkers, which ended in September 2001. (This was a few days before 9/11 and had nothing to do with it. The play's run just ended. A few people in Los Angeles over the next few weeks put their hands on my shoulders, nodded dramatically, and said, "9/11, huh?" And I gently took their hands off and said, "No. 9/7.")

With school starting and a house to reopen, and other little things—like the entire world being different forever—my wife and I settled into the blessings of daily American life we all take so much for granted, and the quiet nights watching the news, and the not-so-quiet discussions concerning what we thought the correct posture for our country was, which can best be summed up in the word "extreme."

For all these reasons, it was nearly Thanksgiving before my wife looked up one evening from her needlepoint and said, "Whatever happened to that Armani outfit?"

I'm serious about the needlepoint, by the way. She took a bunch of lessons a while back, and apparently they were fatal. Every night I would sit downstairs reading next to her, and we'd build a fire, and she'd poke away at that little hoop. All I needed was a long, curved colonial pipe, and a jug from the Whiskey Rebellion (still my favorite war), and anyone who glanced in would've sworn we were Henry Fonda and Claudette Colbert in *Drums Along the Mohawk*. (Wait. Make that Theodore Bikel and Shelley Winters in *Drums Along the Mohawk*.)

Giorgio was back in play! Yikes! I did a spit-take of scotch and told her it was still balled up, uh, that is, hanging in my closet (there's an idea for Clint Eastwood's next movie: *The Unreturned;* or *Million Dollar Outfit*), and that, of course, I was planning to exchange it soon, very soon, amazingly soon, throwing in the move to New York for the play and 9/11 for ballast. She nodded absently and returned to stitching her seascape, and I wistfully realized I would never have two excuses like that again. *Merde! Tabernac'! Drat!* It was time to go back to Saks.

Not right away, though. The weeks blinked by, and Thanksgiving quickly turned to Chris—sorry, I mean Winter-Term Ice-Break—and then to New Year's. January takes time to assimilate, and all this bought me a few more weeks of sweet inaction. Besides, who knows, February might bring the offer of another play, or a movie in Mongolia or some other region unlikely to be high on Saks's "Opening Soon" list.

Back to Signore Armani. Winter became spring, and spring became summer, all of which is nearly impossible to prove in Southern California without the use of a naval observatory. Plenty of acting jobs came up, but none in North Asia, and luckily, no one I was sleeping with mentioned the clothes.

She remembered them again in July, and I interrupted instantly and said, "There's a funny coincidence, honey. It's on the top of my list for tomorrow." This wasn't a lie, technically. I have every right to make up any list I want, any time I like, right on the spot, as long as I use the present tense: "It's on the top of my list." Well, at that moment it was, in fact, exactly on the top of my list. (Don't look at me like that. I learned that trick the same place you did.)

The jig was up, and the next day I was off to Saks with six slick sacks of slacks. (Sorry again, but I never met a pun I didn't like. Consider yourselves lucky I didn't mention the cookies I brought along. You know, the snacks. Forgive me. At least I didn't load everything into two piles, or stacks. Uh-oh. Sometimes I can't pull out of this and have to move the family to a bunch of small cabins. That's right, shacks. I'm so, so sorry. I avoided this problem for a long time, and it fell between the cracks. STOP IT. I saw several therapists, but they were all quacks. Help me. It comes like this in attacks. I'll have to stuff my ears with wax. Even Dr. Seuss would slap me once, slap me twice: smacks. I hate myself now, and might as well lie down on the tracks, and pin myself down with tacks, and—)

Maybe a break would help. I'm getting up.

Okay, it's the next day, and I'm writing again. Whew, that was a bad one. I promise it won't happen again, at least in this chapter. If I think of any more of that rhyme, I'll send them personally to each one of you over the wires, you know, the international messages that have revolutionized business for years. That's right: e-mail. OR FAX. FAX, FAX, FAX, TAX, PAX, LAX, SAX———

(Please stand by.)

Wow, I had to take it on the lam for a week that time. Spent it hiding out in a farmhouse in Indiana run by a lonely widow-woman. Good kisser. Spectacular cherry pie.

Anyway, I pulled into Saks with my . . . stuff. I won't bother making fun of the parking lot, the clientele, or the gauntlet of salesladies poised to lunge with their atomizers. Not that I've suddenly grown forbearance, but because each of these deserves its own chapter. (Not in this book, but someone else's.) I was pleasantly directed to the men's department and met a fine salesman, handed him the zillion-dollar bag, and told him what the problem was. Problem, said he? Not at all, said he. Classy store, Saks, and I waited while he took it in the back. Into the back. Oh, skip it.

When he returned and offered to stroll me through the Armani ward for more meds, I hit on the kind of brilliant idea that changes the world: Why get more stupid clothes I don't want? Why not put the dough onto a credit from the store and use it there to buy my wife something shiny on the next Day of Obligation?

God, I'm smart. Whatever money she's spent has already been spent, so why not think of it as money I won't have to spend more money on? Are you still with me?

The salesman was, and he acknowledged my genius with the same flattery I believe I've portrayed effectively in several movies. He grabbed the blower and piped up the next fellow in command, and the forty seconds that followed were a textbook example of the kind of conversation we've all participated in many times: "Uh-huh . . . Yes, sir . . . I see . . . Uh-huh . . . Yes, sir . . . I see . . . Uh-huh . . . Ohhhhhhh . . . Uh-huh . . . Yes, sir . . . I see . . . All right, sir. Perfectly, sir. Thank you, then."

He replaced the phone gently and said, "Tell me, were the clothes bought on sale or at the regular price?" Well, I don't know, it was a gift. "Is there some way you can find out?" Without hiring Pinkerton's? "Can't you just ask her?"

No, I said, because if I do, she'll ask why, and I'll have to tell her, and she'll make me buy more clothes. Worse, she'll make me wear them. I'll be honest with you—what was your name again? Alan. Well, that's the thing, see, Alan, I don't want to wear the clothes. No, they're terrific clothes—And they look great on you, by the way, but . . . What? Fine, Zegna, whatever, the point is, you look grand in them, but I don't believe they're made for a heavier, bald version of you. Look, can we avoid all this? I just want to turn the dough over and get something for my wife.

"The thing is," he said kindly, "Without a receipt they'll just give you a credit for the sale price, and if she bought them at the regular price, you'd be losing the difference. Can you check your bills? What credit card was it on? Was it a check? Is it billed at the

[51]

beginning or the middle of the month? We need a record for the store to credit you."

Suddenly, I felt very tired, and my head was spinning. Bills, records, cards, *what*? Oh, Lord, it was twenty months ago; she has two credit cards (that I know of); our checks are sent out by the people who do the taxes and the mortgage; all I do is come in every few months to sign the . . .

I looked at him weakly and said, "I'm an actor."

"Yes, sir, I'm a big fan."

"No, I mean . . . I'm an actor."

"Got it, sir. I know what, why don't you have your business manager check your records, and he can get back to me personally?"

We looked at each other for a few seconds, the store silent except for the ceaseless breath of perfectly conditioned air through unseen vents, and a few elegantly hushed voices over in the Bill Blass cul-de-sac. I let a breath out, closed my eyes, slowed my pulse . . . and suddenly I was in the car, heading back to wife and children, home and hearth, day into night. The clothes I'd left behind, and Saks itself, were just abstractions once more, back in the sepia-toned past where they belonged, like photos of Eamon De Valera on a very old wall in a very old bar.

In one of the rare nods of my adult life to the concept of "following up," I actually called our business manager, Marty, and in preternaturally short order for me, too: just under twelve weeks. Marty deals with far bigger and wealthier clients (but none crankier) and, like me, is a founding member of the Jews Who Drink Club. At any rate, I apologized for dumping something this petty on him, and he said not to worry, he'd check it out. His assistant, Diane, got back to me the next day, and she smartly passed it on to Rowena, who was a specialist at this sort of thing, "this sort of thing" being stupid show business husbands—what a *Jeopardy* category that would make, huh?—since it involved digging through the records of what turned out to be six credit cards, on a purchase that went back OVER TWO YEARS, YOU KNOW. (Emphasis hers.) Rowena was very nice, as you can see, but understandably distracted, since she was busy doing things that were more important, at least to her, and she gently averred that the only way she could possibly free the rat from this Skinner box was if I were to raise my butt a hair or two and help out the weenchiest bit by letting her know WHICH CARD WAS USED. (Emphasis, again, hers. She was an emphasizer.)

Which meant I was back to asking my wife. I'd had it. Cooked. Cornered. Collared. Clothed.

By the time I got home, I was ready to throw in the Perry Ellis, three-hundred-count, Egyptian cotton towel, and willing to wear an Ann Taylor, A-line, above-the-knee cocktail dress if she got it for me. I kissed her cheek, patted the kids on the head, and sat down wearily on the bed to unlace my Allan Edmonds brogans, when suddenly a GE Soft White lightbulb went off in my head that put me right back in the game—an idea that wasn't even mine, a foolproof approach I had learned from years of observing the U.S. State Department at work: Keep grinning and pretend nothing's wrong.

It was just crazy enough to work.

AND DID IT EVER. MONTHS PASSED, THEN YEARS. YES, years. My wife forgot. I told Rowena to abandon the search, and she grunted something just before I heard a loud plastic click. Saks and Alan and Giorgio were just ancient memories, like tort reform. No worries. The perfect crime. And then the strangest thing happened.

I felt bad. And a little guilty. And rightly so. I mean, come on, my loving wife, the mother of my children, my partner through thick and thin, who never scolds me for drinking too much (although that hardly ever happens), had the audacity to want me to dress a little better, and cared enough to take the time to go to a fancy store and put a whole outfit together, one she thought might just possibly make me look good. And what do I do, crabapple that I am? Stomp on it, kick it to pieces, and stroll away whistling. Nice going, Cranky. I had betrayed her sincerity by not being honest, and felt as bad, in a way, as if I'd cheated on her. Hmm, wait a minute, as long as I feel that way . . . What? I'm just looking at it. Lighten up, why don't you?

My course was clear. The very next day, just a week more than five years after she gave it to me with such happy eyes, I drove back over the Trail of Tears and down Wilshire Boulevard to the heart of Beverly Hills, and pulled into Saks Fifth Avenue.

I joked with the valets, and they laughed in return, which was really very sweet of them, since there's not a comedy writer's chance in Hamas they had the slightest idea what I was saying; nodded to a pride of hard-eyed lionesses on their cell phones at the front door smoking (and telling their bored friends in bored voices about recent elective surgeries, which, by the look of things, had all been completed that morning); glided through the heavy doors past the guard who would never be buying any of the things he was protecting, smiled benignly at the women stretching out their wares (which is a lot of smiling, unless you're running for office), and wound through the now-familiar gullies and donkey paths up to the men's department. Alan wasn't there, having retired some time ago, but another polite salesman was, a young fellow named Charles. I skipped the snappy banter and told him why I was there.

"All right, sir. And when was the purchase?"

"October 2000."

"I beg your pardon?"

"They didn't fit, so I brought them back. But that was a little later, in October 2002."

"I beg your—What?"

"But instead of exchanging them, I thought I'd buy something for my wife. Anyway, are they still here, do you think?"

"Are they still—I'm sorry, you want to know if your clothes are still hanging on a rack in the back? After all these years?"

"Not hanging. Stacked. Here at Saks."

"Say again?"

"I'd like to know if my slacks are stacked on a rack in the back of Saks. Never mind. Could you take a look?"

He left puzzled and came back sheepish, partly because in the high-fashion business, I guess new designs come out every few hours, and asking for clothes from five years ago is a little like going to a car dealer and asking for one that cranks. Which is another reason I like Brooks Brothers, by the way—it never goes out of style. But let's not start that again.

I had seen the light. I was a changed man. My clothes weren't in the back, or the front, or the side, but I didn't care, and he was nice enough to say he'd take another look and call me. And that wasn't all. I was on such a manic upswing, I stopped on the way out and bought my wife a pricey bracelet, and when she asked me why later on (and a little suspiciously, I thought), I said, "No reason. Actually, the best reason in the world. I love you." How do you like *them* apples? I felt like Alastair Sim at the end of *Scrooge*. Delightful store. Remarkable store.

I've given Charles a couple of weeks now and haven't heard back from him, but I didn't expect to. Hell, that outfit's probably so far out of style they're wearing it to Halloween parties.

So, sale price or not, having lost the dough on the outfit, and then the outfit itself, and after buying The Divine Mrs. M. a piece of big-time jewelry on my own dime for no official reason, I now promised myself and God that I was going back to get the fanciest rig they have. And why? Because she wants me to. Come to think of it, why stop at one outfit? They're well-stocked, and I'm well-heeled. Armani's not the only rummy at the track. If you're going to eat pork, let the grease run from your mouth. What about Calvin Klein, Ralph Lauren, Joseph Abboud, Tommy, uh . . . Somebody give me another name. Oh, who cares, I'll ask when I get there. Say your prayers, Beverly Hills, I'm coming over, and I'm loaded for bear.

Not right away, of course. I mean, you can't rush these things. You people don't understand style, that's your problem. Maybe in the spring. That's when the new stuff comes out, right? Yeah, the spring. Definitely.

Not this year. Or the next. But soon. Before Charles retires, anyway. After all, when you're on the cutting edge of haute couture, who has the time to break in a new salesman?

FIVE

THE FIELD

OUR SONS PLAY BASEBALL IN ONE OR ANOTHER OF THE nearly year-round Little Leagues available here in Southern California. I don't know how kids in Brooklyn or Chicago ever become such great baseball players with no grass and long, cold winters, but of course lots of them do and always have. Anyway, ours play almost all year long and love it. We do, too. Among other positive effects, it's brought back something I had forgotten: what a truly great game baseball is.

The regular Little League season starts in February and ends in June. Then there are summer leagues and clinics; then fall ball, which starts in September and goes to early December; then more clinics. Every holiday has organized games, and we join them all, from the one or two on Native Justice Day in November ("Thanksgiving" in the old invader-calendar) to the relaxed two-week splendors of Winter Solstice Pagan Break or Rite of Spring Fertility Fest. (You remember: the one that used to include that Sunday with the egg hunt the Awful People used to celebrate before they were finally outlawed and sequestered, thank Odin.)

All our league games are played at four beautiful fields of increasing size, joined in the middle by a snack bar and a parking lot. The diamonds are sumptuously kept up by dues and fund-raisers, umps are hired, tryouts and drafts are held, schedules are made, coaches coach, different divisions accept kids from five to twelve, and all the while parents watch from the bleachers proudly, or anxiously, or joyously, or hatefully (or all four if you're me, but more on that later). The grass is gorgeous, the dugouts are real, the bleachers are shaded, and I think there are probably one or two professional Single A teams that wish they had facilities as nice.

Each field has bright blue, padded vinyl outfield walls with ads from local car dealers and sponsors and families, although none, so far, as witty as the old "Hit This Sign and Win a Suit" days. (I'd put one up myself if I had a business that fit, but somehow "Hit this Sign and Win a Cranky Essay" doesn't have the same ring.)

My favorite part—seriously—of the whole operation is when foul balls hit parked cars. No kidding. It makes me howl. (Mine's been hit, too, by the way, several times. I just don't care, and I can't stop laughing.) It's just our cars, the Little League parents; the kids can't reach the street, so it's never a civilian. That wouldn't be cricket, as it were.

Still, every time a popup goes straight back and over the cage, all the decent, respectful, law-abiding parents in the stands, including my wife, cringe waiting for the worst. Except me. I follow each arc upward and downward with the same glee as Madame De Farge waiting for the next blade to fall, and can't stop laughing for half a minute after the unmistakable metal-bass-drum sound of impact. I've teared up sometimes, I've laughed so hard. One of these days I'll probably go all the way and start knitting the license plate numbers into one continuous scarf.

ONE OF THE GREAT PARTS OF THIS COMPLEX IS A COUPLE of cages in the middle that houses an outfit called West Coast Baseball School, the caps of which proudly bear the letters WCBS without a trace of irony. It's run by Nick and Steve, and my wife and I send our boys to anything they do, for three reasons: They're wonderful coaches who really bring the kids along; they call them by their last names, which is especially adorable for the ones who are still skipping around the bases; and they don't coddle anyone. Their manner is so refreshingly brusque, my wife nicknamed them Camp Shake-It-Off, because whenever a kid gets beaned or mashes a finger, they don't run over to hug him while speed-dialing a grief counselor. They just set him on his feet, clap once, and growl "Okay, shake it off." Usually, they don't even move from the sidelines. We love them.

A few weeks ago, our oldest caught a hot peg from third with his face, and immediately grew a fat lip, his first. He cried a little, but there was no blood, and Nick dusted him off. My wife and I took a look, I told him it was beautiful, and we asked what he wanted to do. He said he wanted to keep playing, so we glanced at each other and shrugged, and he ran back out and had a great game. I was as proud as a Mohican father whose son had just killed his first antelope and eaten the heart.

Well, that's not completely true. He did get beaned, and he did have his first fat lip, and I did tell him it was beautiful, and he did run back out and have a great game, and I did feel proud, but . . . I also freaked out *just* a wee bit and whipped around to my wife, voice cracking like Mr. Haney, and sobbed, "Maybe we should take him to the emergency room." She was the unflappable Chingachgook who said, "Oh, he's fine." Ten minutes later, after her flappable husband flapped for the ninth time and asked why we hadn't yet called a specialist from Vienna, she sighed and suggested/insisted that I take the little one back and start dinner.

This was clearly the most masculine thing to do, so I clicked my heels, bowed like Kaiser Wilhelm, and went off to do it, musing on the ride home at how pleased my rugged ancestors must be as they watched the whole thing from above. Yes, that's the old pioneer spirit, I thought with pride back in the kitchen as I set out the salad forks and mixed the dressing, spending only four out of every five minutes panicking at the possibility of one of his hawk-eyed teachers taking the boy aside the next day to ask if Daddy had popped him one the night before. Some Mohican I'd make. If Fenimore Cooper came back to write a book about me, he'd have to call it *The Last of the Untethered Fathers*. Not for the first time, or the last, it was I who needed to shake it off.

THE FINANCIAL AND CULTURAL EPICENTER OF THE operation is the snack bar, the place where Thy glory dwells, and all the kids, parents, umps, and coaches make a beeline to eat and crow, or eat crow. It's stocked with the usual mawkishly sweet kids' crap, featuring phony-berry powders and rollups, costarring unsettling pacifier rings and sugar-coated churros, with special appearance by tobaccoesque pouches of oversweet gums, and starring radioactively colored energy drinks that might as well be twelve ounces of cold insulin (and are, for all I know). How surprised we are when our children find it difficult to sit still in class.

The joint has remarkably good chili dogs and fries, too, not that I've noticed. The first games are early, and the last games are late, so the snack bar is open about ten hours, staffed solely by volunteer parents. (It's currently managed, and beautifully, by our friend Mike, who's literally made it in his own image: He's put his picture on the snack-bar-bucks. People dig them and spend more.)

The Divine Mrs. M. has spent many an entire weekend in there, and I know I'm biased, but when she and her cronies run the joint, it's immaculate, well-stocked, and efficient, and makes a lot of dough for the league, which you might not think would be incidental. Of course, as in every other institution in the Western World, a committee periodically takes collective control and more or less instantly runs it into the ground. It's never stocked, the fries are cold, the variety vanishes, the place is dirty, and they make nothing. There's a lesson in that, but if you need me to point it out, good luck in your run for the European Parliament, and I hope you enjoy Belgium.

Just days before writing this, my wife was in Las Vegas for a weekend high school reunion (or so she said), and during her absence the snack bar had: no hot dogs, no chili, no Icees, and no change. I returned from one foray with a warm Pepsi, a bag of dark, dry popcorn that looked very much like the petrified evacuate one sees on field trips to the Museum of Natural History in third grade, and forty-seven pennies. They also had no plates, and served the icy-cold French fries in oval hot dog holders. Of these there was a great surplus since, remember, there were no hot dogs.

Well, it's only food, and no one there, starting with me, is in immediate danger of starvation. The games were still dandy, and my wife's day in Sin City afforded me an opportunity to sin a tiny bit myself by rotating my head like a periscope and oh-so-subtly checking out several of the team mothers I find, um, compelling. You know what they say: What happens in Little League stays in Little League.

I take a moment now, aristocratically, and condescend to say that I, myself, have oft' times worked in the snack bar, in the spirit of fellowship (and good cheer in't), much like George VI periodically being driven down to the East End to remove a few small pieces of rubble with the rabble during the Battle of Britain.

Just being silly. I love it in there, and the parts I like best are the knowing eye-check of the drink supply in the cooler; the between-customers, arms-crossed, sideways-rest against the wall (and its cousin, the hands-clasped, toothpick-in-mouth, elbows-on-the-counter lean out the ordering window); and my favorite, the professionally bored "Next!" you get to shout. Preparing nachos, filling sodas, making change, and even cleaning pots are all cool, in their way, especially if it's only for a couple of hours and your living doesn't depend on it. It's like painting your own house, which we've all done once. It's fun for three minutes, and then you're ready to blow your brains out.

Anyway, almost all the parents volunteer, and on any given day you see quite a range of folks working the deep-fryer and sweeping up. Cops, accountants, teachers, and doctors all do their bit, and there's even the occasional jaw-dropper: Last Saturday, team mom Annette Bening worked in the morning shift. I don't know if sales were any higher, but the lines were unusually jammed with grinning fathers who'd lost an average of eighty IQ points apiece, all silently rehearsing a few minutes of spontaneous blather. I know, because I was one of them. (The obviousness of men continues to be epic, to the great shock of no one.)

Annette was an exceptionally good sport, by the way, and laughed sweetly with each bonehead as she handed him nachos and he handed her drivel.

The woman has been a great actress many times, but never better than that morning.

· · ·

SPEAKING OF MY WIFE AND THE SNACK BAR, SOMETHING happened there a while ago I still haven't made my peace with, and I don't expect I ever will.

The hot dog man insulted her. She was working a full shift again in the snack bar—away from her family on a weekend, remember, and for no pay—and, also, recall, she runs the place magnificently. She's tireless, and they ought to kiss her behind for doing it, although they can leave that to me. So this guy swaggers in and starts yelling at her and everyone else in there (all women) about how stupid they are in the way they're treating his precious wieners, and then he takes whatever sodas and candy he wants and doesn't pay for it (*everyone* pays for it), and takes more stuff and passes it over the counter to his kid, who doesn't pay for it, either. Then, for good measure, he yells at a volunteer's twelve-year-old daughter who was also helping out. Nice.

My wife wasn't even the one who told me about it, probably intentionally. One of the other mothers told me, and I saw red.

Everyone has his flashpoints, and this sort of behavior is one of mine. As Van Heflin said to Lizabeth Scott in *The Strange Love of Martha Ivers*, "I don't like to get pushed around. I don't like people I like to get pushed around. I don't like anyone to get pushed around."

Abso-blanking-lutely. I wanted justice, and all I needed to do to get it was convince this sausage seller to join me in reenacting a forties noir potboiler.

Now, I'm no tough guy. I'm not a yeller, I almost never confront anyone about anything, I can't even send bad food back in a restaurant, and I'm not trained in any of the martial arts, unless you count smoking and drinking. Most importantly, I don't think I've punched anyone since the eighth grade (a fight I lost, by the way, although I did get in one good shot). Coincidentally, that was my plan: one good shot.

Really. I was so incensed at this so-and-so (that right there shows you how mad I was: *so-and-so*) that I was ready, willing, and able to drive back down there in my Saab, march over to him in my Dockers and Topsiders, roll up the sleeves of my Brooks Brothers summer-weight pinpoint Oxford, throw my *Law & Order* 100th Episode cap on the ground, spit on my Lubridermed hands, and tell him he either had to (a) apologize to everyone in the snack bar and, in the future, pay for what he took, or (b) close his eyes and prepare to be punched in the nose.

That's right, my friends, I was going to lay my haymaker on him, a.k.a. Big Bertha, the Fist of Fury, the Flying Fortress, the Schnozzola Express, the Fabulous Five, the Pink Avenger, Knuckles McBlood, Evander Holymackerel, a Two-Cents Pain. Prepare, villain! Ah, but that was only the first part of my careful plan.

The second part centered chiefly on him turning around and giving me a tremendous beating. Why? I figured there was roughly a 92 percent chance that my middle-aged writer's punch would bounce off him like a pink ball off a concrete wall, and that he'd look puzzled for a second before shrugging, putting down his Coke, and pounding me like a drum. This guy has a lean, ropey, worked-out look, like Scott Glenn with more veins, but I thought, I don't care if he twirls me like a baton, I'm going to do it. I'm going to tell him off, stand up for my wife, and bop him one, even if he's some kind of big-deal, black-belt guy (which I'd talked myself into, and easily). I analyzed the possible outcomes as best I could, and thought I ought to be able to survive one giant, roundhouse Bruce Lee kick to the squash before dropping like a puppet.

And even if the damage was worse, I didn't care. I was perfectly prepared to see stars, and I knew that didn't mean Scarlett Johansson, although one can always hope, don't you think? Fear wasn't on the menu.

By the time I got down there I must have looked like a locomotive in a cartoon, because one of the coaches—our friend Russ—saw me, blanched, did a quintuple-take, and asked what was wrong. I did a few takes myself (just to keep my hand in) and told him my plan, bowing like Edmund Kean at the end. Russ did a few more takes for good measure (throwing in a very creditable Fritz Feld mouth-pop) and told me to take it easy. I responded with a devil-may-care laugh and a perfectly executed Edgar Kennedy face-wipe. Whereupon he pleaded with me to think it over, and Shuffled Off to Buffalo.

Well, there's only one good answer to that, and you all know what it is: I turned around to him slowly like Frank Nelson and said, "Mrs. Ricardo, did *you* pull that brake?" He knew what that meant, by golly, and walked off like Charlie Chaplin, which isn't easy for a man who's six-six and two fifty. I respected him so much for it I saluted like Gunga Din before skulking off and continuing my hunt.

Now, you can ask any big-time action hero you want—Chuck Norris, Steven Segal, Jean-Claude Van Damme, Montgomery Clift—but in order to take revenge on a bad guy, first you have to find him, and this I couldn't do.

I checked the snack bar—just women. Then the batting cages—no luck. Next I decided to go field by field, but he wasn't there, either. In every place, at least three people jerked back in alarm and asked what was wrong.

Revenge is thirsty work, so I left the trail to walk back to the snack bar for a large lemon-cherry striped Icee and ran into my wife—who, it turns out, had been hunting for someone, too, but not the hot dog man. (Although, in a sense, she was. Heh-heh-heh.)

In short, she'd found out what I was up to and was mortified. Russ had told his wife, Marcelle, her close friend, who works in the snack bar, too, who told their other friend, Rochelle, who also works in the snack bar, who told Ellie and Rhonda, who both work in the snack bar, who told Susie, Rabbi Bernhard's wife, who wants to work in the snack bar as soon as she can find someone to run the Spring Carnival for her, who called home to tell her husband, who doesn't eat the hot dogs anyway, because they're not kosher, even though he's heard they're pretty good, who called back to the field to tell Eileen Reinhart, who used to be the principal and does eat the hot dogs, who told our coach, who isn't Jewish but considered calling the rabbi anyway, and settled for telling Dave, the chairman, who told pretty much everyone left who hadn't heard. And, no doubt, many who had.

I think it was one of this last group that dropped the dime on me to my wife, but at that point, who cares? That's the thing about a small community. All I'd done so far is walk around glowering a little, and it was the lead item on the six o'clock news. The reason it scared my wife was that by the time the story got down to her, it had grown slightly to include me stalking the bleachers armed like Rambo and driving erratically around the parking lot in a Hummer loaded with plastique.

In short, she wanted me to cut it out. She didn't need standing up for, she said, and even if she did, she didn't want me to jeopardize the league's relationship with the guy.

What are we jeopardizing here, I said, hot dogs? Is that the relationship at risk? He's a bully and needs to be told so, and, by the way, let him keep his damn hot dogs and stick 'em where the mustard don't shine. I'll buy the hot dogs myself, and donate them, and I'll get Hebrew National, too, so the rabbi can try one.

I'll skip the gristle and get to the filler: She said a defiant no. I took a breath to speak, and she said no again, louder, but with a different inflection. Then I said, "But . . . but . . . but . . ." a few times (something I'm pretty good at). She set her jaw, and I held my hands out like St. Francis. She folded her arms, which is international semaphore for "This discussion is over." I looked for wiggle room, didn't find any, gave her my word, and sulked off with my now-slushy drink (or slushed off with my now-sulky drink). All of which are, if you think about it, the exact same steps of any argument in marriage.

Oh, but it was hard. I saw that guy several times over the next few weeks (sure, *now* he shows up), felt my gorge rise, caught my wife looking over at me, grinned weakly and waved, and went to get another Icee. A couple of times I saw him without her around, but a promise is a promise, and I limited myself to sitting down right next to him in the otherwise-empty bleachers and glaring, or, once, standing directly behind him as he watched a game through the fence. I was very close, fists clenching and unclenching, breathing hard through my teeth. Each time he looked back at me oddly for a second and walked away shaking his head—because, let's be honest, I was acting like a lunatic.

And so it stands, but I have a long memory. (Bad, but long. I can't remember the names of people I just met, but harboring a grudge is no problem.) Besides, it's better to let him think he's off the hook. You know what they say: Revenge is a hot dog best served cold.

So, you see, these fields are lovely, dark, and deep, and, yes, I had promises to keep; but they're actually not the fields I want to tell you about. It's others I'm thinking of, just now. Our home fields aren't the only ones the kids play on, and I found one far more beautiful, in the oddest way, and in the oddest place.

IN ADDITION TO LITTLE LEAGUE, THERE ARE TOURNA-
ments all over the city, county, and state. Many of them involve long drives, but the ones we're in so far are all within ten or twenty miles,

which, in California's car culture, is a roll around the block. They're essentially just more chunks of year-round games with different uniforms and fees and trophies, but this is to the good: more chances to play, and usually with better players, since tournaments are by invitation only.

The places where they play are off the beaten path or, more precisely, on the beaten path—that is, on paths that are often terribly beaten down, far less fancy than our affluent, vinyl-walled stadia. Some, in fact, are positively shabby. The bleachers are rotten and creaky, the infields pitted and pocked, the grass yellow and weedy, overgrown or undergrown (usually both), and the unpainted dugouts have more mold than the average Scottish castle. If you were dropped onto one of these fields on a late, chilly twilight, long after the games were done and the people gone, you might think you had accidentally traveled through time to a post-apocalyptic era where kids hadn't played baseball for hundreds of years, and no one even knew what it was anymore.

In other words, I loved them. Fancy things are dandy, but these scattered diamonds are gorgeously un-dandy, and it's just a tiny way for the kids to see that baseball doesn't always have to be played and learned and loved on grass that's been tended like a fairway at the Masters.

The Dominican Republic has produced some of the greatest professional baseball players of the last fifty years, and the kids there don't have spikes or uniforms, or new, regulation balls and bats, or dugouts or bases. Or anything. But they love the game, and they sure are good at it.

If Kevin Costner ever makes another future-shock, *Waterworld*-ish, *Postman*-type movie—I'm not saying he should, I'm just saying if—and somehow the plot is centered around him giving people hope by rediscovering baseball and coaching Little League, these are the fields they could shoot on. (Come to think of it, Costner's baseball movies are among his best. He's a natural, so to speak.)

One tournament weekend, the handful of games was played over two days on one of these *Mad Max* diamonds a ways north of us, and my wife and I were in the tiny, splintered stands with our giant coffees and our younger son, who didn't need caffeine to drag himself through an early Sunday. He was playing with a few of the other brought-alongs, and they all ran off screaming onto a field behind us. (Watching the instant friendships and play of children is a perfect lesson in how much paradise we leave behind in childhood.)

The stretch of earth the little ones ran out onto wasn't another baseball field. It wasn't anything, really, just a huge hunk of scrubby land. I'm not the best judge of measurements unless I'm mixing cocktails (and I'm a little heavy-handed then), but I guess it was several football fields long and about the same wide. There were no fences around it, just what looked like a woods at the far end, but whatever else was on the sides was too distant to make out: roads, maybe, or a bridge, or maybe nothing at all, just horizon. I glanced behind me periodically to make sure I could see them, and that no little-boy-grabbers were heading their way.

The oddest thing: Each time I turned around and looked across that field, it reminded me of something, and I didn't know what. Not déjà vu exactly (whatever that is, anyway). It wasn't that I'd been there before, it was just that . . . I couldn't tell. Something kept lapping at the back of my mind. It looked like something, or it used to be something, or it was something, but I couldn't place it. The feeling was there, though, and with each glance back it got stronger.

One time, turning around, the kids had run off a little farther than screaming distance (mine, not theirs), so I got up and trudged out to track them down and tell them to—oh, you know how it is with kids. You never really have anything specific to tell them, you just catch up and say something brilliant like, "Don't kill yourselves, okay? Anyone dead? Good, try and keep it that way. If you hit your head on something, and think you're going to die, come and get me first. We all on the same page?" They paid as much attention to me as was normal, which is to say none at all, and went back to playing, and I strolled back to the stands, stepping in ditches every few feet, but only seriously turning my ankle three or four hundred times.

It was a long way back, and I could just make out the game and the uniforms and the muted cheering as I got closer. Every so often there was a patch of weeds, or a broken Coke bottle, or the torn piece of a raggy coat. There were two old shoes, fifty feet apart, and not from the same pair, which is, if you think about it, remarkable. And once I passed an old door of a pickup truck from the fifties—just the door, its glass broken out. I wasn't certain at all it came from a pickup truck, and I probably know as much about off-roading as Gore Vidal, but it just looked like the door from a pickup truck: curved, rusted handle showing flecks of chrome and still housed in blunt, ugly metal that covered mechanisms almost indecently revealed by the absence of leatherette panels long since ripped away.

I stopped, looked, and walked on again, a hundred feet more, and the feeling came back again, much stronger this time. I hadn't been here before, but I had; not here, but someplace like it, and it reminded me of . . . What? What in the world was so compelling about this place?

Closer and closer to the game, laughs and chatting clearer now, parents clapping and coaches yelling for their outfielders to shift (or at least to stop staring straight up at the sky and spinning around), but each step also brought me closer to this feeling, to the memory of something—what, I didn't know—something, something, very strong now, and then my pace began to slow, more and more, until I stopped entirely. My mouth opened a little, then a little more, and it hit me. I knew what it was, where I was, and slowly turned back out to the scrubby field, smiling now and shaking my head. Oh, for goodness' sake . . .

Somewhere behind me, in the official game, an aluminum bat pinged. (What a pale, unsatisfying sound! God bring them back to their senses and ash wood.) Our side cheered, but I didn't even look, and stayed fixed on the giant, borderless land. It was the oddest thing; silly, really.

No, not silly. Not silly at all.

This pocked, weedy, pickup-truck-door-strewn field was . . .

Just that.

Just a field.

Nothing but a field.

No organized, parceled, chalked purpose, just a big hunk of field.

No golden arches in the distance, or colored pinwheels over used car lots, or factory-to-you savings. In a time when every inch of America is spoken for and developed, and planned and shiny, and sold and rented and sublet, and bordered with freeway walls and houses, and hectare-sized parking lots around hectare-sized stores— all great things, in their ways, and signs of a progress I'm part of— this field had escaped someone's notice, and if you took away the Coke bottle and the shoes and the door, it was sitting there the way it had since the nineteenth, and the eighteenth, and the seventeenth centuries, and a great while before that, before even the Indians strolled across the Bering Strait and took it from the wind or who- ever else was there before them, and long before even that, to when places like the La Brea Tar Pits were still learning how to look pretty enough to catch dinosaurs.

Just a field, and it was a very long time since I'd seen one.

And it tugged at me, because I'd played in it, too, like they were doing now—not this one, of course, but ones so much like it you'd need a team of forensics people to tell the difference, in very hot summers and very cold winters, lots of them like this (and lots of lots, too, which is how New Lots Avenue on the east end of Brooklyn got its name), but that was over forty years ago, when boomers were still booming.

My father used to take us sledding on one, at the end of our development, holding up the worn wire fence for us to crawl under, my mind turning it into the barbed wire of Remington's range wars, still an immense, borderless, snowy field, before the houses and stores and schools continued all the way to Peninsula Boulevard and Rockaway Turnpike, past the smelly pond we used to like anyway because it was easy to catch tadpoles, past the tiny, isolated, brick savings bank backed up against a small woods, where the elderly guard always doffed his cap to my mother when she came in, past the marshes and inlets where Jimmy Kaufman was a night watch-man years later, and Richie Kapner and Kenny Nudelman and I used to visit and pile into the roofless security jeep they gave him and fly up and down the dunes like maniacs, playing *Rat Patrol.* All built up now. All gone.

There was another field and woods we used to play in, behind the Adlers and the Smiths, where I stepped on a rusty nail one day, and it went through my white Keds loafer sneaker and into my foot, and I was afraid to tell my parents, and petrified I'd get blood poisoning and lockjaw, but eventually told my mom, who just washed it off.

It was the same woods where we were playing army the day Todd Feuer got shot in the hand with a BB. (Yes, yes, I know it was stupid. Go tell boys not to be stupid. Go tell men, in fact.) We took him back to his house to operate (seriously), to remove the BB with our Cub Scout knives (and his permission, of course). We sterilized the blades with matches, a commonly accepted procedure among ten-year-old cognoscenti, and gave him a pencil to bite on (more shared wisdom, this time from *Gunsmoke*). Then we took him into his bedroom and held him down, one kid on each arm and leg, and began sawing, at which point, in the kind of symmetry that simply cannot exist without a God, Todd's mother walked in with a pile of clean laundry, opened her mouth, and began screaming. I believe she just stopped last week.

There's more to that story, actually, and I might as well tell it now, because it's never going to come up again. Todd's dad was a police detective on the graveyard shift, and he and his sisters were always warned to be especially quiet around the house during the day, which was his father's sleep time.

These were all nice, regular, three-bedroom houses in our neighborhood, and had the same layout. The master bedroom (although perhaps, at twelve by fourteen, it was grandiloquently named) came with or without its own bathroom in those days, depending on how sporty you felt, and was maliciously sandwiched between the kitchen and the first eight-by-ten bedroom, in this case Todd's. So, ten seconds after his mom started screaming, we started screaming in reply, holding up the scout knives in unison by way of explaining our clinic's unique approach—which, not shockingly, caused her to take an even bigger breath and scream louder.

Of course, that's when the master bedroom door flew open, and out ran Detective Sergeant Feuer in the kind of full, striped pajamas nobody has worn since *Good Neighbor Sam*. Miffed, no doubt, at having had his Anita Ekberg dream interrupted, and apparently certain the Russians had attacked, he was brandishing his sap. (For those who've never read Chandler, a sap was de rigueur in those days for the well-dressed enforcer on both sides of the law. It was technically a leather handle with a pouch of lead, but had the easy-to-understand effect of a sock full of nickels. The chances are very good that no one who was ever hit with one was happy about it.)

Mrs. Feuer, a good housewife like all of our mothers, had apparently just washed or waxed (or regrouted) the floor. Either way, her husband's bare right foot shot out from under him like one of the Nicholas Brothers. To regain his balance, his arms pinwheeled briefly, and this caused the hand with the sap to come right at his very own head.

The good news is that his reflexes were A-1, and he very quickly turned his head, missing the sap completely, though not by much. The bad news is that what he whipped his head around into was one of the ex-B-19 fuselage metal doors that framed all of our houses, and the effect of this, at about fourteen miles an hour (allowing for drag), was exactly the same as if he had caught that sap behind the ear.

Up to that point, and not counting the Three Stooges, I'd never seen anyone's eyes actually roll up in his head, nor then seen him pitch straight forward like a tree. Being ten and jerks, we all thought this was pretty funny. The only things missing were the goofy smile on the face of the victim and the cuckoo clock striking four. (Apparently, neither of these things occurs in real life.) His wife screamed, "George!" and caught him, and his rubbery knees firmed up enough to hold things together.

He looked at his wife, though not as if he knew her, then at us, an unhappy recognition returning, tried to speak, thought better of it, hitched up his bottoms, rubbed his face, winced, and made the wise decision of wordlessly going back into his room and closing the door. (It was the smart move. I bet he was a good cop.)

The place with the BB and the sneaker and the snow forts was the same woods that led to another, smaller field, the one that abutted the creek behind Rafe Davis's house, where Jamie Kearns's brother drowned playing Tom Sawyer on a makeshift raft so long ago; a shallow creek, but deep enough, God knows, deep enough. I can't remember his name—Billy, maybe—but I remember his face, and his round glasses, and that day, and coming home to see my mother crying. Never go in the creek, they said, so often after that. Not allowed in the creek.

Just a field, that's what I was staring at now. Like the one when your mother asked where you and your friends were going, and you said, "To the field," and it was just a field.

Just a field, and I was watching kids playing the way kids have always done, without the need of coaches and hats and schedules. I played in Little League, too, when I was a kid, and loved it, but we still had plenty of plain old fields, and those were the best. Boys understand fields as well as they understand candy, and fields understand boys as well as they understand truck doors. That's what I was seeing, and that's why this place was familiar, and that's what had pulled at me so: I was looking at my childhood.

HOW IN THE WORLD WAS THIS HUNK OF LAND JUST sitting there? This is Southern California, not Bulgaria. Undeveloped land here is as rare as a Torah class in Kennebunkport.

As a rule I have no use for the kind of places people have taken to calling "pristine." In fact, I hate the word. (Those who use it are as devotional as any snake handler; how odd that the two groups would never recognize it in each other.)

I like civilization and cities and sprawl, and I don't give a hoot for owls, spotted or otherwise. A hillside covered with houses is more beautiful to me than one covered with trees, because I like the footprints of man and the evidence of humanity's growth and primacy. Birds just wake me up in the morning. It would be nice if we could all drive to work on a drop of water, but until then I'd drill for oil in a patch of tulips, and I actually think a distant derrick on the horizon in the Pacific is pretty next to the setting sun.

Last fall I was working in Calgary, and everybody on the set, from the director on down, said, "Oh, you have to go see Lake Louise. It's only a couple of hours away." So one Sunday the producer called me up and asked if I'd like to go with him. He'd been there several times and said, "It's very spiritual" (another word that makes me gag), and offered to do the driving.

I couldn't think of how to say no fast enough, so I left the warm bed and the remote, took the hangover with me, and we drove two and a half hours, parked, and walked through the trees to Lake Louise. I looked at it for twenty or thirty seconds and said, "That's it? That's all?" And he said, "Yes, isn't it beautiful?" and I almost strangled him right there.

We walked to the gift shop for a cold Coke (for me) and wordlessly headed back to the car, which is when he took a giant bite of a Zone bar and cheerfully said, "You want to take one more look before we leave?" and I almost strangled him again. I had to drive, too, since he was tired, and he snored the whole way, in a small car, and we pulled into the hotel just in time to lose the whole day.

I politely, but firmly, asked the director and the other actors never to mention it again, but you can imagine how well that went. (I'm writing a script now with the same director, Dennis Dugan, and he still laughs about it. I'm thinking of strangling him, too.)

So I am the last guy to get all weepy about untouched land.

But I sure did like that field.

WE'VE BEEN TO PLENTY OF TOURNAMENTS SINCE, BUT not back at The Field. Many of the diamonds are even nicer than ours, some much nicer. Better snack bars, too. Maybe they've stopped scheduling games at the shabby old place. It was pretty run down. I don't know. One of these days, I guess. Maybe.

Of course, sooner or later, it'll be bordered and paved, and turned into something, and that's fine, too. Nobody's going to leave a big hunk of Southern California just sitting there, and that's the way it goes. As my dad said after our sleighing area was turned into houses, "We live here, and we can't blame other people for wanting to live somewhere, too." Absolutely right.

Been a few months now, and I can't even remember exactly where it was. North on, what, Vineland for a while? Ten miles, fifteen . . . Or was it Sepulveda? Memory gets paved over, too, just like fields.

I'm not even angry at the hot dog guy anymore.

The hell I'm not.

SIX

I'M DREAMING . . .
OF A WHITE . . .
CHRI—ER, HOLIDAYS

FIRST OF ALL, I'M A JEW. (NOW THERE'S A GRABBY START for a chapter, eh? Probably cut into sales of the book in France, but what the heck.) The thing is, there are certain subjects in life where it's a good idea to say what you are before giving your opinion. Maybe it's a factor, and maybe it's not, and maybe it won't be necessary in a thousand years, but it still helps in the present as a qualifier, disclaimer, badge, shield, whatever.

Like it or not, one's background affects the way one receives opinions on a given issue. Whether you're hawkish or dovish on war, it helps your credibility if you've ever been in one. (Since my own uniformed service ended with the Cub Scouts, I try to avoid sentiments like, "I say we drop the big one.")

Let's say there's a bill in Congress to give every American under five feet tall a hundred million dollars (and I'll bet you a golf junket to Scotland there is). This may or may not be a good idea, but if someone writes a column saying he supports it—that, yes, the short folk should definitely get the money—it adds at least some perspective to have a note afterward saying, "The writer is four feet eleven inches in height." Therefore, saying you're a Jew is probably the right way to start a discussion about Christmas (or a date with Claudia Schiffer).

Second of all, I use the word "Jew" intentionally. I always use it. I never say Jewish, I say Jew. Being Jewish is easy for me, because it's about responsibility and ritual and worship. Being a Jew is hard, because no one means it as a compliment. So I embrace it. Like all religions, being Jewish is done in private, with others who are the same as you, or alone in prayer. Being a Jew, though, is what I am in the world, and if you're one, too, I hope it doesn't come as a giant shock to hear that it's almost all anyone who looks at you will ever see.

Even if you've never said a prayer and have no beliefs, no matter how hard you try to please others and be invisible, even if you wear sandwich boards that say "Not me!" or "No Jew here!" and become a Buddhist, a Hindu, a Calvinist, a Rosicrucian, or a Wiccan, you're a Jew, so you might as well start loving it. Try getting off the train at Auschwitz sixty years ago and telling the guy there's been a terrible mistake, because you're not religious.

Maybe you're thinking, "Don't pull that concentration camp stuff anymore, it's ancient history." Okay, maybe you're right. Try being a door-to-door salesman in Fallujah, then, and saying to everyone, "Oh, you don't understand, I'm a secular Jew. Thank you, I'll be glad to come in. I mean, we go to temple on Yom Kippur—hi, guys!—but most of the time I'll have a cup of coffee and a cigarette as soon as we get home. Okay, okay, I'm kneeling, take it easy. Anyway, the most Jewish thing I ever do is the Sunday *Times* crossword puzzle, but have you noticed they're getting harder? I had an uncle who did it in ink. Say, those sure are some weird banners. Can I go now?"

And maybe you're thinking, "Don't pull that, either. The only reason they're so angry is that we invaded their country and ruined all their kite flying." Okay, maybe you're right again. Try it in Egypt, then, or Saudi Arabia. Or Chechnya.

Try it in Paris.

No, if you're Jewish, you either know you're a Jew, or you're an idiot, and if you're an idiot, don't worry, I've been one, too, lots of times. We all have. Perhaps, though, now would be a good time to stop, since the world's not going to change anytime soon.

Of course, you may be a resident of that rarest of wards in this asylum, the incurables, the ones who say, "The only reason any of this is happening is Israel." Then I can't help you. Your soul is so torn you wouldn't know your own head's been cut off after the video takes Best Newcomer at the Al Jazeera Emmys.

Speaking of which, "I'm a Jew, and my parents are Jews" is the last thing they made Daniel Pearl say before sawing off his head. When they first snatched him and called their bosses to ask what to do, they didn't say, "We have a reporter," or "We have an American," or "We have a capitalist from the *Wall Street Journal*." They said, "We have a Jew." If that's still not enough, you might as well go all the way, like one of us did, and become the attorney for Hamas. This follows my long-held theory that every Jew is just smart enough to be his own worst enemy.

Which, hooray, finally brings us around to . . . one more word about Jews. (I know, for a chapter on Christmas there hasn't been an awful lot of it so far. Hold onto your yarmulkes, I'll get to it.) Actually, this next point brings us right to December 25, because Christmas, you know (unless you've all forgotten, which is increasingly possible), celebrates not the birth of Santa but the birth of

Jesus, and Jesus was a Jew. That may sound like overstating the obvious, but it's not. You might say, *Yeah, we all know that, let's move on;* but think about it. Jesus wasn't a Christian; all that came later. He was born, lived, and died a Jew—a rabbi, in fact—and it's worth taking a good look at it: Jesus was a Jew, his parents were Jews, everyone he grew up with and knew was a Jew, the disciples were Jews, St. Paul, who built the church, St. Peter, James, Mark, Thomas, Mary Magdalene, the guys crucified next to him on Calvary—they were all Jews, everyone sitting on the grass listening to the Sermon on the Mount, and the first ten thousand Christians. John the Baptist wasn't a Baptist, he was a Jew who baptized. They were all Jews, and that's a lot for such a small people. In fact, so far as I know, the first non-Jews Jesus ever ran into were the ones with the whips and the nails.

By the way, you may not know it, but thousands of other Jews were also crucified in the same way, in the same era, by the same sweethearts, the Romans, although Jesus was the only one who rose and grew to be worshipped by millions. (Unless you count Miramax.)

We may not know what color Jesus' eyes were, but it's a cinch that Joseph and Mary looked a lot more like Elliot Gould and Lainie Kazan than Brad Pitt and Ann Heche.

Anyway, we're finally on to Christmas.

After one more point. (Come on, don't be mad.)

Here's the thing. Every ethnic group, tribe, people, and race has its bragging rights, but I think the Jews have had a vastly disproportionate effect on the world over the centuries to their numbers. For goodness' sake, take just three: Jesus Christ, Karl Marx, and Sigmund Freud. Can you think of any other trillion people added together who have so shaken up Heaven and Earth? Put us down anywhere in the world, and one generation later you've got the best hospitals, furniture stores, schools, libraries, delis, and 97 percent of anything funny that's ever been written.

Be honest, if you needed an emergency heart operation in ten minutes, and you had to choose your surgeon right there, right then, that second, and the list they handed you had only six names, and you were in a strange place and didn't know any of them, and the six names were: Dr. Bush, Dr. Kennedy, Dr. Giuliani, Dr. Arafat, Dr. Sharpton, and Dr. Lieberman . . . which one would you pick? Yes, yes, I know, it's a terrible question. I feel awful; I don't know how I'll ever get over it. All people are obviously exactly the same, and I'm certain each one of them is a magnificent scholar, but . . . *which one would you pick?* Hell, bin Laden would probably pick Lieberman.

ARE JEWS OVER-REPRESENTED IN ALL SORTS OF IMPORtant fields? Yes, but isn't that an amazing thing? You'd think that, through the years, folks would look at the Jews and say, "These people are astonishing. Let's be more like them." The actual response has been, uh, slightly different, more along the lines of "These people are too good at everything they do. Let's kill them." It's another of life's ironies that the England in which William Shakespeare created Shylock had very few models for The Bard to go on—close to zero, actually, those of the Hebrew persuasion having been invited to leave Her Britannic Majesty's realm just a hair before Elizabethan times, in 1290. They weren't asked back again till the Restoration, when Cromwell looked around and realized that no one in England had had a decent argument for four hundred years. (Incidentally, I not only have nothing against Shakespeare, but consider Shylock a candle lit in the darkness.)

I'm a short-run pessimist and a long-run optimist; I believe deeply that one day, for all peoples, the lion will lie down with the lamb. When that will occur is anyone's guess, maybe even God's. (That'd be a kick in the head, wouldn't it? You get to Heaven and God says, "Me? I was waiting for you.") The odds for universal brotherhood hitting the charts in the next short while are not good, but whether it's the long run or the long, long run, we'll just have to wait and see. It'll probably come somewhere between the United States winning a World Cup and the sun burning out, both of which are going to take millions of years, anyway.

In the meantime, I think Americans have made great progress embracing tolerance of all, and we're often highly skilled at adopting aspects of other cultures into our own. So much so that sometimes it gets a little silly. A few years back a national fast-food chain added a snappy little item to their breakfast menu: ham and cheese on a bagel. I still don't know whether that's a giant leap forward, or the dumbest thing I've ever heard in my life.

Anyway, I have a modest proposal concerning the Jews: Any group that survives thousands of years of attempt after attempt to destroy them, and can still consistently pop out people from Pushkin to the Three Stooges, should be let into the party, and maybe even allowed to keep their own country the size of a book of matches in the middle of a football field. Folks: When Jesus comes back again, where do you think he's going to come from?

And now, if no one has any further interruptions, I'd like to talk about Christmas.

The issue, as you know, is what we should call it. "The Holidays" has become a popular dodge, which is interesting considering that the word "holidays" comes from a contraction of "Holy Days," which is the one thing the people who insist on using it don't want to acknowledge in the first place. And you've all heard some of the eye-rolling contortions—Winter Solstice Break, for instance.

I guess I'm in the group that shrugs and says, What in the world is so wrong about your dry cleaner, and (gasp!) the evening news, and even (double gasp and grabbing of chest!) your senator saying "Merry Christmas"? I don't get it, I swear I don't. Ninety-two percent of the country (or thereabouts) is actively or inactively or nominally Christian; they all celebrate Christmas. Does that make America a Christian country? Not officially, maybe, and it never has been, but doesn't it kind of make it one unofficially? The main thing is . . . WHO CARES? I don't. In fact, it's fine with me. Look, folks, in case this little fun-fact has passed you by, the United States was started by Christians, thought up by Christians, and grown by Christians, and I can't speak for you, but I'm glad they did.

Personally, I like being The Other, the guy on the outside of the whole thing. Besides, every time I get too assimilated and start thinking I'm Alistair Cooke, Christmas comes along to remind me I'm probably closer to Sam Cooke. This keeps me honest, and I love the dissonance. As a kid I adored *The Nutcracker Suite,* and finally saw it onstage a few years ago. It was dandy, but as Tchaikovsky's gorgeous music unfolded, all I could think of was what my ancestral Russian brethren were doing on the night it premiered. Probably not dressing for the ballet, I'm guessing. As the wonderful comic Richard Morris used to say, "My grandfather had a very rare job for a Jew in Russia at the time. He was a liaison between the soldiers' horses and the ground."

Forget, for a minute, whether someone thinks America's a Christian country. Forget Christmas, or Snow Time Pagan Fest, or The Thing with the Gifts, or whatever you don't want to call it. How many people have to do a thing, or be a thing, or support a thing, or celebrate a thing, before we say they *are* the thing? Look: Men like to make love to women, right? Not *every single* man on Earth likes to make love to women, but I think it's still fair to say . . . Men like to make love to women. Yes? No? Kind of? Move on to the multiple choice?

I don't mind being silly—it's part of how I make a living—but sometimes we all get a little too silly and need to think about it. One of these days (soon, probably) a major American city is going to have a black mayor, a black police chief, a black fire chief, a black school superintendent, a black city attorney, and a 100 percent black city council at the same time—and yet, if they all come out in favor of something like vouchers, you can bet someone (and probably someone white) will step forward and call them racist. Now, that's not true, any more than having a host of black city leaders makes it a black city. It's just a city in America.

But some of my black friends call Atlanta a black city, because it has a large black population. (I've worked there at least twenty times, and the only characteristic I've come away with is that their late-night drinking population is huge. Or so I'm told.) Can my friends call it black? Why not? Is it an American city? Sure. Wait, though— what if 2 percent or 6 percent or 10 percent of the people who live there aren't American? Does calling it American offend them? If it's over a certain percentage of noncitizens, should we stop calling it American? Can the noncitizens call it something else if they want? Brussels, maybe? If so, there ought to be another set of stationery with the city seal. Even that might not reflect every group, though— so why not have ten types to choose from? Fifty?

In other words . . . How dumb are we prepared to be?

By the way, I've been saying "African-American" instead of "black" for a long time, but the last two paragraphs just used it too often, and I had to go back to "black." I mean, "African-American" has seven syllables. Trust me, if you reread the last half page and replace them all, you'll see what I mean.

I DON'T NEED ANYONE'S HELP KNOWING WHAT I AM, OR how to tell my kids what they are. When they ask, "Do we have Santa?" I say, No, that's for our Christian friends who celebrate Christmas. When they ask if we could put up lights, again I say, No, we don't do that, it's for our Christian friends. Same with a tree.

The point is, I can handle that, and I don't need anyone's help by forbidding people to mention it. And I don't need the White House to put anything on their lawn next to the Christmas tree. I'll take care of my own holidays just fine.

Besides, those questions give me the chance at home to point out that Jews are only a tiny group in the world, and not everyone is thrilled we're still hanging around banging out Marx Brothers— but that, on the other hand, America, Christian America, with all its mistakes past and present, has not only given us the best place in the world to live and grow, but was instrumental in creating Israel and helping it survive. That no matter what bones I have to pick with Christendom in the last two thousand years—and there are a few big ones—it wasn't a Christian Germany that murdered so many, it was the explicitly, exuberantly, specifically-required-to-formally-and-publicly-leave-Christianity-and-turn-your-back-on-it-or-you-couldn't-get-ahead Nazis who did; and that the biggest friend Israel has in the world today, by a huge margin, is Christian America.

So far, watching *It's a Wonderful Life* every December and *Easter Parade* every April, as we do, doesn't seem to have hurt the kids' baseball games. (Actually, we only watched *Easter Parade* once, and they were bored stiff by it. Truth to tell, it's not one of my favorites, but I figured it was kind of a classic. You know, Judy Garland and

Fred Astaire, and the colors and the costumes and the dancing. "On the avenue . . . Fifth Avenue . . ." Okay, I hate it, too.)

By the way, I don't give them big fire-hose blasts of this stuff. One of America's blessings is that we can allow all our children to be innocent about evil in the world for a while, and just open their Hot Wheels toys and watch Daddy grumble trying to put them together. And they're definitely too young to need to know that there's a group of folks in the world—a very, very big group, and a very, very motivated group—who would slaughter every Jew—and every American, and every Christian—in an instant if they could, and dance all day when they were done. And that group, whatever else they may be, doesn't celebrate Christmas. No, plenty of time to tell them that in the future. Hell, they know it anyway. It's the adults who don't know it.

So Merry Christmas to all Christians, this year and forever. As far as my family and I are concerned, you're free to say it all you want, wherever you want, whenever you want. I hope you will. In fact, I insist you do.

And to the folks who get all red in the face over that and want to pass laws that forbid it, okay, do what you've got to do, and Happy Hannu-Kwanz-Mas to you, too.

For myself, I believe this year I'm going to try to find a bar with an old jukebox and that great Bing Crosby's "White Christmas" on it.

"White Christmas," by the way, in case you didn't know, was one of thousands of hit songs written by a guy born in Russia named Isaac Baline, who moved here as a boy and changed his name to Irving Berlin, and was, in addition to many other things, a Jew.

Of course.

SEVEN

NEVER? EVER? FOREVER?

IT FINALLY HIT ME THAT GOD IS A WOMAN.

I don't know how long it's taken for that bulb to flicker on, but it's so obvious to me now, I feel like saying it again: God is a woman.

Of course, religious followers have prayed for thousands of years to "God the Father," and "Our Father our King," and "Master of the universe," and "Our Father, who art in Heaven." In fact, I'm one of them. (That's right, I'm one of the stupid people.) But I'm telling you, God is a woman.

And I hate the lame, politically correct sound of it (like someone using the word "Goddess") that makes any self-respecting crank want to throw up. It certainly has that effect on me.

I also know that the wisest scholars of the God-based religions would probably say that putting the Creator into any specific gender is pointless. But I insist, one more time, that God is a woman.

And the reason is, let's be honest:

If God were a man, adultery would not be a sin.

Thank you. Drive safely.

Think about it. If God were a man, the commandment would read, "Thou shalt not commit adultery—unless she's really hot. Then, what the heck."

That's not what it says, though, does it? If you remember your Bible—and I know you do—Moses went to Mount Sinai (the mountain, not the hospital) to get the Ten Commandments. Remember how long he was up there, though? Forty days and forty nights, right?

How long would it take *you* to write down the Ten Commandments? Ten minutes? (If that. Remember, they're short. Strict, but short.)

Then why'd it take him forty days? I'll tell you why. I'll bet you thirty-nine of those days were spent just hammering out adultery.

And why not? Why wouldn't they be? Isn't that the one you'd pick to ask about if you had a chance? The rest aren't that bad, really. Most of us don't want to kill anyone, or steal anything, or lie; most people like their parents. And I don't know anyone who wouldn't be willing to keep the Sabbath holy, as long as that included football. (The only other potential sticking point seems to be that no one knows what "graven" means.)

But being told, in the middle of the desert, for the first time in history, that there's no sex outside marriage? At a time when any guy with two nickels to rub together could have as much as he wanted? I'd expect a few raised hands on that one.

Wouldn't you? If there was one thing you could ask God, one cud you could chew, one nit you could pick, would you really waste it on "Why can't New York pizza be made in Los Angeles?" or "What is it with kids and poop jokes?" or "How about just a few cigarettes a day?"

Uh-uh. I know what I'd ask.

Well, I think that's what Moses did, too. So here we go, Moses and God, one-on-one, mano-a-God-o. And as the old comedians used to say, it might have gone something like this . . .

MOSES

Hello? Anyone there? Hel-lo? Always makes me wait, this guy. No ego-tripping there, nooo. Surprised he doesn't make me sit in a lower chair, too. No trees, sun shining straight down, very nice for an old man. Helloooooo . . .

Whoa, jeez, hi, there you are. No, just give me a second, here, catch my breath. You scared me, that's why. I don't think you know your own strength. Why do you always have to sneak up on a person? Can't you yell something in advance, let someone know you're on the way? I don't know, "Ready or not, here I come," or "Watch out, don't look up." What do I care? Blow a horn, whatever you like. All that lightning is fine for the new people, but I'm already with the program. You're preaching to the choir.

Anyway, I know everything's settled and we're all done here, but I just had one more question. Let's see, where did I put that . . . By the way, I thought about it again, and I completely agree—Commandments is the way to go with what we call them. I was tossing around Hints or Suggestions or Guidelines. Pointers, maybe. You know, the soft sell. But Commandments definitely has that "Because I'm God, that's why" feel to it, and a lot more pizzazz than The Ten Tips or something like that. And frankly I think we're going to need some of that punch when it's time for me to go back down and tell everyone. It certainly helped with circumcision, and that was no cakewalk, let me tell you. Scared the bejeezus out of them. "Bejeezus." I don't know, figure of speech.

Now where in the world did I . . . Oh, here it is. Isn't that silly? Right on the clipboard the whole time. Anyway, I just had one teeny thing on number eight . . . beg your pardon? Yup, adultery, that's the one. Say again?

Well, there's nothing wrong with it at all . . . per se. I love it. I just wanted to—No, no, it's absolutely clear. Couldn't be clearer. Hey, take it easy. Boy, it's like dealing with a writer. Look, it's clear as a bell, okay? I mean, Thou Shalt Not Commit Adultery. What's not clear about that? No flab, no gristle. Adultery, boom, you don't do it, and that's that.

What's that? Get to the point? All righty. (CLEARS THROAT) So, it's no women, ever? I mean, you get married, and that's it? I see. Okay, let me just get that down: No . . . women . . . ever. Hmmm. Yeah . . .

For how long? Well, I mean, how long do you expect— Certainly for the honeymoon, I'm guessing, that's only fair. But after that, are you picturing, I don't know, a few months, a year? How are you seeing this play out, timewise? Oh. Forever? Okay. Hang on: for . . . ever . . .

Meaning. . . ? Forever. I see. Got you. Uh-huh. For . . .

Can you define forever? Well, what I mean is, being as you're God and all, forever is probably very different for you than us. Sometimes here on earth things go on for a while, and it seems like forever. You know, like speeches at a benefit. Is that what you mean? Help me out here, and give me a ballpark. Doesn't have to be a bottom line; we can revisit it another time, like the Patriot Act. But what's your general take so far? I see. Uh-huh. For-ever. Okey-dokey. No exceptions. Never. Ever? Okay. Got it.

Now, does that include the road? The road. You never

heard of the road? Get outta here—really? The road. Traveling, out of town, away from home. On the hustings. Well, I don't know, let's say—and I'm just spitballing here—let's say some of the fellas are on patrol, out in the boonies, and maybe they have a high-ranking official with them, too, and—No, not *me*, I'm just saying, a high-ranking official. Aaron, Joshua, anyone. So they're far away, and some of the local gals come out to draw water from the well, and you know how it is, there's a little, "Hey, can I help you with that?" and "Where are you guys from?" and "Wow, nice camel," and "That's a funny question, but, no, I don't have more than ten brothers," and "Are you a model? You should be," and "Did you hear that, Ari? She's never met a circumcised man." The usual stuff, and one thing leads to another. The road. No? That's it, just no? Wait a second, give me a chance to develop my idea here.

What if they're not married? I said, what if the women aren't married? Same well, same girls, same water, but they're all single. No one's engaged, no serious relationships, nothing. Just a big bunch of happy, healthy, single . . . eager, mind you, not just willing. Dying to do it. And remember, as I said: unattached.

What guys? *Our* guys? What about them? Is who married? Oh, I see, gotcha, the women are single, and you want to know if the men are single, too. Good question. Well, now, first of all, as I said, they're on the road and away from home, okay? And let me just underline that, I don't mean the next tribe over, I mean far, far, far from—Excuse me but, please, you interrupt, and I lose my train of thought. What was the question again? Right, are the *men* married. By the way, if I may say, you've cut right to the heart of things once again, which is one of the reasons I love working with you. I mean, you've posed a very trenchant question there: *Are the men married . . .*

(CLEARS THROAT AGAIN) Well, yes, they are. In this hypothetical case. The girls aren't. The girls are single, but let's say, for argument's sake, at this particular time, the guys are . . . mrrd. Marrd. *Married.*

Hold your horses. I did not leave that out, okay? I was getting to it in my own way. No, excuse me, but I didn't gloss over anything. Have I ever glossed over anything with you? In fact, if I may, I think you've done a little glossing here and there yourself. Oh, really? What would you call parting the Red Sea, being up front? Sure, go ahead, everyone walk across, no worries, but you never bothered to mention it might still be a little moist, did you? You ever pick up twenty thousand old people slipping on fish? So let's please not bring up glossing things over. Then why don't we just say we've both got a few skeletons in the closet, and leave it at that. Fine. No, I said fine first. Okay, *you* said fine first. *Fine.*

Boy, it's like arguing with my wife sometimes with you. Look, these things are going to be around for a long time, so what's wrong with spending another two minutes on them now? I'm just trying to make sure we're on the same tablet.

Now, let me go back and recap so there's no misunderstanding: Guys on the road. Very far from home. Married, yes, but they're soldiers, remember, very brave, very loyal, do whatever you say, and never a complaint. No cracks about the food or the money or the sandals, either. And beautiful, single girls who really want to. No, huh? Who's surprised to hear that? Can I please finish before you jump in and cut me down? Jeez, Louise . . . Huh? *Jeez, Louise.* How do I know where these things come from?

Wait a minute, you just brought up a very good point: where things come from. Let's say their culture is very different from ours. Who? The girls at the well, who else? So their culture is very different, see, and maybe it's a big insult to the village if you turn them down. So *not* doing it with them causes not only a big diplomatic flap, but maybe a war. Oh, please, let's not be naïve, my Friend, shall we? There are lots of places like that, and we both know it. There are some very touchy people out there, and if not doing it starts a war, you could say our men having a fling with their women saves lives. And maybe spending time with our guys even helps convert the other village away from idol worship. You know, the kind of stuff you *really* hate. Saves lives, ends idol worship, and everyone's happy. I don't know, sounds pretty good. It's a win-win, if you ask me.

No? That's it, just . . . no? All right. Whew.

Hey, here's a thought. I—What? What's so funny? Me? *I'm* funny? How am I funny? You mean, like a clown? I *amuse* you? No, no, I'm just glad you're enjoying yourself so much. That's why we're all here.

Okay, let's say we have to negotiate a big treaty with a very tough tribe, and naturally we send one of our top guys—No, not *me*, I'm just saying, a top guy. Again with the top guy. . . .

So let's say this top guy, whoever he is, concludes the deal—very successfully, by the way, as always, very good for you, One God and all that—and they all go downstairs to the bar afterward, and he feels like cutting loose a bit and celebrating. Have a couple. Why not, right? And maybe there's a woman in there—I don't know, newly divorced, say, and feeling a little low about herself, and could really use some attention to help put her self-image back together. So this might be great for her. And the guy's like, Hey, I don't know what your husband's problem is, but you are one hot lady, and she's like, Wow, really? And he's like, No, I mean it, and she's like, You're so sweet, and he's like, No, you are, and she's like, It feels like I've known you a long time, and he's like, Yeah, me too. And they've both had a few, and, you know, maybe a stroll upstairs would be just what the doctor ordered. Just one night, by the way, that's it—never see each other again, it's there and it's gone, hello, goodbye, bang, boom. And it had a very positive, healthy effect for both of them.

Ooh, wait, wait a second, you could even wipe the memory of it out, too. The whole memory, so he doesn't even get to tell his friends. How about that? You can't ask for more than that. So, it's good for her, good for him, but no memory, and it's like it never happened. What do you say? No, huh? Just no. Okay, I'm with you: nothing, no women, on the road, off the road, no one, ever.

What about actors? Actors. I'm just asking. *Actors.* Oh, stop, they do *not* all think they're you already. Some, maybe, but you find that in every profession, don't you think? Is that so? You ever hang out with a surgeon? You're darn right I'm right. And let's not even start with lawyers and senators. Do I want to hear what? (SIGHS) Sure, why not? Go ahead.

Uh-huh. Uh-huh. Uh-huh. Wait, so the lawyer goes to Heaven and gets the nicest room, yeah. . . . Uh-huh. Uh-huh. Oh, that's great. Ha-ha-ha-ha-ha-ha. Funny. That's a good one. "We almost never get lawyers." I love that one. Actually, you did, but it gets better every time. No, really. And you know, it's never the joke, anyway, it's the guy who tells it. "Never get lawyers." Good one.

Look, I think I can see the handwriting on the wall here, but I've got one more question, okay? Handwriting on the wall. I don't know, just picked it up somewhere.

Anyway, are there any extraordinary circumstances that would make a difference in your mind on this adultery thing? Something we might call an Act of God clause. I don't know, something crazy, long odds, never going to happen.

Well, what about twins? It's not something that would come up a lot, but it's always in a fella's head—you put it there, so I'm not telling you something you don't know—but just the possibility, see, just that crazy chance would give everyone something to shoot for. Or never mind twins. Just two at once. Any two. How about that? You can't pass that up, am I right? No one could. Two at once, come on. Make an exception if a guy has a shot at two women, and if that's the only way out. They'd all be happy with that, I know they will. Just . . . give them that hope. Please. Be a regular guy for once. How about it? An asterisk and a little clause at the bottom: "Twins or better, go ahead. Knock yourself out." How about it?

What do you mean you can't do it? It's your rules, you're the guy. You can do anything you want.

All right, then—three. Come on, *triplets*. Who's ever going to hit that? And only once the kids are out of the house, like a prize at the end of the guy's life. How about that? Not around here . . . a thousand miles. Make it ten thousand, what do I care? Only blondes, then. We never see them anyway.

All right, four, then. *Five.* SIX.

"It's too likely?" Are you crazy? In what universe is that ever gonna happen? *When in the world is an old man ever going to wind up with six blondes who look exactly alike?*

(THE OLD PROPHET SITS DOWN ON A ROCK SHAKING HIS HEAD.)

MOSES (cont'd)

Well, that's it. I thought there might be some wiggle room here, but . . . What's the big deal on this one? We'll never understand women, but they'll never understand us either. The one thing everyone wants from the second he wants it, and you say no. You point at every one of us and say, "That's right, buddy, you. Never again will you slip another toga off a new shoulder. Never, ever, forever." That's right, I said us. Yes, me, too. Here we go again. I'm glad you think it's funny. Well, maybe you haven't heard lately, but six hundred's the new four hundred.

It hurts the wife? I know that. What am I, an idiot? That's why I said far away, so no one ever knows. They always know? On some level they always know? Oh, come on, no they don't. They do? Really? And the kids always know? No, they don't. On some level they do? Really? And you. Yeah, you'd know. And I'd know. Okay, okay.

Boy, the others are more obvious, but this one is . . . I don't know, it's deep. It's just deep.

I'm sorry. Look at that, I'm apologizing to you, too, just like—

Hey, wait a minute. You're not a woman, are you? Well, I

just always assumed, I guess, but a lot of things fall into place if you're—What? Oh, hold on.

(HE LOOKS AROUND THE GROUND AND STOMPS A FOOT.)

MOSES (cont'd)

Yeah, I got him. I said I got him, didn't I? If I said I got him, I got him. Here, look. All right, don't look. Gee. You know, considering you're the one who invented spiders, you're awfully afraid of them.

That's it, I'm heading down. Yes, I promise I'll check the rest of the path. Don't I always? You know, I hate to end on an argument here, but if you hate insects so much, why don't you do it? I don't know, zap 'em out. Point your finger, wiggle your nose, whatever you do. Then I don't have to chase the bees, and the June bugs, and the spiders, and every other damn thing whenever I come over.

Excuse me, but I hate it when the webs get on my face, too, all right? Who doesn't hate the webs? I just don't understand when it became my job to—Oh, forget it. Every time. Every time with the bugs.

(HE GOES A FEW STEPS, TURNS AROUND, AND SHOUTS . . .)

MOSES (cont'd)

Hey, just for the record, if I'm ever on a desert island with Rosanna Arquette, we're just doing it, and I don't care what

[99]

happens, okay? I get on that island, and all bets are off. You understand? Hey. I know you hear me, so don't pretend you don't.

Oh, there you are. At least we're both laughing at the same thing. I know it's never going to happen. What? It is? Really? It's okay? All right, just a desert island, and just Rosanna Arquette. I can live with that. That's great! I know it's stupid, but, yeah, it makes me feel better. Okay, just a desert island, and just Rosanna Arquette. Beautiful.

(HE STARTS DOWN BUT TURNS BACK.)

MOSES (cont'd)

How about Vegas? No, I'm just saying, you said the desert, but Vegas is in the desert, so I'm just asking. Just the island? Got you.

Does it have a hotel?

EIGHT

GODFATHER III: THE QUICKENING

I SAW *GODFATHER III* AGAIN THE OTHER NIGHT, AND IT'S still terrible.

I always see it. It's got to be, I don't know, dozens of times already. Twenty-five, thirty, forty times. I watch it whenever it's on, and it's on a lot. And for the life of me, I don't know why since, as I just said—and as I'm sure you know—it's terrible.

I've seen it far more than the first two put together; twice as much, five times as much. This puzzles me, too, because *The Godfather* and *Godfather II* belong in the smallest group of the greatest movies ever made, spectacular and gripping art in every sense. They don't interest me, though, and I don't watch them. It's the third one I can't keep my eyes off of, the one that's unremittingly bad.

Please understand that each time I see it I don't want to. There's no pleasure in the act, perverse or otherwise, only sadness and detachment. I feel stupid when I finally turn the set off, like yet another vital part of my life has been stolen. Worse yet, I know all this beforehand with perfect certainty, and that it will all occur in the same order.

But I do it. I watch it every time. Not like a train wreck, either. I don't want to see train wrecks; I don't watch accidents on the side of the road; I won't listen to serial killers luxuriate over their confessions in court; I despise all voyeuristic leering at tragedy or evil, and try to avoid giving it one more entry into the temporal world through my eyes.

I'll tell you what it is, though, and maybe you'll know what I mean. It's not that I want to be annoyed and disappointed yet again. It's that whenever I'm flipping around and *Godfather III* comes on, I think to myself, "Wait a minute. It can't be *this* bad. I must be watching it wrong. All those other times were a fluke. That's it. It's me. All I have to do is give it another try, and then this time it'll be terrific."

So I do. And, of course, as I walk slowly upstairs turning the lights out afterward, I think, every single time, "Nope, I was right. It's awful. Oh, well . . . maybe next time."

We're drawn to it like bugs to a zapper ("No, Hermie, stop! Don't go into the blue light!") The good news is that if you've been zapped by it over the years, I have an idea you might find interesting. I've thought of a way to—believe it or not—fix it. That's right, I have a way to fix *Godfather III*. But first . . .

AS HINTED AT IN THE TITLE OF THIS CHAPTER, I CALL every movie sequel *The Quickening*. I don't know why I love it so much, but I do.

I've crowbarred *The Quickening* into conversation and writing every chance I get since I first saw it a few years back on a poster for the sequel to *Highlander,* which was a pretty good goofy movie, as far as pretty good goofy movies go. The first one, starring Christopher

Lambert and a bunch of hardy and hearty Scottish pagans (are there any other kind?) is loaded with magic and fighting and immortality, along with lots of giant, thick, shining, glistening, dripping, always-at-the-ready swords. (Hmm, I wonder what the root of that image is?)

In case you missed the original *Highlander,* the always-hacking-anyone-with-a-different-kilt-to-pieces Scots suspiciously toss Lambert out on his ear one day when his battle wounds magically heal. (Apparently, being the only one in the village with a French accent from birth never raised any eyebrows, but there you are.) The movie was profitable and bred another—the one called, yes, *Highlander II: The Quickening.* I didn't know what it meant then, and I still don't.

Come to think of it, I do. It meant the studio didn't have the nerve to call it *Highlander II: What Did You Expect?*

Of course, every so often a sequel is just as nifty as, or even a hair better than, the original. *Godfather II* is an example of this, and so is—actually, that's the only one, isn't it? Wait, no, it's not. I think *Kill Bill: Volume I and Volume II* are both neat, gripping, original, and super-cool movies, and that wasn't the first time I left a theater thinking, boy, that Tarantino is an interesting cat.

For the most part, though, as you know, sequels drop in quality like a blind man off a cliff, and that's probably why for years I've been adding those two silly words: *Rambo II: The Quickening; Police Academy IX: The Quickening; Chucky XII: The Quickening.* (Some of these franchises have higher numbers than Pope Johns or Ptolemys.)

Incidentally, to stave off the trivia tsunami of rage I sense rising among that very special 1 percent of you, let me say now that yes, I know, technically, *Rambo II* was actually called *Rambo: First Blood, Part II,* but deconstructing that would take a chapter in itself, and leave us all lunging for a bottle. Hold on. Not a bad idea, that. Shall we? Okay, let's all grab a quick one and meet back in five.

Ah, much better. Additionally, *The Quickening* can be used in all sorts of other ways, like describing a friend's second marriage (although probably not to his face), or a senator you don't like who's been reelected (although probably not to his face, either). For that matter, wouldn't it be nice if particularly brutal institutions came with subtitles of their own? *Sudan*: *The Final Chapter*, for example. Since that won't be happening anytime soon, we'll just have to keep noticing their little peccadilloes and folksy charm ourselves.

I'M NOT A SEQUEL SNOB, BY THE WAY—AND NOT JUST because I've been in a few myself. (Well, not entirely.) To be perfectly honest, I would've taken a part in *Death Wish V* in a second, or any other movie, no matter how cheesy, provided it gave me a good role and a chance to hit the ball. As you know, good character actors show up all the time in bad movies, because actors, like everyone else, get used to eating. Everyone runs his career differently, but I've always felt that in the world of character acting, which I define as anyone in the picture not kissing Renee Zellweger, the best approach is to be as good as you can, as often as you can. Or, as one of my agents, Leigh Brillstein, used to say, "You don't want to be the funniest guy in your own living room."

The concept of sequels never bothered me anyway, and one reason is that Shakespeare used them all the time. After all, there would never have been a *Henry IV, Part II* if *Henry IV, Part I* hadn't made money, and the only reason there was a *Henry V* was that *Henry IV, Part II* made money. The same goes for *Henry VI, Part I, Part II, Part III, Part. . . .* You get the point.

Show Biz has always been, at least in part, a commercial enterprise, and sometimes that's not such a dirty word, especially if you're the one getting the billion-dollar check. "Oh, you like Falstaff?" reasoned The Bard. "Fine with me. Here he comes again." Once more unto the breach, indeed.

(N.B. For those who went to public schools after 1980, William Shakespeare was a playwright and poet many years ago in a very bad place called England, and, though sexist, racist, xenophobic, nationalistic, unilateral, and fascist, he used to be considered, by isolated pockets of other awful people, as a fair-to-middling writer. Still, it's probably best never to say his name again. And, while we've paused for useless arcana, "N.B." stands for *nota bene,* which means "Note this well." It's Latin, which, I know, is just another offensive language used by horrible men. Like Ovid. Latin, though, is also the root of the Romance languages, one of which you're reading. Not romance as in Brad and Angelina, but—oh, skip it.)

The fact that entertainment is profitable doesn't, by definition, make it unworthy. Lots of movies today may stink—in fact, let's leave it there: lots of movies today stink. The problem, though, isn't the money that comes out, it's the money that goes in.

Money can't make stupid people smart, but it often makes smart people stupid. Given the choice today between making one movie for a hundred and fifty million dollars, or ten movies for fifteen million dollars each, every executive in Hollywood will make one movie for a hundred and fifty million. This is because the goal is not making good movies, but being able to strut into a restaurant and have everyone think you're a really powerful guy. (We've changed so much since cave days, haven't we?)

Oh, and they're wrong. It's anti-art. If, instead, you gave ten writer-directors fifteen million dollars each and sent them off to tell their stories, it certainly wouldn't guarantee anything, but you'd be far more likely to have at least a handful of them turn out to be a

Sideways, or *Remains of the Day,* or *House of Games,* or *Animal House,* wouldn't you?

But that's not what most people like to do. Most people like to spend money.

Sadly (for us, for you, for me—for movie fans), when a movie is made for a hundred and fifty, or a hundred and eighty, or two hundred million dollars, you know as well as I do that dollars to donuts (whatever that means) it will come out overproduced, overwrought, overstarred, overwritten, overdirected, overdesigned, overlit, over made-up, over-dressed, and over-everythinged. At best, it'll be okay. More likely, it'll stink. You'll still go see it, because it's either that or *Scooby Two: The Quickening,* or *Knife in the Eye IV: The Sickening.* Any way you slice it, after twelve bucks a ticket, times-two-times-three-times-eight for popcorn and soda and parking and a sitter, you'll wind up walking out of the theater like an old cartoon character whose head morphs into a giant lollipop that says "Sucker."

Charlie Chaplin didn't spend hours and days and weeks on "authentic" backgrounds for his movies. He spent hours and days and weeks trying to do something funny. I can't stand movies where the camera dotes endlessly on the elaborate décor of the daughter's bedroom, and the wallpaper and the vases in the hall, and the perfectly designed shirts and ties, and the excruciatingly pressed suits on the gangsters. Great directors don't shoot scenes so their other director friends can lean over in screening rooms and say, "Beautiful shot there with the sun right between the houses, and the birds going by exactly over the train. It's amazing how you timed it all when the car jumped the sidewalk as the building collapsed. Must've taken weeks." Great directors try to get their actors to move the audience. And the audience desperately wants to be moved. That's why they come, and that's what they're looking for: laughing and crying. In case we've forgotten—and we have—that's the point of the whole exercise. Not the hundred thousand obviously fake "soldiers" drawn in by computer.

Every time I read about a star who worked out with a team of trainers nine hours a day for a year to have the right look for a role, I think, You know, maybe if you'd spent a couple of those weeks on the accent, the movie wouldn't have stunk.

This tin ear and lunatic spending in Hollywood goes on and on, over and over in the executive corps, until the guy above you finally realizes you're an idiot, and you get fired. Since you really are an idiot, the only way out is to beat the guy above you to the punch, and convince everyone above *him* that he's an idiot first. Since he is, this isn't that hard. Then you can move up and take *his* job. At the same time, of course, you'll get to pick someone for the old job you just left. Naturally, you'll want someone you can trust—and, in this case, "someone you can trust" means someone who's no better or smarter or more talented than you, but who wants to go along and get along and not make waves, and will be loyal enough not to try to assassinate you the same way you just assassinated the guy before you. At least not right away.

Remember, none of this gets any movies or television shows made, but that's not the point. As my friend, the writer Jim Vallely, observes, "The point of the job is not to make something good, or to make anything at all. The point of the job . . . is to *keep* the job."

All this must sound at least a little familiar to you, because whatever business you're in, your bosses are dumb, too, aren't they? They may not know it, but that's okay, because you do, right? Everyone above you is stupid, and below you, too. Guess who that leaves? That's right, look around. There's no one else in the room, is there? And let's be honest, since you're no great shakes either, this means that starting with you, everyone, at every level, in every organization in the world, is a moron.

Thankfully, of course, now that women have finally emerged in far stronger numbers in government, entertainment, corporations, and universities, things in this regard have changed quite a bit: The pool of idiots has doubled.

I don't know about you, but I'm more or less constantly agape that civilization moves forward at all; but it does. Every so often there's an Aristotle, or a Bach, or a John Paul II (fill in your own favorite men and women), and we all get dragged along in their slipstream for a while as they reach for the stars. But on a day-to-day level—and not even worrying about the places where the guys are out-and-out crooks—the most successful stewards of the biggest institutions in America are turnipheads. You know it, and I know it. On some level, even they know it.

Next time you're flying one of those giant, old-school national airlines that are losing money like a drunk at the track, look in the front of the complimentary magazine in the seat pocket at the little picture they always have of the president of the airline. Got it open to the right page? Yeah, the guy in the suit, smiling. Okay, look at that face. Closely.

Now: Is that a schmuck, or is that a schmuck? No offense (of course not—why would anyone take offense at that?), but, you know, that guy wasn't picked because he has any idea at all about how to run an airline. He got the job because the other empty vessels who picked him think he'll sit there quietly with the same vacant smile until they can all retire. And *their* pensions can't be stolen by anyone above them, can they?

MOVIES MAY NOT HAVE TO BE GOOD TO HAVE SEQUELS, but they do have to make dough.

Entertainment is very personal. There will always be some

movies you or I like so much (and against all prevailing opinion) that they still couldn't make enough of them to suit us.

I like all the *Star Trek* movies, even the ones everyone said stunk. I dig Shatner's Kirk above all the other captains, and always have, and that's that. It's possible, of course, to like many different kinds of movies at the same time. You can enjoy both *Octopussy* and *Howard's End*, just not necessarily on a double-bill; although, come to think of it, those two titles go together pretty well. (Or, more precisely, don't.)

Well, I like the *Star Trek*s. I don't care how old they are or who got killed, they could make another ten and I'd see every one. I don't care if Chekhov's in a wheelchair, or Sulu can't lift his sword (or goes back to being straight, or decides he only likes Vulcans), or Uhura looks like Moms Mabley. If it were up to me, I'd make them forever and, not incidentally, give the cast work. These days, you know, you could even bring back Scotty and Bones: James Doohan and DeForest Kelley may have passed away, but with today's computer graphics they're just a few clicks away. Hell, they could stitch two or three of the old TV episodes together and just call it a movie, and I'd probably go see that.

On the other hand, I have no particular interest in the last few *Star Wars* episodes, but millions of people do, and what's wrong with that? Good luck, and God bless, and I hope they keep coming for you.

Every so often there's even a movie where you want them to make a sequel, you *need* them to make a sequel, but none ever comes. It's a shame when that happens (or, rather, doesn't); it's like losing the chance to see friends you miss, in a setting that can never be real again without them.

Silverado was such a movie for me. Who knows why that didn't happen: time or schedules, money or desire. But every time Kevin

Costner and Scott Glenn ride off into the sunset, and Costner turns around to shout, "We'll be back!" I think, "Oh, fellas, I wish you had."

WHICH BRINGS US BACK TO *GODFATHER III*, A MOVIE I've come to think of as, "Oh, fellas, I wish you *hadn't*."

It has such a weird pull to it, like watching the tape of two old-time trains slamming into each other, over and over, and each time thinking, "Maybe this time they don't crash?"

Oh, but they do. As good as the first two were, that's how bad the third one is. It's like building another Washington Monument next to the original, but straight down into the ground. Remember the guy who plays the assassin dressed as the priest at the end? I don't even think it was in the script for him to shoot the daughter. I think he just snapped and screamed, "I'm a disappointed fan."

By the way, this has nothing to do with Sofia Coppola, who caught much of the flak when the movie was first released. She's doing just fine, in case you hadn't noticed, and not just because of her Academy Award. She's a fine writer-director, and so, of course, is her dad. They may be the most talented family in Hollywood, not counting the Olsen twins. But casting your daughter in that role wasn't love, Francis. I love my sons, but I wouldn't toss them out on the field to pitch in the World Series, or take the pole position at Indy. And not just because they're seven and ten.

It wasn't her, though. It was everything.

The rub on this will never go away, because art never goes away—bad or good. *Godfather III* didn't just blow a franchise. Who cares about a franchise? It hurt those who cared about it. It hurt those who needed it to be wonderful. It hurt everyone transported by great storytelling. Moviegoers can take an endless stream of stinkers in their lives, but the beloved ones, the magnificent ones, the truly great ones destroy us when they're awful. That's why it still tears. If movies are art—and they are—the worst disappointments stick with us like a piece of inoperable shrapnel: forever.

And *Godfather III* is not only inoperable, it's still ticking.

The movie has all the right pieces, but they don't fit. It's like watching a parallel universe where things look similar but nothing is good. This is a lesson about life as well as movies: Sometimes even Babe Ruth struck out. *Godfather III* had the best actors, the best writers, the best director, the best setting, characters, stories, fan base, money, everything. From time to time, we all just forget how hard it is to hit a baseball.

The real drag is, it's not even bad enough to be good-bad.

You know what good-bad is—the kind of movie that's so bad it's fabulous. So stupendously terrible it becomes hysterical. *Plan 9 from Outer Space* is the nonpareil, the gold medal winner of "brilliantly bad," but in recent years a couple of new outrageous stinkers, *Showgirls* and *Glitter,* have crept up on Ed Wood's magnum opus. One woman at work tells me she's been to *Glitter* parties where people dress up like Mariah Carey in different scenes, and act it out, like *The Rocky Horror Picture Show.* (Is that thing still playing somewhere? Probably—if only in places like Shanghai and Kurdistan, where people love it for real, without irony.)

Godfather III is NOT one of these. It's as bad as anything can be without crossing the line into so-bad-it's-fun. It goes right up to the line and stops, and stays there, and pitches a tent and plants a flag.

But don't worry, because, as I said before, I've figured out how to set things right. I know how to bring back the Corleones, give us the movie we wanted, and fix *Godfather III.* Here's how:

Make it again.

Hold on. Don't sputter. That's right, I said it: Make *Godfather III* again. One more time. Pretend it didn't happen, and try again.

You and I wouldn't care, would we? Just the opposite. We'd be thrilled. We all need the Corleone family to continue in the American storybook as mythic, iconic art, and the only way that's going to happen is if they call a do-over, take a Mulligan, and make it again. Think about it. There's precedent. It's happened before in American cultural life. When, you say? Name one, you say? Glad to.

New Coke.

Remember New Coke? Of course you do. It was a weird couple of months, but so what? They saw what they'd done, and went back to Coke, and pretended it never happened. And so did we.

Not right away, of course. First they tried to convince us with testing, remember? "But all the blindfolded people like New Coke better." Uh-uh. Then they tried to placate us by keeping the new one and flogging it, but bringing the old one back and calling it Classic Coke. "Now you can get both!" Thank you, no. The wrongness touched something in all of us. It wasn't just a soft drink at stake—it was the order of the universe.

Then a very rare thing happened in corporate America, or any other part of the world throughout history. They realized they were wrong, and that there's no shame in it; and they picked everything up and went back to where they were before.

Americans, you know, will always forgive someone who apologizes.

And the whole thing drifted off like a smoke ring. They went back to Coke, and that was that. Brilliant. If you don't remember New Coke, or were too young, that actually proves the point: It's as if it never happened, like a family that never mentions the crazy aunt in the attic. "We won't say anything if you don't. Come on, everyone, let's all have an icy cold Coke and pretend nothing happened." And they did, and we did.

So how hard would it be to do the same thing with *Godfather*

III? Take it off the shelves of every Blockbuster in the middle of the night, get some tech-wizard busy wiping out every Internet site, and pretend nothing happened. The CIA may not be very good at figuring out who's killing us, but sneaking in and grabbing every *Godfather III* in the world? They could handle that. Might be right up their alley.

Look, someone has to know Coppola. Tell him everyone makes mistakes, that he's a great artist (which is true), that we love him (which is also true), and we'll forget the whole thing if he makes another one. He can call it *Godfather IV* if he wants, or *3½,* or *8½,* or *9½ Weeks.* (Wait, not that one. That's going in the wrong direction. Another movie that's not bad enough for good-bad, and not dirty enough for porn.) Tell him he gets to start again, with any story he wants. Tell him we *need* him to start again. And—dare I say it?— make him an offer he can't refuse.

With three conditions (there are always conditions):

1. Please make it good this time.
2. Please, please, *please* make it good this time.
3. Don't use anything from the old one.

Here's what I mean by number 3: We need Al Pacino back. He's old enough now to play Don Corleone at the same age Brando did. He's great, and that alone will make the whole thing worth the trouble.

I know what you're thinking: "Look, idiot, don't you remember? Pacino's dead. Michael *died* at the end. He got sicker and sicker, and probably lost his mind as well, and slid off the chair in the sun, and there was no one there to find him. Just like his father."

No, he didn't.

"Yes, he did."

Um, no, he didn't.

"Yes, Larry, he did."

You don't get it. He couldn't have, because . . . none of that happened. He never got sick, and he didn't die. Because there's no *Godfather III*. See?

Remember: New Coke.

In fact, let's not even say *Godfather III* anymore. We won't even mention it. If it ever has to come up again, we'll call it *The Thing Whose Name Must Never Be Said*. Okay? Okay.

Now. Just a few more suggestions, and we'll be all set.

As long as everything's up for grabs, this time around what do you say we skip the Vatican plot line? It more or less didn't work at all. I'm sure it sounded great around the table and all, but I think we can let it go.

So Michael's back, and we lose the Vatican. Good. We're making progress here.

Talia Shire's always good; she's in, too. Too many black outfits, but never mind. Oh, yeah, and Andy Garcia was fabulous. He's perfect for the part. Cool, strong, violent, just right. Definitely bring him back. A little older now, but who cares? Remember, you just reintroduce the character like nothing happened. "Hey, everybody, look! It's Sonny's boy, Vincent! He's a grandfather now. Been running the mob for us in Hong Kong for thirty-two years, but came back just in time to take the big picture in the beginning."

And while we're on the subject, Eli Wallach is one of the greatest actors in film history, but *will you please pay Robert Duvall whatever he wants and get him back?*

Sheesh. How in the world do you make a *Godfather* movie without Duvall? Whose bright idea was that? If he's booked up, *wait* six months. It'll be worth it. And please, *please* don't tell me that George

Hamilton was brought in to fill the same role. I actually dig Hamilton, going back to *Home from the Hill*, with Robert Mitchum, but no; oh, no; oh-no-you-don't.

What else? Oh, yeah, the son being an opera singer didn't work, either. If that's what you want, just go all the way and make him gay. That should provide some interesting tension in a mafia family, although *The Sopranos* probably got most of the good stuff out of that already.

You need the great Diane Keaton, too. But you've got to do better by her than you did in . . . *The Thing Whose Name Must Never Be Said*.

"Michael, Anthony is having his big-time, international opera debut and wants you to be there."

"Wow, Kay, where's that? Paris, London, Moscow?"

"Oh, no. Those places are pretty good, too, but our son is starring in the hub of classical music in Europe . . . Sicily!"

"Gee, what a coincidence. I have to be there anyway to get killed. When's opening night?"

"The first weekend my heavyset, new, not-at-all-Italian husband can't make it. You know, so I have to be there all alone at the ancestral source of your immense power, drinking thick red wine on very warm days, and you and I can be forced to reconnect."

You could hear eyeballs rolling all across America.

THE WHOLE THING WASN'T EVEN COPPOLA'S FAULT, YOU know, in a larger sense. Not his, not hers, not theirs. It's ours. The blame belongs to us, the American audience. Because for a long time now—and more so every year—we're so guilt-ridden we can't allow our myths to reflect sorrow felt from a position of strength. Our artists feel this self-hatred, too, and they give us what we want:

weakness. "I'm bad," they cry, "We're bad, our history's bad, and none of us should ever win. Thank you, sir, may I have another?"

Troubled characters can make for thrilling stories, but only as long as the protagonists return to strength. We won't admit this, but sometimes we need our heroes to be awful and win. We don't want the Corleones to be chastened by their immorality, we want them to use it even more extravagantly, to move confidently through their challenges and conquer the world. We ourselves would never act that way, of course, but we like to see *them* do it. We want to see them do it. We need to see them do it.

We don't want Michael Corleone to learn his life lessons. We don't want him to look at Diane Keaton with doe-eyes and say, "Gee, honey, I'm sorry. I was wrong. Can you ever forgive me?"

We want him to slam another door in her face.

We don't want him to get sick, lose his abilities, seek forgiveness, give up his power, and die. We want him to get sick, lose his abilities, seek forgiveness, give up his power . . . *and fight back. One more time. And win.*

We want ominous music to throb, and his eye to get fierce—not Pacino's, you understand: *Michael's.* Pacino is not what's real to us, *Michael* is real—and we want him to make a plan and carry it out, no matter how horrible; triumphant in his world, more and more, worse and worse, unopposed and honored—

And *then* leave him empty and alone at the end staring out at a lake. Or a tree, or a wall, or a TV. Not crazy. Perfectly aware. Not dead. Perfectly well. Not vanquished. Victorious.

But without self. Without love. Without hope. Without God.

Until the next time. When it all happens again. *Made it, Ma. Top of the world.*

That's what I want. I want my Godfather back. I want ten more of them.

THIS LIMPNESS INFECTS AMERICAN ART AT THE HIGH-est levels, and movies—the greatest delivery vehicle of grand themes in human history—have lost their way. We're adrift at sea, no breeze or motion to carry us on. And it is we who have stopped the wind.

I don't want my Wyatt Earps to be sensitive and say, "You don't ever want to know what it's like to kill a man. You don't ever want to know!" *You and I* are the ones who don't ever want to know what it's like to kill a man. Not Wyatt Earp. Kurt Russell was a great Earp—but only when he was killing people with Val Kilmer, not when he was worried about the meaning of it all.

I don't need to hear how conflicted Earp is, or see six hours of backstory about the death of his one true love and why he's closed off emotionally, or see all the brothers' wives get together and say, "*Ooh,* you're a hard man, Wyatt." I don't need to be told that, Gee, maybe they could've walked away from the fight and talked the whole thing out.

It's worse than boring. It's trite.

For a truly great Wyatt Earp, check out *My Darling Clementine* one of these days, with Henry Fonda, Walter Brennan, and Victor Mature (a far better actor than he thought he was, and someone who didn't have to lose eighty pounds to be Doc Holliday).

God save us from art that wrings its hands.

The Alamo wasn't a relativistic swamp of tortured fops and ego-maniacs. For art's sake? It was a lean, mythic sacrifice, two hundred heroes against five thousand Mexican soldiers without choice or mercy—which, incidentally, is something every schoolboy knew forty years ago anyway. A movie that doesn't understand this has set out to be terrible before the first frame is shot. And will achieve its goal.

I want King Arthur to be King Arthur; I don't need him to "learn" and "understand" that his beautiful young girlfriend in the perfectly sensible forest-leather bustier is just as good with a sword as he is, so we can have "Take Your Daughters to Camelot Day." I don't need Robin Hood to say, "Golly, Marian, you're strong, too, and smarter than me!" If one more skinny nineteen-year-old Brit actress stands legs spread with a tough look on a billboard in her high-heeled boots, I'm going to go get a crossbow myself. (For a great King Arthur, see *Excalibur*, for chivalry, try *Ivanhoe*, with Robert Taylor, Elizabeth Taylor, and the always wonderful George Sanders; and if you haven't seen Errol Flynn's *Robin Hood*, you have no business saying you love movies. All of these are nearly perfect myth-as-truth-as-parable art.)

There are plenty of ways to have true female warrior-heroes in great movies, and anyone who says there aren't is a fool. Jodie Foster was one, in *Silence of the Lambs*, and Uma Thurman was another, in those *Kill Bill* movies. Greer Garson was, too, in *Mrs. Miniver*, but from a different time with different premises. The question of whether or not someone is heroic in a given story depends on how she's made, and what she's asked to do.

And how she's dressed.

I'm like any other man, and I'll always be drawn to cleavage, but if that's what you're selling, you can't have heroism as well. Beauty, always, sexiness, great, but nudity can't coexist with real drama (or comedy). All the women I mentioned above are gorgeous and sexy, but you can't have soft, medium, or hardboiled-porn with a real heroine. I'm not a prude—I've seen both—but movies are either erotica or stories. Maybe you can think of one that blends them, but I can't.

There's always someone being interviewed at a film festival saying, "I wanted to make a porn movie that was also a great movie with a great plot." This is an idiot.

Look, the instant the heroine's blouse is ripped off in a movie, and she's naked, and her hands are tied over her head in a dungeon, you've left the part of the brain that reaches for the stars, and entered the part that reaches . . . a little lower. Adolescence and vulgarity—two words that will certainly be on my family crest, if I ever get one (and a great toast, if you add exclamation points)—have an important place in entertainment and show business, and that's fine. But you can't turn around and call it heroic art.

Plus, these movies reflect an unintended and unnoticed irony. I mean, come on, everyone, please: savage, voracious, scantily clad, English women with leather push-up bras? These aren't feminist icons. They're letters to *Penthouse*.

All this applies to nonfiction as well. I don't want revisionist stories of Lincoln, or Patton, or MacArthur, or Roosevelt, or Churchill, or Washington, or any of them. "But the Alamo was a lot more than just a brave last stand." No, it wasn't, you pinhead. The truth may sometimes be gray, but art isn't, and when it tries to be, it teaches neither history nor morality. Worse, it doesn't entertain. And it's no fun. The John Wayne *Alamo* is a little knuckleheaded, but it's fun.

Keep your troubled souls, and give us back our heroes.

WAKE UP, FOLKS. A CULTURE THAT TURNS ITS HEROES into villains isn't asking the world for forgiveness, it's asking for help holding the sword while we run on it. Have we emasculated our storytellers as much as ourselves?

It was great storytelling to keep the Bat Signal flashing in the sky in the Batman movies—even though, if you think about it, it was pointless and redundant in an age of instant communication. But it was an important metaphor. There's nothing heroic about calling him up on the cell phone. "I'm sorry, Commissioner, one sec. I've got another call coming in—I think Robin needs a lift home. He's the designated driver. After that I'll be right over. Oh, and tell Chief O'Hara I got his e-mail."

The Bat Signal in a dark sky is poetic and timeless; that's why it's Art. It's a primal call for someone to save us in a dark world. Lose the Bat Signal, and you lose that need and that scream. Lose the Bat Signal, and you lose that Art.

The loss of heroic Americana doesn't just concern movies. It's not only *The Godfather* that needs to turn around and go back to what made it great. There's broken but fixable art everywhere in American culture if we'll just look for it. For instance . . .

Why don't we start making '57 Chevys again?

Seriously. Cars today are reliable, but they've got the soul of a vat of paste. They move us without moving us, and can't hold our interest more than three blocks after driving off the lot. Practicality is fine, but we used to have that and style, too. And they blended together perfectly in the '57 Chevy—the coolest, best-designed, most confident, flashiest (yet dignified) car ever made.

So why don't we make them again? Those plans have got to be sitting on a shelf somewhere, right? Update them for safety, and roll 'em out.

Think about it. Who wouldn't jump at the chance to buy a brand-new '57 Chevy? I would. You would. We all would. There wouldn't be one unemployed man or woman in the United States. They'd all be building '57 Chevys. Make some electric if you want, hybrid, hydrogen-based, traditional combustion, whatever you like.

We'd all be riding around honking at each other, and the whole country would look like one massive, multicultural *Happy Days*.

It might even be the answer to our problems in the world: '57 Chevys are a lot cheaper than missiles, and everyone wants one. Let's send all the UN folks who are looking to win back their reputations to all the hot spots of the world with tanker ships full of Bel Airs, and every time a suicide bomber comes running up, they could say, "Hold it, my hot-blooded friend. Before you do something you can't take back, why not harness some of that passion, grab a virgin, and hop into the back seat of this thing?"

We're going to be trying a lot stupider things before it's all done. Isn't this one worth a shot?

Then, when we're back home in America, our wives can pull their hair back in ponytails, we can toss a few eight-ounce, real glass bottles of Coca-Cola into a Coleman chest, our kids can climb into their pajamas (with feet) so they can go to sleep in the back, and then we can all drive our Nomad wagons to one of thousands of newly built drive-in theaters, and hang one of those old, forty-seven pound pig-iron speakers onto the window just in time for the opening credits of *Godfather IV: Michael's Revenge*.

Yeah, I know none of it's ever going to happen.

But it's a nice thought, isn't it?

NINE

ADULTERY II: THE QUICKENING

THAT'S RIGHT, I USED *THE QUICKENING* AGAIN. I KNOW it's annoying, but as I told you, it tickles me. Besides, it could always get worse. If this book sells well, I'm seriously considering calling the next one *Larry Miller: The Quickening*.

Anyway, that little imaginary chat between Moses and God a few pages back may have popped the cork on the subject of adultery, but it needs to decant. (I have no way of knowing if that's a proper metaphor, since I've never decanted anything. I'm a guzzler; niceties puzzle me. Once, when The Divine Mrs. M. and I were dating, we were seated at a restaurant far above both our stations, both of us trying to look like people we weren't. The waiter suggested decanting the wine, and I immediately said, "Of course." About thirty seconds later, as he stood slow-pouring it from the bottle to that gravy boat thing they use, I drummed my fingers, glanced at Eileen, caught the same vibe from her, and turned back to him and said, "Yeah, you know what? We'll just drink it now, thanks. No, you're doing great, but I think it's ready." And Eileen said, "Even if it's not, we are." (Come to think of it, I believe that was the first night, later on, she and I ordered Chinese food together.)

You could get an entire book's worth of material out of adultery—Flaubert sure did—but I think it boils down to this:

The thought feels wrong . . . but then we think about it.
We're told we can't . . . and then we want to.
We feel strong, then weak; immune, then susceptible.

This loop plays over and over for roughly the rest of your life: Want to. Can't. Won't. Wow. Want to. Can't. Won't. Wow. Every so often it starts with "wow" and goes in reverse.

One thing is pretty clear to me: If you haven't cheated yet, don't. I have a feeling once you cross the Rubicon, everything is different forever. (Look what happened to the first guy who did it. And those were his *friends*.)

Let's begin by assuming there's no God. That's not what I think, but just go with it, okay? So, there's no God, it's all made up, no before or after, no reward or punishment, no one watching, no rules of any kind. (I don't know about you, but as far as adultery goes, if there's no God, I'm going to spend eternity feeling like a moron. Then again, if there's no God, there's no eternity, so there's no feeling like a moron. In fact there are no feelings, period, good or bad. Consequences—or rewards—exist only if there's a God.)

But let's assume there isn't. Are there any earthly, temporal, secular reasons not to have sex outside your marriage? Ever? Let's go back to my made-up Moses hypothetical: You're away from home, meet a woman in the hotel bar, she just wants to do it, and that's that. And you do.

Let's further say the woman you met has no diseases; she's perfectly sane (except for liking you); she doesn't want anything from you (no *Fatal Attraction* stuff); you both leave with a fond wave; and your wife never finds out and never suspects. In other words, the perfect crime.

No, let's change those words. Let's not even call it a crime. Let's call it . . . the perfect affair. So remember: No God, no rules, no disease, no hurt, no guilt, no harm, no foul.

But is it wrong? Is anything about it wrong? Well, I guess if you put it like that—and I'm the one putting it like that—no. With all those qualifications? No. I guess it wouldn't be wrong. . . .

Except for one thing. My friend Mike Langworthy got married before I did, still in his twenties, and a few years later, with my single-cylinder bachelor libido still chugging along like Thomas the Tank Engine, I asked him one night over a drink if he ever cheated on his wife, and he said, "No."

And I asked why not, and he looked at me for a few seconds and said, "I promised I wouldn't."

That's the best answer I've ever heard, and it moves me every time I think about it. I thought it then, and I think it now, and I've told him so since. No one's perfect, and you and he and I could always make mistakes, but we haven't so far, and that's the right earthly reason not to: I pledged my honor; I gave my word.

I promised I wouldn't.

That's why it's wrong, even if there is no God. Even if no one ever finds out, and everything is perfect. Besides which . . .

Perfect? *PERFECT?* What's perfect? I'll tell you what. Nothing. Nothing's perfect. The concept is inhuman and stupid to begin with, which is why I chose it. "A perfect affair"? Hell, that's not a hypothetical; it's a male fantasy. The oldest rule in the world is still true, the one that predates the Ten Commandments by millennia and is known to anyone who's ever walked around on two legs and isn't an idiot:

There's no free lunch.

I don't think I ever fully understood that saying till about ten years ago. Actually, I disagreed with it. "Yeah, there is," I used to say. "There's a free lunch."

No. There isn't. There's no free lunch. Everything has a price, up front or later. That's not cynical, it's liberating, and a big step toward individual accountability, responsibility, and loyalty—which, if you think about it, is the whole point of the Ten Commandments to begin with. In fact, "There's no free lunch" is a pretty good secular reduction of numbers 1 through 10 right there. If you had to pick just one saying to carry around in your wallet for the rest of your life on a laminated card next to the metric conversion table you've never used, "There's No Free Lunch" wouldn't be a bad choice at all.

Ah—but what if, in addition to that ancient, streetwise dictum, there's a slightly inconvenient, eenchy-weenchy P.S. on the other side? In other words . . .

What if there *is* a God? Just suppose. I know it's crazy and could never happen, since that would make your parents right about something, but let it sit there and seep in for just a second. What if? Not an old guy with a beard, but as real as your desk; as impossible to picture as a goldfish (or me) trying to read Faulkner. Times a million. Times a trillion. Times infinity. What if "Thou shalt not commit adultery" was written intentionally—and in lightning, not magic marker? "You're in for it now, mate," as one of the Brit soldiers says to the Boers in *Breaker Morant*.

The problem with sex is, I still can't stop thinking about it. Can you? Well, nothing wrong with that, eh? We'll always have our fantasies, right? We can always stroll out of work with slightly glazed eyes thinking about the girl at the coffee cart. Hmm?

Not so fast. We're not off the hook then either, because some religions believe just thinking about it is a sin in itself.

If that's the case, I'm in tremendous trouble.

I remember reading Jimmy Carter's interview in *Playboy* when he ran for president—at a time of life when my glands were lit like an all-night warehouse—saying he had lusted in his heart, and that a sin of the heart was just as bad as the sin of doing it.

This doesn't appeal to me. I don't want to spend a million years having to listen to Hugh Hefner talk about all the women he's had, and only being able to mumble, "Oh, yeah, I did that one, too. In my head, anyway."

Can you imagine the ribbing you'd take? "How about you, Larry? Got any good stories? Don't be shy, we've heard it all, two or three times at least. The fat guy in the tights look familiar? That's right, Henry VIII. It's hard to tell, since he's on fire, but that's him. And *his* stories are, like, way sadistic. So what'd you do to get here?"

"Me? Oh, it was the woman in the next office."

"Yeah? You two do it all the time?"

"Nah, just . . . thought about it. A lot, though."

"Oh, one of those. You can't sit with us. You gotta go over there with the Enron guys. Hey, Mick, you and the Stones have any good stories?"

It doesn't seem fair. I think the guys who only thought about it should at least get a couple of levels above, where it's more just like living in Panama.

I THINK THERE SHOULD BE DIFFERENT LEVELS OF ADUL-tery, too. A guy who did it once shouldn't get the same sentence as a guy who did it all the time.

George Burns, a famous comedian in the twelfth century, used to tell a story about his one dalliance. In the fifties he went to Las Vegas for a night for some awards dinner with all his friends. "All his friends" meant, in this case, all the other big comedians of the day from movies, television, stage, and radio. And it was just a boys' night out, so the wives stayed back in California.

So far, so good, but you can probably see this coming. They all got drunk, and a bunch of, uh, chorus girls were sent over as a gift from a prominent, er, hotel owner, and the whole thing took on a bit of a Roman feeling, and one thing led to another, and Burns wound up taking a riding-school alumna back to his room. Or she took him, or they both took each other. Somebody took someone, that's for sure, and she stayed the night; and not in a sisterly fashion (not in my family, anyway).

The next step is both unbelievable and predictable at the same time. The sun comes up and into the room pops his wife, Gracie, with a bellman and all her luggage, to surprise her husband, which I think it's safe to say she did. She turned around and stormed right back out, and went back to L.A. Burns and the woman got dressed. We don't know what happened to the bellman, although waiting around for a tip was probably out of the question.

Anyway, by the time Gracie walked into their house back in Beverly Hills, there was a $10,000 diamond necklace on the dining room table and a note saying, "Please forgive me." This was ten grand in the fifties, remember. Probably a hundred grand today.

The upshot is that for the rest of their lives neither one ever mentioned it. Ten years later, though, Gracie was talking to a friend and said, "I wish George would fool around again. I need some earrings."

Now was what he did right? Maybe not, but it never happened before or after, and it doesn't seem as bad as the guy who does it all the time with different women, or the same woman, or bunches of women. More to the point, I don't think anyone should end a marriage over it.

I hope they just made George scrub floors or something for a few weeks before letting him in—and not just because he played The Boss in the movies.

THERE'S ANOTHER KIND OF ADULTERY THAT I THINK IS amazing, though—a kind of superadultery, like the flu and the superflu.

You know how every so often you read about a guy who dies, and it turns out he had another, completely different family somewhere else? You know what I mean?

I'm not talking about polygamy, where everyone knows about it, and all three houses have a common courtyard, and everyone goes shopping together. I'm talking about two whole marriages in different places, and no one knows anything. It just amazes me when someone does that.

Have you noticed the guy always has, like, four kids in each one? And neither of the women ever knew. Each of them thought good ol' Bill just, you know, *traveled* a lot.

When one of those guys strolls in on Judgment Day, I'll bet even God stands up, closes the door, tiptoes back and sits on the edge of the desk, offers him a mint, and says, "Okay—I just need to know. How'd you pull it off?"

I'd like to know that one myself. How did he do it? Never mind why. How? I can't even get out twice a year. I mean, I could if I wanted, I just can't get it together. You know how it is: you come home after a long day, watch a cartoon with the kids, eat your dinner over the sink, brush their teeth and get mad during it, read to them and get mad during it, say their prayers and get mad during it, storm out, count to ten, go back in, feed the fish and get mad during it, apologize to everyone including the fish, finally lie down in your bed . . .

Only to get furious all over again at not being able to watch the Isela Vega top-ripping-off scene in *Bring Me the Head of Alfredo Garcia* because your wife has to/wants to/is just plain going to watch the last twenty minutes of her favorite, stupid Redecorate-the-Den-for-Fifty-Dollars show, which is unwatchable on its best days, but is now completely impossible since they stopped having the little Scottish blonde on, so you're forced to pick your way through the Hot Wheel–covered living room in order to clear a space on the couch to read your new copy of *The American Grump* with the dog, who's still the only one who understands you completely. As long as you feed him.

And this yutz does it all twice? Two full, separate families? What does he do, drive to the other place and brush *their* teeth? Or does he just spend a couple of weeks in each joint for thirty years? I seriously can't imagine the logistics.

These fellows are never rich, either, or handsome, or anything. They're regular, chubby guys who work for Aetna, or the post office, or Delta; they have regular names like Ed, or Burt, or Carl. It's not a hot affair, it's a whole other marriage, with torn underwear and arguments, and wives of the same age—meaning over fifty-nine.

I just can't imagine how they do it. "Joan, I've got to go on another business trip tomorrow for a couple of weeks."

"Oh, Bob, not again? That darn company. That makes two weeks out of every month for the last forty-seven years."

"I know, honey, but it's our busy season."

Have you noticed it's never the women who have the other family? That has to tell you something right there. At least a few reasons are obvious, but the guy would still have to be as dumb as a hammer, wouldn't he? "Say, Lillian, I just remembered something. Weren't you pregnant last year?"

"Yes, Jim, twins, but to be honest, they're with my second family in Portland. Technically, my first. Or at least *they* think they are."

"Say again?"

"It had to come out sooner or later. I have another husband."

"Really. Are you any nicer to him?"

Somewhere in history there's got to be a case where the guy has another family, and the wife has another family at the same time, and neither of them knows it. So whenever he leaves the house, she calls *her* second husband and says, "Ed, darling, it's Barbara. Vince just went to Baffin Bay for the Steamfitters Convention. I'll be right over."

But if Ed's married, what does he tell *his* wife? "Bad news, Carol. That was the office, and they need me to come downtown now. For two weeks. Again."

Hold it, I'm getting confused. Let's start again. Say a guy has two families, but they each have another family, and then each of *them* has another family, and—do you realize we may all be related? The first guy out of the Olduvai Gorge was probably just going one gorge over.

Plus, I've only got two kids, and I'm constantly mixing them up. How do these guys keep any of it straight?

"Merry Christmas, everyone."

"Uh, Dad, we're Jewish."

"Just testing you. What address is this? You're not mad, are you, Margaret?"

"I wasn't, but I'm about to be. My name's Jeannie. You're lucky I have to get to my other family."

"*Your* other family? For Christmas?"

"No. Kwanzaa."

"Well, that explains all the Mingus albums."

Many exotic and faraway parts of the world still legally and enthusiastically practice polygamy, and their wealthiest men often have five, ten, twenty wives or more, and dozens and dozens of children, but since these places are just lately a little guarded on the subject (and a wee bit touchy in general for the last thousand years), that's all I have to say about that.

There's a lot of plural marriage in the United States, too, you know—and I mean all over the United States, not just remnants of sects in Utah. It's not legal, but apparently there are plenty of people who get around it, and I'll bet you a dollar we'll see a lot of test cases play out in the next few years. The wives not only know about each other but are, at least on the surface, as pleased as punch about the whole thing. I'd like to see that guy in the mall on Valentine's Day. "That's a pretty one. Can I get seven?"

I guess we've all seen group photos of these folks, and one hates to generalize too awfully much or paint with too broad a brush. But the faces of these women and their bull man in those shots are always—always—just plain spooky.

THE OTHER BRAND OF MULTIPLE-PARTNER FONDLING while married is known as "swinging," which has to be the all-time, world heavyweight champion of irony.

I'm sure you've seen documentaries of swingers' clubs in mid-sized American cities with cold winters, where three or four couples of average-looking-to-powerfully-unattractive people get together in each other's basement dens on alternate-side-of-the-street Wednesdays, and set their folding chairs and their occasional tables along the walls, and put their sad three-bean salads, and their patterned bowls of pretzels, and their earth-tone place settings out on the checked plastic tablecloth—and then, after a little small talk about schools and paneling, they roll up the carpets and bring out four horrifying, inflatable mats covered by nubby, low-thread-count sheets and topped by jelly-soft pillows with fading stripes and tiny, tiny feathers visible in the seams. If those mats could talk . . . we'd all beg them not to.

Folks, swinging is what Duke Ellington and Count Basie did in the forties and fifties, not what sweet, lost people do in *their* forties and fifties. (Perhaps premium cable channels could fill some of this void.)

Which all brings us back around to regular, old-fashioned adultery and a definition. As far as I understand it, adultery is when a married person has sex outside of the marriage. Technically, the strictest religious view often includes *any* sex outside marriage, even between singles. But this, let's be honest, is nuts.

Let's leave it at that, though, which is a very reasonable understanding we all have: a married person, man or woman, who has sex with anyone other than his spouse.

And yes, I know I said "his." Like hand towels from the fifties, adultery is often marked "His" and "Hers," but for the sake of ease, I'm just going to use the male pronoun, and I hope that's all right. It gets a little clunky to keep saying "his or her" spouse, or "his or her" anything, and I've never been comfortable using the plural—and incorrect—"their" with a singular noun, as in "Everyone has to live their own way." Cheerful commentators in our brave new world use "their" all the time, and no one notices or cares anymore, if anyone ever did. But for as long as I'm alive—which, I have it on good authority, will be forever—I'm going to stick with "his." Remember: It'll make the book shorter, and that saves trees.

Also, I know as well as you do that men have begun marrying men, and women marrying women, in various civil and progressive religious contexts. The next few years will see a good bit of legal wrangling on it, and it will eventually be accepted or rejected, and commonplace or rare, but that's not what this discussion is about. Perhaps the dynamics of one partner cheating on the other in heterosexual relationships are exactly the same as homosexual relationships, or mostly the same, or somewhat the same.

I don't know and don't much care; for now, I'm going to force us to stay on topic—that is, a typical married couple, man and woman with children, where one strays on the other. Everyone okay?

Whew. Two disclaimers in a row—I'm exhausted. Like a two hundred–word version of "Your actual mileage may vary." What delicate moves we must all undertake in the Third Millennium, hmm? Makes *Swan Lake* look like a clog dance.

You know, covering your bases may take a little extra time, but it's worth remembering that politically correct speech guidelines began with the best of intentions: so that dumb guys—or rotten guys—didn't get to casually hurt someone's feelings anytime they felt like it. A whole culture stood up and said, "Excuse me, but you don't get to say that anymore." And that was a good moment in human history.

Since the American pendulum swings only to extremes, though, these noble efforts have since gone completely bonkers. As it stands now, one concerned citizen with slightly thin skin (in other words, a complete lunatic) can affect events, textbooks, board meetings, movies, art, names, titles, and anything else he feels like putting his pea brain to, just by getting his dander up at the right moment. If your instinct is to disbelieve this—or even pooh-pooh it—well, perhaps I'm wrong and you're right. Give me a call, then, won't you, the next time you see a Charlie Chan movie on TV?

I don't think you'll ever find anyone with better "We Are the World" credentials than the ex-president of Harvard, but he certainly got a valuable appendage caught in a wringer a while back, and the line of folks waiting to turn the crank (even though he resigned) is still around the block. Actually, I think he's dead academically but doesn't know it; he'll probably get hissed wherever he speaks for the rest of his life. Ah, well. Even the alpha-male runs the risk of the other coyotes looking at him funny when the pack gets too far from town. In fact, that fellow might want to take Arianna Huffington's lead, toss the last few chips he has into the middle, hit the bar in the lobby, wake up early the next day, and drive himself over to the Hoover Institution.

BACK TO CHEATING, AND NOT AT SCHOOL. WHAT ABOUT women, then? Do they cheat the same way as men? I recently saw a movie with Diane Lane and Richard Gere. (They were in it, that is; we didn't all go out to a movie together.) It was called *Unfaithful II: The Quickening*.

Heh-heh.

Sorry, it was called *Unfaithful*. So, they're married in it, with a fabulous house in the suburbs and a great kid, and Gere's the sweetest guy in the world, and the best father, and a great provider, or, as a friend of mine says, all that and a bag of chips. They're rich, too, incidentally, and in case you've forgotten, he's RICHARD BLANKING GERE.

Pardon.

Still, life's a little dull for Mrs. Blanking Gere, and one satanically windy afternoon she takes herself for a day trip to the city and bumps (literally) into a handsome young man in front of his gorgeous downtown apartment on her way to buy party favors (for her kid's birthday, no less). You know, hours away from her house, in the hippest, coolest part of the city. Because that's where all the best party-favor stores are.

Anyway, she skins her knee in this donnybrook, and he invites her inside for a Band-Aid and some meaningful looks. Oh, and he's from a foreign country, too. (In Europe. Just guess. Uh-huh.) The appropriate sidewalk demurrals follow, and a lot of maidenly "Oh, I couldn't, really, I'm fine, thank you. No, no, I like blood and limping." This Texas Two-Step having made its full circuit around the floor, the fly goes inside with the spider, where he really hits below the belt by reading to her from a book. (Guys with accents reading *books*? Aw, man, she never had a chance!)

Nothing more happens in that session, but the virus is already coursing through the host, and back home that night in Boring Hills Estates, she decides to return the following day with a nice bottle of wine as a thank-you gift to Pierre the Impaler, for saving her leg. You know, the way we'd all be so grateful we'd put on special lingerie and take a car to a train, to a rope bridge across a canyon, to a Huck Finn raft down rapids, back downtown again with a gift the liquor store on the guy's corner could've sent over in three minutes with a note.

But the die is cast and—consciously or unconsciously, or both— she returns to the scene of the scent, and after a little initial shyness, the skilled hands of her sophisticated, fancy-free, Gallic lover (Yay!) relax her oppressive, Puritan, American inhibitions (Boo!) enough that, quick as you can say Jacques be nimble, she's presenting like a gibbon.

And, as my mother would say, they're off to the races. *The Quickening*, indeed.

The rest of the movie doesn't quite matter. It's a good story, with some nifty twists, but for this discussion we're only concerned with the part about how an otherwise happily married woman could slip just enough that her libido leaps out like a starving crocodile and eats itself from the tail.

I asked several women about this, two of my wife's friends and two of mine here at work. And I make no pretense about that being a scientific survey. You and I are perfectly capable of having opinions and chats around the water cooler without first doing eleven years of research on a Genius Grant, and our results may be just as edifying. In fact, whether the issue is men and women, schools, health care, foreign policy, spiked hair, or anything else, anytime I see someone on TV introduced as an "expert," all it does is guarantee to me that the guy's a moron. I guess "expert" or "Ph.D." on the crawl underneath is more polite than "Dr. Farko Hollis, Utter Fool Without the Sense God Gave a Squirrel."

I remember when *Time* reported the results of a decades-long, top-shelf study revealing the shattering conclusion that little boys tend to be different from little girls. What a cultural quake that must've been for our deep thinkers. Naturally, it's the kind of jaw dropper any mother from Finland to Cambodia could have told you for the last eighty thousand years in exchange for a bowl of milk. After which, I'm sure the wilier among them would quietly take you aside and offer to sell you some other terrific ideas: for instance, had the Great White professor noticed that the sun tends to rise in the same spot almost every day?

ANYWAY, THE WOMEN ASKED ABOUT *UNFAITHFUL* ARE all single. (This was intentional on my part.) They range from mid-twenties to early thirties. One runs her own business, one is a producer, one runs the billing department for a business, and one created and runs an important charity.

And, by the way, they're all seriously pretty. Crazy pretty. So pretty it makes your eyes water. I wasn't trying for this, but in L.A. it's almost unavoidable.

I have a theory about Southern California—that for the last

eighty years the prettiest girls in the country moved out here in droves to get into the movies, and when most of them didn't, they married instead, settled down, and had families. As a result, the gene pool from San Diego to Santa Barbara clicks like a Geiger counter in *Silkwood*. This, in turn, has bred a two-hundred-mile blast zone where any randomly chosen handful of women looks like the high school cheerleading squad you've been carrying around in your head since ninth grade.

Women have become so unfairly pretty in California that the average twenty-three-year-old receptionist at the Department of Water and Power in Ventura County could out-point the most beautiful girl in the history of Moscow.

This also explains why the first thing every athlete says after winning something is, "I'm going to Disneyland."

So these four women had all seen *Unfaithful* and knew it well, and were pleased to talk about it—in fact, anxious to talk about it. Actually, it was as if they'd been *waiting* to talk about it.

They all thought it was good, but of no particular enlightenment to them—an interesting story, but not very real for their lives. And not, according to them, because they weren't married. "Women don't want that," one said. "We want the walks on the beach and the hand holding." "I can talk like the women on *Sex and the City* with the best of them," said another, "but it's not what I'm looking for. I'm looking for the guy who wants more." Good luck on that one in Hollywood, I told her, but she was way ahead of me.

The only time men know what they want is when a woman is strong enough to tell them. If you're waiting for a man to figure things out on his own, you're going to have a nice wait on your hands.

The third felt she had Diane Lane's number. (Make your own puns there.) "Oh, she knew what she was doing," this one said.

"Maybe not consciously, and I'm sure she would've denied it, but, please, getting dressed up for the guy? With special underwear? That's what made it interesting. You could see each step as the slope got more slippery. But she was kidding herself the whole way. She was gone from the start."

The fourth said something I found interesting. She knows women, she said, whose husbands had cheated, more than once, or for longer periods. The affairs were ultimately discovered, and the wives forgave them, and they put the pieces back together . . . but it was never the same. Not for the woman, not for the man. Their lives changed forever, and not for the better. What was lost? Trust and faith, love and support. Comfort. Relaxed mutuality. Even the arguments changed. Worse still, the laughter vanished, which is far more important than you may think. Ultimately, they just separated, then divorced, and that was that.

I know a guy from work who cheated, and I like him a lot. He's not a demon, he just slipped and gave in. But after that it wasn't the last time, and it cost him his marriage. It's like walking a few yards into a big forest—it's easier to get lost than you may think.

The pull of sexual desire is amazing, though, and who doesn't know that? I disagree with those who call it a need, like air and water, but it sure can become that if you get addicted, and I know people who are.

You know how lots of artists and musicians over the years have tried heroin because they think it helps tap into their talents? The great Charlie Parker comes to mind, but I know people who've done this, too—friends I'm thinking of now. There's not one who didn't learn a terrible lesson. It doesn't help your talent. It kills the talent. It snuffs it out like sand shoveled onto a campfire. It doesn't just destroy the body, it destroys the soul and everything it was capable of.

Sometimes I think adultery has the same effect on a marriage. Maybe you can dabble in it a little and walk away. But if you can't, it'll kill the magic you take for granted. And I don't think that's what you want.

That's why I say to us all, including myself, if you haven't done anything yet, don't. Is there divine punishment later on? Maybe, maybe not, but it doesn't matter. Never mind later on. If you're caught, your punishment starts right now, pal, by your own hand. It's in the look on your kids' faces when you say goodbye to them. (If you're still sane enough to notice.) I hope seeing that new nipple was worth it.

I asked my research team if they knew a woman who'd cheated on her husband first, before he cheated on her. They all did, but their answers were almost the same. "Oh, yeah," they said, "but those were bad marriages with awful stuff." "Those were bad men." "I know someone," said one, "but her marriage had been dead a long time already. He wouldn't go to counseling, that kind of thing." "I don't think women in good marriages do that. Not on their own. Not first." Never? They didn't know anyone who did. I guess there are, but they didn't know any. "What do you mean by a good marriage?" I asked the last, and she smiled and said, "Well, Richard Gere in a mansion with a kid? I could weather a few boring patches."

How strong is that pull, though, for both men and women? How strong a drug is adultery even for those who've never injected it? Strong enough to be very afraid of.

ON BEHALF OF THOSE WHO HAVEN'T SLIPPED, I JUST want to say that no man out there who sleeps with a different woman every night has a stronger sex drive than me. I think about it just as often, and would like to do exactly what he's doing (at least for a few weeks). I'll bet every husband who doesn't cheat feels the same way. We just don't do it. I'm not a saint, and could fail anytime. That's why I'm afraid of it. I want to be the kind of man my father was with my mother, and not just because he was bald.

And for those of you thinking, "You know, Larry, you're not exactly George Clooney." First of all . . . Sez you. Really, though, it doesn't matter. As you know, anyone who wants to fool around can; and show business is a crazy place. I could go to this or that place with friends if I wanted. It's not that I can't; I won't. At least I haven't.

I promised I wouldn't.

What if I were George Burns that night in Vegas? What if it happens tomorrow, or next year, or the year after? What would I do? I don't know.

What would you do?

In the end, there's only one thing I think I know for sure. A marriage is a fire that has to be stoked, or it goes out.

And you can't stoke it by putting your log in someone else's fire.

TEN

DEBBIE DOES DALLAS II: THE QUICKENING

I SWEAR, I THOUGHT I WAS OVER SAYING THAT, BUT I guess not. Don't hate me, though. I'm admitting there's a problem. Think of it like quitting smoking, caving in, and running out to get a pack. Yes, there've also been a couple of lapses with puns along the way, but that's not so bad, is it? It's this other thing I need your support on, and I agree with you. I mean, *The Quickening*. It's sickening.

Sorry. Don't worry. No problem. Pardon me while I get up to stir the sauce. It's thickening.

I'm okay, I'm on top of it, no biggie. It's not as if I'm suddenly going to run out and become a witch, and start Wiccaning.

Let's change the subject, that'll do it. We could maybe, I don't know, raise our voices in praise of *Great Expectations*. You know, a Dickens-Sing. Help me. It's starting again. I . . . I . . .

It's no good. I've got to get out of here.

OKAY, I'M BACK. IT'S ALL OVER. I TOOK A POWDER AGAIN for a couple of weeks and went back to that farmhouse in Indiana. The wistful widow was remarried by this time to a stereopticon salesman from Wagon Gap named Chaney (no relation, different spelling). He was pretty amiable about the whole thing—considering—and they put me up in the spare till the spell passed. (Turns out they both like puns well enough, but can't abide limericks.) We played cards together on the porch, of a night, and I stole a look or two, but what the hay. Still makes a heckuva cherry pie, she does. As for pitching woo, well, I couldn't—and wouldn't—say.

LET'S AWAY. IT TURNS OUT THERE REALLY IS A MOVIE called *Debbie Does Dallas II*, and let me just say I know that for a fact. How? *And* how. That is, here's how.

Like most things in life, pornography can be used to one extreme or another, and I don't believe either one is healthy. Five percent of American men have probably never seen naked pictures at all, not even once; another five percent probably do nothing but look at it twenty-four hours a day, seven days a week. I think both of these groups are very likely an inch away from going on a three-state murder spree.

The rest of us are in the middle. One of the ways men respond to women is visually, in case you hadn't noticed, and that's, of course, what porn is.

So far as I can tell, the first thing people did when photography was invented was take a picture of Lincoln. The second thing, right behind it (so to speak), was to think, "Say, I wonder if Miss Brightenbecker over at the Cattlemen's Association would let me take a few shots of her without the bustle?" They probably wondered whether it would even print out on the paper, as if the chemicals might make a value judgment—the way some people used to think the sky would explode if a plane broke the sound barrier.

Well, Miss Brightenbecker had no objections, and the sky didn't explode, and here we are. Like all of us, though, every time I pass a Calvin Klein billboard with the kids in the car, I wonder if our culture has gone too far. There are three possibilities: we haven't gone too far; everything's about the same; we've gone way, way too far.

My wife was talking about Internet porn at work with friends, and she said it made her angry, and that our kids were never going to have the Internet in their bedrooms. And one of the guys laughed and said, "Oh, you probably don't even want them to see *Playboy*." And she said, "No, that's exactly wrong. *Playboy* is fine with me. I expect them to see it. I want them to see it. In fact, I expect them to hide it. That's in the normal range. But the Internet is too much; it's constant, it's far more graphic, they can get into a bad habit, and, by the way, that's how predators find them."

I agreed with her so much when she told me, I turned it right off.

Kidding. But I'm actually glad I know almost nothing about the Internet. In case you think I'm lying, I sent the first three drafts of this book to the publisher by hand—hard copies made on a machine and FedExed at the Kinko's on Laurel Canyon and Ventura. I can write on the computer, but I use it like a typewriter, indenting and paging manually, without any interference from that snotty software. Each time I called the publisher in New York to say I was sending something, and that it should be there in a few days, Cal Morgan, my editor, gently said, "You know, Larry, it's also possible to e-mail it. Might be easier for both of us." After the first few long silences, he stopped asking.

But my wife and I agree completely on this one. It's one thing for a thirteen-year-old to have a tattered *Playboy* in his night table drawer under an old math workbook, and it'll make me smile when I find one and realize ours have gone from "Yuchhh" to "Oooh . . ." (I had one that Larry Fink lifted from his dad and gave to me when we were twelve; I wish I still had it today. You know, for old times' sake.) But the Internet is too much, too fast, and has no limits.

The point is, though, I've seen magazines plenty of times. I'm no prude—in fact, just the opposite. It's like fistfights at a hockey game. We think they're an outrage, and they are, but as soon as one breaks out we all leap up laughing and say, "Ooh, look, a fight!" If someone walked into the office right now with naked pictures of a woman, I would look at them like any other guy. In fact, let's just wait a second and see if that happens. All right, it didn't. One more minute. No. Huh. Typical: never around when you need 'em.

It's ironic that what's not shown about a woman is often sexier than what is shown. Especially so the wilder they get. Leno used to do a bit in his act about the more graphic ones: "A friend of mine is a gynecologist, and I showed him a picture from *Hustler,* and he looked at it and said, 'Gee, I have no idea what that is.' "

I suppose, like all things in life, it would be the images and lighting and fashions of my youth I'd find most appealing in a centerfold. I guess I really do wish I had the one Larry Fink gave me.

The thing is, I could never buy one in public. Not then, not now. I could never just walk into a store and get one. Never.

Well, that's not completely true, because I did. Twice. Both times I was drenched with sweat, and not from the pictures.

THE FIRST TIME WAS FOURTEEN YEARS AGO. THIS WAS before I was married, although I'm not sure why I added that.

I had done an interview with *Penthouse*. Not one of the big interviews, but one of the single-page question-and-answer things they used to do with comics and actors and sports guys. I was on the road, in a hotel, and my agent called and said, "Hey, it just came out, and you're in it. It's great—go get one." I was all excited, so I went downstairs to the gift shop.

I went to the magazine section in the back. There they were, several bundles of the new issue still tied in their yellow plastic bands, and one stack, loose, just waiting for me. I'd been looking forward to this for a long time. So I picked up two copies—my folks were still alive, and I was going to get one for them—and turned to the counter.

And stopped dead. And thought, "Oh, no. How am I going to do this?" There was a Little Old Ladies with White Hair and Spectacles convention in the hotel—or at least it suddenly seemed that way, since five or six of them were milling around the gift shop like guards at a bingo tournament. Just as bad, or worse, the clerk at the register was a young woman. "Stop it," I thought. "Don't be an idiot. Everyone buys these things; it's no big deal. Besides, you have a fabulous reason. You're in it. You're in the magazine, and you want to see how it came out. Just walk up and buy it, and stop being stupid. There's nothing wrong with buying a *Penthouse* anyway."

All of this is true, but it didn't matter. I turned around, put them back on the stack, and walked out of the shop, head down, very, very fast.

Halfway through the lobby I stopped again. "Oh, you really are nuts," I thought. "You're *in* the magazine, for crying out loud. And even if you weren't, who cares? Just go get it."

But I tried again, couldn't, and walked back out. This time I stood at the entrance and waited for the other customers to leave. It took a while, and I couldn't have looked more suspicious if I were a drug dealer hanging around a junior high. The place finally cleared out and I went back inside, scratching the right side of my face as I passed the clerk, went to the back, picked it up again (just one this time; let my parents get their own), got to the counter, put it down, looked up, and immediately burst open like a pomegranate.

"I'm in it," I said. "I swear, I'm in it, they do interviews with comics, and I'm a comic, and I'm here working . . . not here, there's a club in town . . . well, not in town, it's more like on the perimeter. To be honest, I don't know where it is, they just pick me up, but I'm buying this to read the interview. You want to see it? I'm sorry, I don't know what page it is, and you don't need to see. I'll probably throw it out after the interview. If you want, I'll bring it back, and you can sell it again. Sorry, forget that. You know what? I don't need the change. You keep it, or give it away. Either way, I'll just be going now."

Naturally, at this point, she finally looked up for the first time and took a good, long look at me, because I was acting like a suicide bomber.

I still have that magazine in my dresser drawer at the house. I haven't looked at it in a while, but I might again. If I do, I don't think it'll be for the interview.

THE SECOND TIME WAS TWO YEARS AGO, AS I WAS ON MY way to work. I have an office for writing, and stopped off at a 7-Eleven on the way for a cup of coffee. I had just dropped the kids at school, and it was early. As I filled the cup and put the lid on, I noticed several things in the store at the same time, in the tiniest fraction of a second.

Two house painters had just bought a box of donuts for break-fast, and they were the only ones in the store. The clerk, a young girl, gave them their change and spoke to them in Spanish. When they left, the store was empty. *Empty.*

I walked up to the counter, put the coffee down, took out my wallet . . . and felt my heart starting to thump: There was a rack of *Playboy*s behind the counter. (A rack of *Playboy*s? What an etymological coincidence. You might even say it was a rack of racks. I'm not saying you should, but you could. In fact, when the store was first being built, and they were putting those shelves in, before even one magazine was on display, you could've run inside and yelled, "Hey, nice rack.")

The point is, the store was empty, and a rack of *Playboy*s was hanging there. I mean, stacked there. Sitting on—on top of—pressed against—oh, forget it. They were there, okay? And the clerk had spoken Spanish. Empty store, *Playboy,* Spanish! What a parley! Who could pass this up? I looked around one more time, shrugged, and thought, "I'll never have a chance like this again." So as she tapped in the price of the coffee, I said as evenly as I could, "And do me a favor, please, let me have a copy of *Playboy.*" She turned wordlessly, no reaction, picked one up, and placed it on the counter.

It worked. Unbelievable! First-time robbers in a convenience store were probably less terrified knocking over the place, but I held my voice steady, pronounced every word within an inch of its life, and she understood me perfectly. I handed her the money, she made change—all very quickly, but without rushing—took out a bag from under the counter (yes, a plain brown wrapper), and I thought, *This is going to work. This is really going to work.*

Then, of course, disaster. Defeat. Calamity. How could it be otherwise?

As she slipped the magazine into the bag, she looked up at me, smiled sweetly, and—in perfect, native, unaccented English—said, "By the way, I just have to tell you, I think you're really funny."

If I didn't have both hands on the counter, I would've slid to the floor in a dead faint.

YOU KNOW HOW SOMETIMES IN BASEBALL IT'S THE bottom of the ninth, two outs, home team down by three, no one on, and the game's in the bag? The visiting team is confident, their closer is firing heat, the crowd is silent, and the last batter steps up, ready to lose. He takes two strikes, and even the diehards are leaving, and some of the players in the dugout glance longingly into the locker room, sorry for their teammate, but hoping for a swift, merciful kill. The batter pulls it together to weakly swing at the third pitch, another strike, and just manages to tap a weak, easy grounder to third. Well, that's it. Game's over, right?

But then the third baseman makes an error—not even a big error, just the tiniest lapse in concentration. Maybe he double-pumps the ball, or can't get it out of his glove. And the runner's safe. Whoa. That was weird. But no big deal, right? Just get the next guy. Right?

Wrong. The universe has shifted, and when the universe shifts in baseball, everyone can feel it. The fans sit back down with tiny smiles, because they know. The fielders set themselves, pound their gloves and shout encouragement, but they know, too, that with that one infinitesimally small mistake, everything has changed, and the momentum has gone over completely.

And suddenly, very quickly, like the blink of an eye . . . base hit, walk, home run. Grand slam. Four runs. You lose. Game over. 'Bye.

One tiny thing.

When that girl at the 7-Eleven said, "I think you're funny," I knew it was all over. And, of course, it was.

She slipped the *Playboy* into the bag, but it was a little thick that month, or the paper bag manufacturers were feeling especially sadistic, because it didn't quite fit in, and tore it down the side. "Oh, darn," she said, reaching for another one. "So, what's it like to work with Eddie Murphy?"

"Wh . . . What?" I stammered through cracked lips. "Oh, great. He's, uh . . . He's really nice, and—"

The second bag tore, even farther, and she laughed and reached for a third. "God, these things. Yeah, so, you were saying?"

I tried to think of what had led me to this horrible moment, and heard a voice screaming inside, "Get out. Just leave. Run."

I licked my lips and croaked, "Listen, you know what? I don't need a . . . I'll just take it. You don't have to—"

That's when the door opened, and a mother came in with three kids, one in her arms. Naturally. "Okay, one bag of chips, and that's it," she was saying, in that titanium-edged, "It's-still-early-but-I've-already-had-it" voice that only mothers have.

I fought off another swoon, looked at the cashier, and said, "I'm sorry," but it wasn't to her I was speaking.

Well, God had enjoyed his little morning laugh and had better things to do, I guess, because suddenly the *Playboy* slid right into the bag, just as it was made to do, and she handed it to me with another smile. I took it weakly, feeling very old, and turned to the door. "Hey, you forgot your coffee," she said, and I shuffled back, picked it up, and managed the smallest of nods. When I reached the door she added, "Say hi to Eddie." I nodded again, even less than before, and tried to wave, but the hand I picked up was the one holding the bag, and I almost cried instead. The last thing I remember noticing was the crook-running-out height chart on the door: I was five inches shorter than usual.

I pulled the car around the corner, turned it off, and sat for a while staring straight ahead. By the time I picked up the coffee, it was cold.

THAT *PLAYBOY* IS IN THE SAME DRESSER DRAWER WITH the *Penthouse,* along with a *Sports Illustrated* anniversary swimsuit issue I managed to purchase last year without too much difficulty at an Indian casino in another state wearing a bowler hat and Groucho glasses. My collection.

Since the aforementioned invention of photography (by a fellow named Daguerre—a Frenchman, come to think of it, which makes perfect sense), magazines have been joined by other methods of delivery of occasional erotica to men. For example, there are, or so I'm told, movies available in most hotels under the category of "adult." (I guess "adolescent" and "pathetic" didn't have quite the ring they wanted.) These "adult" movies—since, of course, none of you would know—are purchasable in rooms across North America. (I've never stayed in Mexico, but God only knows what they have down there.) The "adult" movies are there for you at the touch of the "adult" button, right alongside, say, films from the *Princess Diaries* series. (Terrific movies, by the way, those *Princess* things, with some wonderful recurring character parts. I, for one, hope they make many more.)

Further, and most important: Can I stop putting "adult" in quotes?

Naturally, no one reading this (or writing it) has ever been alone on the road and accidentally clicked one of these movies on while reaching for the Gideon Bible. We can all only imagine how embarrassing it must be for that awful man who's depraved enough even to check the table of contents (if that's the appropriate phrase) and browse the available fare. Embarrassing, I mean, when he's checking out the next day and has to convince the nineteen-year-old female part-time college student behind the desk that the $13.99 was for Buffalo Wings. Unless, of course, that's someone's stage name.

THE FIRST TIME I SAW ANY KIND OF DIRTY MOVIE WAS AT a bachelor party during my senior year at college. My pals and I weren't invited, but we knew the guy and had the proper credentials for admission—we were drunk—so we wandered over and fit right in.

I guess those were the innocent, halcyon days before mean, rich college athletes were worldly enough to hire strippers.

It was 1975, before cable, videos, or anything like that was around, and just a few weeks after breasts were invented.

In fact, the only thing they could get their hands on, so to speak, was what used to be called a stag movie. It had to be sixty years old (the movie, not the actress), and was black and white, silent, cracked, out of focus, and sputtering. They showed it on a sheet hung over the fireplace of their frat house (to complete the cliché), and the combined effect made the whole experience very much like attending a bachelor party during the Coolidge administration.

No offense to Silent Cal, who was once president of that very school I was attending, but the evening would have been vastly more entertaining if we'd just stared at the sheet.

CUT TO TODAY, AND HOTELS IN AMERICA ARE PROBABLY making more on porn movies than they are on the cost of the room. It's a wonder all those leatherette Bibles with the faux-gold-leaf paint on the edges don't just burst into flames in their little drawers.

(Be honest, how often have you ever glanced at a Bible in a hotel? Those night table drawers get opened so rarely they smell like a six-hundred-year-old doctor's bag. One that was buried with the doctor.)

Well, I had a second childhood and ordered one of these things in a hotel exactly fifteen months ago at this writing. There's a reason I remember the time so precisely.

I'd just done a one-nighter in New York. After the job I went back to the hotel and called home; then I turned on the TV and thought about ordering room service or maybe having a drink, and was too tired for either. Okay, I had the drink. Then I pressed "MENU" on the remote to see if maybe *Gone in Sixty Seconds* or *Van Helsing* was on, or some other giant, steaming turd I'd missed in the theaters. That's when I saw the word "adult" flashing. So to speak. Hmmm . . .

I drummed my fingers for a few seconds, or maybe an hour, turned around and looked behind me—I actually did, which is idiotic, looked to the left and the right and behind me, and since I was sitting on the edge of the bed in a hotel room alone, there wasn't a lot behind me except me.

So I pressed it. That's right. I pressed the button for the adult menu. Oh, you impulsive fool! You madcap! You voluptuary! You prisoner of caprice!

But which to choose? There were five or eight or twelve or something, and, as you may know, the promo cards for porn (sounds like a sign at a demonstration, doesn't it? "English Teachers for Peace!" "Promo Cards for Porn!") don't help the cautious consumer a great deal in making an informed choice. Trailers are more or less out of the question, for reasons that may be obvious—unless the producers someday lose their minds and start making ones that just involve the plot.

The titles of these films, however, are refreshingly to the point and often quite clever. As we all know, they're frequently based on the titles of mainstream hits: *Star Whores,* for example. (I just made that one up. See how easy it is? If it hasn't already been made, you're welcome to—oops, so it has, says Cal, my trusty editor, who knows how to use the Internet. Ah, well. You'll have to come up with your own.)

Ultimately, I figured, they were all probably about the same, like Chinese food, so I just picked one, and that was that. (I seriously can't remember which one, but there really was a *Debbie Does Dallas* sequel on the menu, although I also can't remember whether it was II, or III, or IV, or whether there were so many they had Koechel numbers. The important thing is, as you know, that I haven't said *The Quickening* again.)

Whichever it was, I watched five or ten minutes and turned it off. And I'd like to tell you why. I think I learned something important, although it was peanuts compared to what I was going to learn soon.

As I've said, I'm not a prude, and if people over eighteen want to watch other people over eighteen in various configurations and dodecahedrons, it's okay with me. And if hotels make dough on them, that's okay, too.

But nothing exists in a vacuum, does it? And some things have consequences, don't they?

See, the reason I turned it off was that there's an element of pornography men don't register most of the time, but that hit me in that room like a ton of bricks.

It's so *sad*. So terribly sad. So empty. For everyone—starting with whoever's watching it. That's why it wasn't compelling, why it wasn't interesting. But it's saddest of all for the people in it, and that's why I turned it off.

It's just as sad for the actors as for the actresses, by the way, the men as well as the women—and, yes, they absolutely are actors and actresses. I have no idea how they do it. I mean, now *that's* acting. I've missed my mark dozens of times in movies, or been moved over by the cinematographer into the light, or told I was speaking too softly by the sound mixer, or been instructed to get a lot better quickly by the director. How anyone can remember all these things and—well, you know—at the same time is not only beyond me, it's almost inhuman. And do they just do it once? I mean, shoot it once? I mean, make it once? I mean, lay it down once? Seriously, Stanley Kubrick was famous for doing twenty, fifty, eighty takes of everything. Do they have stand-ins or stunt men? Or is that redundant? Let's be honest, even once would involve a level of concentration I don't believe even levitating yogis can match.

Whatever the case, that inescapable, palpable sadness soaks through every frame of the final product—a metaphysical pointlessness, an empty, mechanical quality, an absence of purpose, of soul; a reduced, rutting, technical physicality, a kind of *Is this as far as we've come in six thousand years?* feeling.

And once you see that side of it, you can't ever not see it again. You can't go back and watch it through a teenager's eyes. I wouldn't have had these thoughts as a teenager anyway, which is fine, because I'm not a teenager. I'm an adult, without the quotation marks, and I guess every so often I ought to feel and think like one.

It's like what my friend Dan Pasternak told me about Alcoholics Anonymous. He fell off the wagon once and spent a few nights drinking. "Was it fun?" I asked him. He gave me a small smile and said, "There's nothing worse than a bellyful of liquor, and a head full of AA."

I think the sadness is especially present for the women, though. You can almost feel the hurt somewhere inside. I can't watch them without thinking. "What happened? Something in childhood? Something awful?" Of course, anyone who's seen my act might say the same thing.

On the other hand, maybe I'm wrong. Really. I say that a lot in life, and I mean it every time: Maybe I'm wrong. Maybe all the actors and actresses in the porn business would say, "Hey, nothing bad ever happened to me, pal, and I don't need your sympathy. I like this work, I'm doing very well, thank you very much, and it beats the tar out of the post office. I'm as happy as a—well, let's just say I'm happy and leave it at that."

In any case, right or wrong, I turned it off, read a little of my airplane book, and went to sleep.

I HAD AN EARLY FLIGHT BACK, SO I WOKE UP, WASHED up, packed up, and took my little overnighter downstairs for a quick juice and coffee before getting picked up. I got off the elevator, went to the desk, and the clerk was young and pretty, so pretty, in fact, I remember thinking, "Gershwin was right. A pretty girl *is* like a melody." She was polite, too, and sincere, and that made her even prettier, and then she made the whole thing way, way better—perfect, really—by leaning over and whispering, "We're not supposed to say anything, but I just want to tell you I think you're a good actor."

I know, I know, it's another pretty young woman who likes me, and no, it doesn't happen a lot, it's just this story. Believe me, I'm well aware that my demographic tends more toward chubby guys with bad complexions who can recite the entire script to *Goodfellas*. Oh, wait, that's me.

But there's a reason I'm telling you this time, because, unlike the 7-Eleven, I wasn't trying to buy a *Playboy,* and didn't faint, and had the chance to offer my best smile in return and say, "Thank you. That's so sweet."

She smiled, too, and excused herself to answer the phone, and I remember watching her tear the bill out of the printer and thinking, "I wonder who's lucky enough to kiss this beautiful girl?"

That's when I had a wonderful thought, a joyous epiphany, as I realized I don't need anything else sexual from other women for the rest of my life. We're all vulnerable to mistakes, big and small, but I haven't made any yet—at least not in that department—and I think I'll be okay. I'm the luckiest guy in the world, because I don't need to risk my marriage, or a giant black mark—or break my promise—and every so often a girl like this will lean over and say something nice, and I'll always have those moments. Sex is all just fleeting moments anyway, and I don't need to have affairs, and I don't need to take chances, and I certainly don't need to sit in hotel rooms late at night watching por—

That's when it hit me. The movie. The bill. *Oh, no.*

Then I fainted. Or, at least, wanted to.

Now, it's not what you think. You've probably seen that scene in movies a thousand times where the bill has the name of the porn movie on it, and the clerk shouts it out, and everyone in line knows, too, and people clutch their children and run away, and the guy's embarrassed.

But that's not what happened to me, because that's not what happens to anyone. Not in real life. No hotel prints the name of the movie, ever. They make too much money on them to embarrass the guest. Ever. They never print the title, and no employee will ever know what you saw. EVER.

Unless . . .

Remember, folks, I was only in town for one night. The room and tax were paid for by the people who hired me. I didn't order room service, I didn't have anything cleaned or pressed, I didn't go to the health club, I didn't go to the restaurant, I didn't hire a car, I didn't buy anything in the gift shop. There was nothing on that bill.

So when my pretty, young clerk, my gorgeous part-time student, my Rosalind, my Isolde, my Melisande, my Roxanne (Alexander's, not Sting's), hung up the phone and walked back over to me in slow motion, like the referee in *Raging Bull* crossing the ring to tell DeNiro he's won, and laid the bill on the counter between us so I could sign it, and leaned in again with a smile, we both looked down and saw the exact same thing at the exact same time: an entire sheet of blank paper with nothing on it.

Oh, there was one thing. One lonely charge smack dab in the middle.

Print the name of the movie? They didn't have to print the name of the movie. It would have been more merciful if they had. A title like *Rear Admiral* might be gross, but far worse is the work the imagination does when the only thing they do print is three words more obvious and debased than any title could ever be, three words surrounded by empty paper, not discreetly buried in dozens of items, not unnoticed among three pages of boring charges, but alone with nothing else around them, *naked,* as it were, and impossible to misapprehend:

In . . . Room . . . Entertainment.

Unmistakable. Why? Because those words were followed by a line of dots across the page and a price:

$13.99.

What else in the world costs $13.99? Nothing. Regular movies are $8.99, two for $17.98. $13.99 is some kind of unalterable figure, like Planck's Constant, or pi: It is what it is, and couldn't be anything else. It screams and waves its arms, it points to itself and yodels. It ululates. It is one thing, and one thing only, and that thing is . . .

In . . . Room . . . Entertainment.

Our heads were less than a foot away, and we were looking right at each other. She didn't say anything. She didn't have to.

She knew. I knew she knew. And she knew I knew she knew. Neither of us moved for five or ten seconds, which is a very long time at a moment like that.

Finally, throat drier than it was at the 7-Eleven, I hoarsely said, "I turned it off after five minutes," but her smile had already dropped at the corners. I considered trying to say—

WHAT? SAY WHAT? EXPLAIN MARRIED MALE SEXUALITY to a young girl in twenty words? She won't even understand it after she gets married herself. No one does—not even men.

What then? Tell her I've never cheated, but sometimes I think about it? Say I ordered the movie, but I didn't really want to, but I did, but I didn't, but I did? Make an excuse? "I just couldn't sit through *Troy* again." (That's certainly true.)

Pointless. I summoned every fiber I had, stood (disengaged, if you will), signed the bill, folded it twice (or three times; or twenty), put it in my jacket, turned, took a few steps, stopped, and, after a long, unsuccessful attempt to vanish into another dimension, turned back and nodded my head like a World War I pilot to the foe who's just shot him down. Before leaving I think I said something clever, like "Good luck in your career."

And that's the last time I ever ordered an "adult" movie.

Will I continue to glance over at the covers of *Playboy* on the racks—er, shelves—behind the counters? Sure. I'm a guy, and a guy can be a hundred and three and impotent and still smile at a cheerleader. Will I continue to look at someone's copy of the *Sports Illustrated* swimsuit issue, or even buy one on my own, if the Harpo wig doesn't slip off? I may just do that. (Though they're not quite as good as they used to be, are they?) Will I lean over someone's shoulder backstage to peer at a magazine on his desk? Why not?

But adult movies in hotels? Gee, maybe not. I think I'll just flip around instead. Got to be a *Law & Order* on somewhere. Yeah, that's the ticket. Maybe an episode with one of those terrific guest stars they always seem to find.

But why? Why no more X-rated forays? After all, I'm alone in the room. I'm a big boy; I can do what I want. Men like naked women. I'm a man; *I* like naked women. So why not? Because the films are so sad? Because I've seen some moral beacon in the sky I hadn't seen before? Because I feel a political, or social, or religious pull? Because it's not healing the world and moving it forward?

No, not really. None of those.

No, never mind the guilt or the shabbiness. Never mind putting money into the pockets of the men and women who take advantage of these men and women. Never mind being a pathetic link at the end of a corrupt chain. Never mind any of it.

I just can't go through the billing process again.

ELEVEN

WHAT IT'S LIKE TO BE IN SHOW BUSINESS

"SO, IS ONE O'CLOCK OKAY FOR YOUR FOOT MASSAGE?"

Every so often in life someone utters a line that just can't be beat, and I think that's one of them. A team of writers could work all day, every day, for the rest of their lives, and never top it for pure emblematic idiocy. I picked up the phone in the office, said hello, and that's how the voice at the other end answered, with no preamble: "So, is one o'clock okay for your foot massage?"

I'm guessing this doesn't happen a lot in the aluminum siding business.

There are so many ways to respond to a question like that—all of them inadequate—that I was speechless. I pulled the receiver away and looked at it for a few seconds, returned it to my ear, narrowed my eyes, leaned forward, and finally said, "What?"

True, the initial question was delivered with a splash of facetiousness by the caller, a voice I knew well, my publicist and friend, and noted dueling enthusiast, Michael Hansen. I like people who bring mysteries to show business, and Michael has a pretty big one:

how anyone has managed to be as successful as he is in Hollywood with a name like "Hansen." (Perhaps all the age-old stereotypes are just vicious libels. . . ? No, no, it can't be that.) But he's a great pro and the only one of my crack representatives who gives whiskey on birthdays. This goes a long way toward explaining our friendship.

The call came on a Tuesday, and the appointment was offered to me for that weekend, Sunday, at one o'clock. This was no idle offer, though: This was a business matter, and one that went beyond the normal pampering so casually passed around Hollywood like syphilis at a Fatty Arbuckle party. It was Emmy Awards Sunday, you see—one of the big days and nights here in the Dream Factory— and there were three reasons I looked at the phone blankly:

1. As Hansen knew, I don't spend an awful lot of time in life hunting up strangers to rub my feet. (There's nothing wrong with my feet, by the way: no bunions, protrusions, fungi, webbing, bromadrosis, odd angles or lengths, mismatched totals, broken nails, scars, colorations or conditions of any kind. No surprises or horrors. It's not that. They're just guy-feet. And I don't need them touched.)

2. I wasn't nominated for anything that year (which, more or less, had led to)

3. I wasn't going.

Yet here I was being handed (or footed) an apparently much-sought-after top-shelf amenity, and only one among the dozens of other free gifts available to me at the same time, courtesy of HBO, as part of their annual, pre-Emmy Sunday Afternoon Splasheroo at the Peninsula Hotel in Beverly Hills.

Naturally, I analyzed the opportunity from a strictly professional remove before whining, "Is this something I have to do?" Hansen quickly said, "Call Eileen before you decide." He knows his clients.

The Divine Mrs. M. squealed with pleasure (INSERT YOUR OWN SEX JOKE HERE) when I told her, and her giggling gave me the precious extra seconds necessary to reassess my position, brighten like a sun, do a buck-and-wing on the tenth part of a dollar, and say, "Oh, yeah, honey, that's why I'm calling. I know this is the stuff you like. We'll bring the kids, too, and they can swim or something while you and I play Supermarket Sweep. It took some doing, by the way, but I even got you an appointment for a foot massage. Well, again, I know you like these things, and they tell me he's the top guy in town. I mean, keep this under your hat and all, but he usually only does, like, Kate Winslet and . . . Marjorie Main, but I talked him into it. Hey, and we'll grab a bite with the kids afterward in the restaurant, too. Maybe even a quick one in the bar, just you and me. How's that sound?" Married men are, as a rule, morons, but under pressure we're capable of maneuvering like Octavian at Actium.

Now, I've been on a bunch of things on HBO, and they make, I think, some of the best stuff on television. (If there's anything in the last fifty years better than *The Sopranos*, I'd like to know what.) But as I mentioned, I hadn't been nominated. So why me, then? I was flattered, but why?

Like most things in show business, the correct question is, Why not? As many of you probably know—oh, that's silly; you all know this unless you were raised by Ted Kaczynski—the Emmys (Emmy's? Emmies? Emmie's? Skip it? Who cares?) is a glittery TV special broadcast every year at the same time in September that Lorne Greene used to introduce the new Chevys on *Bonanza*, although this is judged by most cognoscenti to be a coincidence.

I was just telling Hansen to switch the foot appointment from me to Eileen (without letting her know, of course . . . oh, shut up), and then to see if maybe they had also set up a special wing with retired Montessori teachers or something for everyone's kids (no, it's not at all crazy), when she called back, devastated, to say she couldn't make it. There were Little League games and registrations and snack bar duties she couldn't get out of that Sunday, and I'd have to go alone. This was plainly nuts, because here I don't even want to go, and she wants to go very much. So I told her she should go alone instead and get all the stuff, and I'd take her place in everything at Little League (which I'd done several times before, and successfully, too, if you call massive drops in registration and weeks of written complaints about surliness successful.)

Another irony: My wife is a multi-award-winning television writer, with one of those awards coming for a great series on HBO, *Dream On,* and the only one in our family ever nominated for an Emmy (twice). But in this case Hansen told me I couldn't send her in my place to cart off a tumbrel-load of free stuff, and that someone wanted me to do the hauling personally.

By the way, even though my wife didn't win either of those Emmy nominations, I should tell you that it was a glamorous and thrilling evening for me both times, a top-shelf night out with the champagne wishes and caviar dreams set, the most wonderful people to meet and laugh with, in the most wonderful whirl in the world, a personal dream come true, and the sort of Hollywood-at-its-best affair that simultaneously brings tears of joy to one's eyes and great pleasure to so many around the country.

No, none of that's so. (Good Lord, give me a little credit here, folks.) Look, of course I'd be thrilled if I ever won one, but that night has nothing to do with the work done to get there. It's Hollywood at its most impossibly self-absorbed, and I hated every second. I made more trips to the bathroom than a first-time Depends wearer, and walked out onto the side balcony three times to watch the sun go down. (All three times John Goodman was there with a drink. The first time, he glanced over at me, nodded hello, jerked his head back toward the room and said, "Jesus, huh?")

For one thing, I don't know about you, but any time I have to put on a tuxedo I find it impossible not to think of Commodore Vanderbilt's famous last words on the *Titanic:* "We're dressed in our best, and are prepared to go down like gentlemen." We all like to think that we, too, might have said something similarly jaunty on a sinking ship in the North Atlantic, followed by a prayer for loved ones and strangers, and a deep, heartfelt sense that we were, truly, "Nearer, my God, to Thee." In my case, though, I'm afraid it would have been followed immediately by a loud "Aaaaaaaaaaaaa!," an angry "Out of my way, Limey," and a lot of pointless running around in small circles.

So how did I like the Emmys? I love my wife, and I was disappointed she didn't win, and at the big Governor's Ball afterward I danced and smiled with her and told her how great she was, which is true. Then I went back out to drink with Goodman. Like any other sane woman, my wife loves to dress up and go out a couple of times a year, and in this case she was deservedly pretty happy to be doing it at one of the biggest events in our business, where, to boot, she'd been singled out for nomination. She had the best time laughing with friends and colleagues, eating fancy chow, and drinking expensive bubbly.

But me? About halfway through dinner, the woman sitting on my left gushed, "Isn't this wonderful?" and I said, "You seem like a likable person, but frankly, I would kill you to not be here now." (That is a true story. The woman laughed, but her heart wasn't in it. If I recall correctly, those were the last words we exchanged that night.)

Our friend Jim Vallely, who was nominated and won last year for a great *Arrested Development* script, had a very funny observation that goes for the Oscars as well: "Yeah, no one's supposed to know who wins, but please, how do you think the guy with the camera always winds up exactly on the winner?"

Good point.

So, come Super Sunday (Hollywood version), I dropped everyone off at Little League, hugged my wife and laughed with her at the silliness of things, checked out the kids' equipment (and that of a couple of my favorite team moms), and drove off the fields and over the hill to the Peninsula Hotel.

OKAY, FIRST OF ALL, WHY DO SO MANY PEOPLE WANT TO give so much stuff away in the "gift bags" at these events? It's not the studios or networks paying for this, you know, it's the manufacturers. And they're climbing over each other to do it.

Companies with products want people to buy them. This is the beginning and the end of my sophistication in the science of economics. In fact, the only thing I remember from my one economics course in college is that the professor, on the final, looked for the phrase "science of economics" instead of just "economics" in the first sentence of your answer. If you had it, you got an A. If you didn't, you got a C. (I got a C.)

These same companies will do anything, up to and including paying jillions of dollars, to get their products seen in movies and television shows—even ones that stink. You know this. It's called product placement, and you've seen it (or been annoyed by it) thousands of times. It's the subtle revenue-enhancer that occurs when someone in the movie squeezes an obviously visible tube of Coppertone Sunblock onto his kid, or a character in, say, *The Fast and the Furious* stops racing cars for a minute, wipes his brow, and says to his friend, "Boy, I'm hungry and sure could go for a Big Mac and an icy cold Coke," and his friend says, "Sounds good to me, but I think I'll try one of their Chicken Caesar Salads. They're the healthy alternative," and the first one says, "Hey, there's one now. No mistaking those friendly golden arches, eh? Hand me that Bic Clic pen, will you, the one with the smudge-proof, retractable felt tip, so I can write down its exact location next to the name of our fence."

Now, I haven't seen the movie, and I'm just making that up, but we all know it's not that farfetched. Characters sometimes plug products so brazenly these days they're just a whisker away from looking right into the camera, winking, and saying, "Red Bull: You'll Never Sleep Again!"

The opposite of product placement also occurs in movies (product *non*-placement, we might call it), and it's almost as grating. This is where Anheuser Busch graciously declines the opportunity to become a patron of the arts—in other words, refuses to pony up the scratch—and word is immediately passed down to the prop master on the set not to allow the Budweiser cans to read visibly as Budweiser cans. The two options the prop master has are: (1) paint over the name, or (2) change it to Shmudpeiser. Either way, of course, you and I can still tell it's Budweiser from a hundred yards away, making the whole effort just a tiny bit pointless. Martians could land and know what brand it is. (And you know how prissy they are, the sourpussed teetotalers.)

Look, I hate to sound artsy-fartsy, but the occasional, visible use of a well-known product as part of the story being told in a movie or television show is fine—'57 Chevys in *Happy Days*, or packs of Lucky Strikes in a WWII movie, for instance—but only if the studio doesn't ask for money from General Motors or R.J. Reynolds as a condition of showing it in the first place. Once they do that, it changes the storytelling and tramples all over the art. I'd probably do a commercial if it came up (and I thought I could be good in it). Hell, for enough dough, I'd hang upside down in a closet and sleep like a bat. But plays and movies and television shows should be plays and movies and television shows first and last, without someone trying to get the characters to show the brand name on the underwear they're taking off.

Frankly, though, on the other hand . . . I mean, let's be honest, *what about* that question of money? For enough dough, most of us might be tempted to show that brand name, don't you think? Would you? Would I? How about it?

Until it happens, who knows, right? Who ever knows for certain—for certain, mind you, with not even the slightest possibility of wobble—exactly what he or she might do in the face of a gigantic pile of money? "But Larry, your character of the chairman would probably drive expensive cars anyway, right? You said so yourself. So what's the harm in deciding beforehand to make sure they're BMWs, and call the company first, and then put in a line where you say how great they are? They *are* great, right? So you wouldn't be lying. And just for that, they'd pay the difference to make the movie here in L.A. instead of Prague. Of course, we'd call Mercedes first, too, and ask if they want to get in on it. See if we can get a bidding war going. But they're great cars, too, so what's wrong with that?"

I don't know, I really don't. I thought there was something deeply wrong with it a few paragraphs ago, but now I'm not so sure. As my friend Lotus Weinstock used to say, "I'm looking forward to someday saying that fame and fortune did not bring me happiness." I mean, let's not go off half-cocked here and blow a good chance to make a little . . . get a little . . .

What do *you* think?

• • •

THERE ARE MANY OTHER KINDS OF SUCH SILLINESS IN entertainment, but, believe it or not, it's not always the movie's fault. Ever notice character names that sound goofy and klunky and made up? Of course you have. Remember Cole Trickle in *Days of Thunder?* An okay movie, but I'll bet Tom Cruise's character name had NASCAR dads all over the country shaking their heads and muttering. "Oh, Lord. 'Cole Trickle'? Sounds like gonorrhea in Canada." (I know, that's the second venereal disease joke I've used in this chapter, but I like both of them, and that's just the way it worked out. Besides, it took me five tries to spell gonorrhea right, and I hate to waste the effort. Now let's see if I can go for the gold and work in chlamydia before the end of the book. And remember—that's right, it keeps my mind off *The Quickening*.)

The reason character names often sound so dumb is that "Dave Wilson" or "Rob O'Malley" or "Tom Gilchrist" didn't clear, and what "didn't clear" means is that the folks in the studio whose job it is to check these things out couldn't find a name that no one would sue on. Really. So they have to move further and further outside the box, until all that's left are preposterous handles like Chauncy Fastbinder, or Bennett Sinkhole, or Milo Kishka. Or Cole Trickle.

Of course, it's always possible that a particular film's writers or director or producers actually *liked* the name or title they chose; sometimes it's just a matter of taste.

I was in a movie once I still think had one of the best working titles I've ever come across: *Cloak and Diaper*. See what I mean? You probably smiled when you read it. It's clever and witty, and—so rare—even tells you what the movie's about. "Oh, yeah, *Cloak and Diaper*. So it's, like, spies who have a baby?" Exactly. Funny, informative, and compelling, and in just three words. A perfect title. So naturally someone at the studio hated it, and it was changed to *Undercover Blues,* which is not funny, not informative, and puzzling. Other than that, I guess it's perfect, too.

A similar syndrome I'm sure has puzzled you many times over the years is when a character in the movie is being mercilessly tortured to reveal a phone number, and finally screams out, "Okay, you win, I'll talk! The number where the money is buried is . . . 555-1212!" It's perfectly stupid, and always takes you out of the action, but nearly every other number there is will ring through to a real person, and bunches of people in every theater will actually call it. Silly people who desperately need a hobby, true, but they'll call it nonetheless, and that's a lot of people calling the same number at the same time, even on flops like *Gigli*. (*Gigli*, you may remember, rhymes with, "Maybe we should break up?")

SO I PULLED UP TO THE PENINSULA, AND IMMEDIATELY wished I was back in the snack bar, hurting business.

Everyone at these places on event days, starting with the parking guys, is on the lookout for actors and directors and agents. The guy who was holding the front door actually said, "Good luck tonight," to me with a big smile, before receiving a "He's not nominated" touch on the arm by a knowing bellman. (These guys are sharp.) My usual walking pace is no faster than it would be to my own execution, but it's fair to say I was whisked to the gift area by a series of people who said, "HBO?" and passed me on to the next one. It was an entire ground floor wing blocked by a table with five men in blazers and clipboards and earpieces that couldn't have been much more difficult to enter than Camp David.

As I approached the table, two well-known actresses left the area, each leading a beefy guy holding cartons of stuff. Picture

Oddjob with twenty boxes of pumps and bath salts. This was looking to be quite a haul.

My dad used to work for Carling's Red Cap Ale after getting out of the service in the forties, and he told me that in those days they let each employee take home as much beer as he could carry every night at quitting time. Pretty good perk (and I'll bet they don't do it anymore), but I didn't think I'd be as lucky. I wasn't.

The desk guards assigned me a very nice young woman who said she would carry whatever I pointed at, and proceeded to take me around to each station/display/room. The first was for one of the big cell phone outfits, and a tired-looking man shook my hand with a wince and began describing the phone-of-the-future the company wanted me to have. (He couldn't have known that I don't want anything-of-the-future, other than cures for every disease on Earth, and a hangover pill, but never mind that now.)

It was a tabletop model for the home, large enough to have a built-in computer screen, and he showed me how it could get the weather report, music, movies, news, and lions and tigers and bears, oh my. In a pinch, I'm sure the thing could send a rocket to the moon.

I looked up at him halfway through, not understanding a word he was saying anyway, and said, "Have you been here long today?" And he said, "Well, they wanted me to be the one, because I designed it." He smiled weakly and tried to continue, but I interrupted again.

"Wait a minute," I said, "You *designed* this?" He brightened a little. "Yes," he said. "It's my model. I invented the first system to integrate—"

I stopped him again with a shake of the head and a hand on his shoulder and said, "You designed this and built it, and you have to stand here today telling *actors* about it?"

He shrugged and picked one up, boxed, off the table, but I took it out of his hands and put it back down. "But the kids'll love it," he said, a puzzled protest in his voice, and I said, "They play baseball and football." After a beat, he said, "I used to play baseball."

I shook his hand goodbye and said, "Buddy, we all used to do a lot of things before these folks got a hold of us. Good luck with it," and walked on to the next display.

I'm sure most people would think I was nuts for not wanting a free six-hundred-dollar Thing, or whatever it was, but I just don't need another twenty-pound hunk of brushed metal I can't use sitting around the house. The kids would love it, all right. They'd love throwing it at each other. And, eventually, at me.

Then came the sunglasses, expensive designer ones. I don't wear sunglasses, even here in L.A.—not because I have anything against shades, but because I lose them before I get to the car after leaving the store. About six years ago, I finally stopped trying. Squinting through July and August like a Mongol horseman seems to work just fine.

But here I was trying on pair after pair, all of which were way too flashy for me. "How about these?" asked the polite representative, who was beginning to realize she was dealing with an idiot. And I said, "If I ever wore these in public, I'd be the first one to hit me." She didn't speak Cranky, so I took the first pair she picked—it was for my wife, anyway—and thanked her. Ralph Lauren, I think. (The glasses, not her.) Ray-Bans in the mall are sixty or seventy bucks, so I figured these had to be a lot more.

Next came lingerie. This is something I am not immune to, and after demurring on various masks (for whom, I didn't ask), and a slightly unsettling style of robe (Hint: They had belts to hold things, and not shot glasses. Although . . .), the knowing young representative gestured to a rack of diaphanous baby-doll peignoirs, which are right up my alley, so to speak. Now we were getting somewhere.

What size is your wife, she asked?

I don't know.

Is she like me?

No, from time to time she eats food.

How about me? asked another one.

Kind of, but . . .

Bigger here?

Yes. That's why I asked her out.

Back here?

No, but thank you, though.

How tall?

Oh, regular, I guess; girl-size. I could eat pie off her head, although so far that hasn't come up.

What color?

Green.

She's green?

No, it's my favorite color.

We don't have green.

Okay, pink.

You want pink?

No, *she's* pink.

This was as good as it was going to get for the three of us, and they elegantly (but as quickly as possible) folded a lot of things into several bags, passed them over to my handler, and off we went again.

There were a lot more stations, but you don't need to hear about every one, or, at least, I don't need to tell you. It went about the same way at each, and I took whatever I thought might give wifey a smile. Handbags, large for everything and small for some things;

soy lotions for the kids (but not ours); jeans; hats; gloves; shoes. Nothing for men, at least nothing for me, but that's not why I was there anyway.

There was even a jewelry room. Seriously. Real jewelry, big and expensive, and not fake. Very big. The kind of diamonds and emeralds even Joan Rivers would eye and say, "Oh, no, that's too gaudy." And I said to the guy, "Bet you're not giving *these* away. Heh-heh-heh." He momentarily looked as if he'd eaten something very sour before saying, "No, sir. But we'd loan them to your wife for the night to be seen on television," and I told him I wasn't nominated for anything, and he said, "Yes, I know. The bellman told me."

Just kidding. He didn't say that (although the bellman might well have told him). But he didn't loan me any jewelry, either, not even after I showed him the lingerie and asked if I could have a necklace to go with them. You know, for the night.

That's when I said to my young friend with the bags, "You know what? I think this is enough. Let's call it a day." And she started to say that there was still this and that to go, but I just smiled, and she smiled, and we understood each other perfectly, and she started to lead me back out toward the table in the front with the guards.

Just down the hall, though, she stepped over to an open doorway and gestured into a posh suite with soft music playing, and I froze and thought, "Wow, these HBO guys think of everything," but before I could say something stupid like, "That's very sweet of you, but I'm married," she pointed inside and said, "It's one o'clock. Time for your foot massage."

Oh. Uh, well, no, thank you, I said, I really don't need one. But she said, "He's the best. He's done Kate Winslet." I looked closely at her for a trace of irony, found none, and thought, "Well, I'm probably going to write about all this. Maybe I should at least look in." (My capacity for research and sacrifice is second to none.) I checked my watch, thought about the lines at the snack bar, shrugged, and followed her inside.

There were two men and three women, not counting the two clients already being soaked (and soaked), and the main guy was just finishing up someone's feet, a woman I didn't know. It wasn't Kate Winslet. Everyone looked up and said hello with relaxed, wealthy, Southern California smiles, and the man, the owner-operator-originator of this particular technique, gestured to a chair.

"No, thank you," I said, "I don't need the rub, I just wanted to say hello and take a look around." One of the women with her feet up said, "You really must. It's Heaven." "She's right, you know. Heaven," agreed the other soaker. I was turning this fresh take on the afterlife around in my head for a while, when the owner said, "Please. Let me show you what we do," but I said, "Again, thank you, but I've got to be back at the . . . my kids have a . . . I can still catch the last few . . ." One of his assistants was already leading me in, and handed me a glass of something cold and clear that, aggravatingly, wasn't gin.

"Conflicting obligations today, hmm?" the owner drawled with a smile, looking up from his work, and I said, "Aye, there's the rub. Get it? Rub?" regretting it the instant I saw seven blank faces staring back at me. He implored me once more to sit, and having yet again in life committed ritual sepuku with a bad pun, I took a last look around for my handler, who had wisely stacked the booty and split. Then, after one more shrug, I sat down in a terrific chair and put my feet up.

The rubber was gently toweling off the rubbees, who fairly glided out of the room. Then he turned to me, nodded at my Topsiders, and said, "Come on. Don't be shy."

•   •   •

THERE WAS ONE OTHER TIME IN LIFE I WAS TALKED INTO being rubbed against my will. About eight years ago my wife was given a free weekend for two at a big-time resort out here in the desert called Two Bunch Palms. (There are no words missing from that name, it's just . . . Two Bunch Palms.) The gift certificate came from someone in show business as a thank-you for my wife's help on a script; it was the centerpiece of one of those giant wicker baskets, surrounded with marmalade and stupid Danish cookies. (Who uses blue tins for food anymore? It's like pressed meats from the Boer War.) She made the reservations, and off we went for three days. I'll skip the part about me not wanting to.

The first day at breakfast she told me she'd made appointments for us that day for their world-famous salt rub. My knowledge of salt rubbing up to that point had been limited to the kind Captain Bligh ordered for you as dessert following the main course of two or three hundred lashes. (Although those were, in their way, world famous, too.)

Anyway, I didn't see a way to get out of going. (It's like what they say about battles: At that point, it'd be harder *not* to do it than to do it.) I tried sulking about it back in the room, and sighing loudly, until I realized she was intentionally not looking at me. So I accepted my fate, took off my clothes, put on a monogrammed robe so thick it could've gotten me through the Shackleton Expedition, and headed down to the health club.

The scent of eucalyptus nauseates me, but, then again almost everything does, except the planks behind a bar at closing time. I entered the spa—a dim, acoustically hushed area hot enough to grow orchids—and met my young, attractive masseuse, who, it turns out, wasn't a masseuse at all, but a young, attractive masseur. In other words, a guy. A blonde, muscular guy. A tattooed, blonde, muscular guy. Anyone want to guess what symbol from World War II was one of the tattoos?

Oh, this was just getting better and better.

I don't think I'm a stick in the mud, I swear I don't, and anything people want to do is fine with me, but the thought of getting a deep-tissue massage from someone who looks like Brian Bosworth (or a guy in *Oz*) was only slightly more palatable than having the same fellow do a table dance for me, and I was rapidly growing less sanguine about this operation. Tick-tick-tick . . .

He told me to lie down naked on my back on a rubber table—naturally—and I did. Although not right away. Then he spent a couple of minutes hosing me up and down with a gentle flow of warm water. I think I peed, but it was hard to tell with so much else going on. Tick-tick-tick . . .

Well, after all, the thing was called a salt rub, so the trickle-down dribble was followed by The Boz covering me with salt. Not Morton's, of course (you know, the "When it rains, it pours" stuff) and not the large, kosher brand far more popular with margaritas than on Passover. It was a rough, grainy, chunky, gooey, pasty salt, and, not to put too fine a point on it, it was revolting. Tick-tick-tick . . .

Then—how could it be otherwise?—he began to knead it and rub it in. Tick-tick-tick . . .

The thing was scheduled for an hour and a half, but about three minutes in he paused and said, "You feel a little tense. Is something wrong?"

Now I finally breathed out and said, "Look, pal, what's it cost me to get out of here right now?" Ten minutes and twenty bucks later, I was all hosed off again—I did my own hosing this time, which made it much easier to tell when my bladder let go—and another five after that I was strolling back to the room in my giant robe, whistling "Arrivederci, Roma."

And I remember thinking, "Maybe Eileen was right after all. I feel fantastic."

That was the first and last time, until the guy at the Peninsula with the feet.

I'M NOT IMMUNE TO SWAG, BY THE WAY. IN FACT, JUST the opposite. Every jacket and hat I've owned in my adult life has some movie or television show or radio station printed on it. I'm not proud of this, and it's actually mortifying, but Los Angeles is warm enough most of the time not to need a coat, and if I have to go to New York in the winter, I grab the heavy tweed thing I've had since college. I'm not cheap, I just don't care.

Every ten months or so, my wife and I throw dozens of Tri-Star sweatshirts and Sony Pictures coffee mugs and Warner Brothers down vests and KLUV wristbands into crates and ship them to relatives back East who are (I think, anyway) thrilled to get them.

For twelve years, to this day—no exaggeration here: every single morning, seven days a week—I have worn an Arsenio Hall bathrobe while shaving. I was on his show a bunch of times (and always liked him), and they used to give you a nice gift basket in the dressing room, and it always included these great robes. All cotton, not too fluffy, just right. I mean, *terrific* robes. I sent a few to nieces and nephews, and kept two for myself; to this day I alternate between a white one with a purple silhouette on the back of him pointing up with one hand, and a black one with the slogan "It's a night thing" on the breast pocket. Great robes.

Last winter we were planning to make up a box of stuff to send to a soldier in Iraq. I was in the office writing. This is at Universal, and I went down the hall to ask Jim Brubaker (who's produced dozens of seriously good movies, like *The Right Stuff*) if I could throw in some movie stuff. He was off on location somewhere, but his assistant, Gina, said sure, and she unlocked a storage room, and we just started throwing in whatever was there—caps and visors, ski goggles and gloves (I know most of it was useless, but what the heck) and wristbands and sweatbands and socks, all with the names of movies on them. There were a few winter coats left, too: nice, long, roomy, insulated ones, shiny green. I had one at home they'd given me (that I had already since given away), and asked if I could throw one of those in, too, and again she said sure.

A month after we sent them, we got a nice letter from a sergeant in Iraq. The stuff was great, he said, all of it, and sent his thanks, and mentioned how he'd given the winter coat to his local interpreter, an Iraqi who lived in the village who was so important to their work, and served as his ears and eyes. And the guy was so deeply thrilled, he said: It was the nicest thing he'd ever had, that anyone in his family had ever had, that anyone in the village had ever had, and he was so proud of it.

Even the crustiest of us must close our eyes for a moment when we hear this kind of thing, shaking our heads with gratitude at how much we have, and shocked at how little others have. This I did, and wished them both well in my heart, until . . .

My eyes shot open, and I sat up at the desk, and it hit me. Oh, no. Oh, my God.

Folks, let's be honest. To people in that part of the world, especially these days, anyone putting on something obviously from Hollywood might as well be wearing sandwich boards that say, "I have Jewish friends," which I can't imagine is a terribly popular thing in the Arab world (as opposed to the rest of the world, or Mars, for that matter), and I was suddenly petrified this poor Iraqi was making a target of himself, both by visibly working for an American soldier in the first place, and now wearing a shiny winter coat to boot. Why didn't I just send him one with a bullseye on it? Nice gift, all right. Thanks a bunch, pal.

And I'm still terrified that one day I'll see an item in the paper about some roadside bombing and read, "The only clue Iraqi police have to the identity of the victim is that apparently he worked on *Bruce Almighty.*"

WELL, I TOOK THE FOOT RUB. I DIDN'T PLAN TO, BUT WHY not? I'm here, he's here, and my feet are here. Why be a jerk and pass it up, right? He slid my shoes and socks off and pointed to the pre-rub soak-softener, which was a special sonic electro-dip he had invented, too. (This joint had more inventors than a patent office.) It took a little coaxing to get me to put my feet into the thing, though, because it was plugged into the wall and *whirring,* and the whole setup looked like that scene where Sean Connery throws the bad guy into a bath, tosses an electric radio in after him, watches him jerk and jolt for a few seconds, and then strolls out muttering, "Shocking."

"Do you feel the tingling?" Dr. Scholl asked with a giggle after I finally dipped. I did, and told him so. "That's how you know it's working. And look! Look at the water!" Sure enough, the water was getting darker by the second. Much darker, too, and fast. "Those are the toxins being released by your system." Okay. This was certainly impressive, but I suddenly felt like an aristocratic mark in a four-teenth-century con: "Look, m'Lord, look! I put the lead and base metals in one end, and, sure as the world's a pancake, out comes *gold* from the other. How lucky you are that I have just one of these miraculous machines left before selling it to the French!"

Well, the foot rub was okay. How bad can any massage be? Neck, back, hands, feet, it's always going to be good, right? Like the old saying about sex, even the worst is pretty good (unless, of course, you're the one who's terrible and your partner isn't telling you). Your feet get very clean, and the mysterious hydro-electra-solution gets very dark, and I could take it or leave it, but it's a decent enough way to spend time, I guess, if you're looking for ways to fill the day. I wasn't even annoyed when he asked if I wanted to buy the thing that *whirs*. I didn't, but took a few bottles of his nitro-fuel-burning water as a consolation prize—at ten bucks a pop. He invented that, too, and, after all, remember: There's no free lunch.

When I walked out front for my car, things were really heating up for the Emmys, with limos and flowers, and publicists barking orders into cell phones. I loaded the bags into the trunk, and rolled slowly down the driveway of show business and back over the hill to the sunny world of Little League.

My wife was in the stands watching one of the kids, and she kissed me and told me he was really hitting the ball hard today, and how the little one had made a great catch earlier, and how a pitch bounced up when he was catching and bonked him in the cup, and he yelled, "Holy Mackerel, it hit my jock!" and couldn't stop laughing, and that the game stopped while everyone else laughed, too. She asked how it went at the Peninsula, and I handed her the sunglasses, and she put them on and smiled, and I told her there was lots more, but, boy-oh-boy, just wait'll she sees my feet.

And who knows, maybe next year I'll be pulling up at the Peninsula in a limo, and the same guy will open the front door and say, "Good luck tonight, sir," and the bellman next to him will smile and say, "That's right, sir. Good luck tonight."

The key to show business—at least one of them—is not needing that. It's doing the work and loving it, and if you win something along the way, so much the better. But anyone who needs anything better than coming home to a healthy family on a sunny day is missing the point of life, no matter what business he's in.

LATER THAT NIGHT MY WIFE AND I HAD A DRINK TOGETHER downstairs, and she put on one of those lacy things, and it fit just fine. Turns out we didn't need a diamond necklace after all.

TWELVE

TEACH YOUR CHILDREN THAT LOU IS FUNNY

WE ALL TRY TO TEACH OUR CHILDREN WELL. THAT WAS the first line of a wonderful Crosby, Stills, Nash, and Young song, remember? "Teach Your Children," it was called, or "Teach Your Children Well," maybe, and it went, "Teach . . . your chil-dren well . . ."

Okay, that's all I remember, but it was a good song. (Has anyone in history ever learned the second line of a song? I'll settle for someone who knows what Auld Lang Syne means.) Wait a minute, I should know it, I listened to the stupid thing enough. Hold it: "Teach . . . your chil-dren well . . . da da da-da . . . some something some-thing . . ."

Nope. I guess one of the things we should teach our children well is better memory techniques.

Sometimes we disagree on what good teaching is, though, don't we?

One of the received and accepted truths of parenting used to be, "Children should be seen and not heard." Remember that quaint little dictum? Perhaps not, since it's been neither seen *nor* heard for quite a while. The more current version might be, "Children should interrupt any adult whenever they feel like it without even the slightest regard for manners or self-control. Further, they should be encouraged in this self-absorption, and patted on the head every time they give voice to any random, vacant, or tendentious thought that flies into their (by definition) childish skulls on anything, anytime, anywhere. To do otherwise would crush their spirits forever, and ensure refusals in ten years from every college in North America, except the one Tom Wolfe wrote about."

I guess that wouldn't fit very well on a bumper sticker. On the other hand, with careful penmanship, it might be successfully painted onto the fender of a Navigator.

Another previously well-regarded piece of advice that's become antique: "Spare the rod and spoil the child." It's generally agreed these days that corporal punishment results in emotional scarring. This is true—but for the parent, not the child.

I spanked one of our kids a few years ago. He was five or six. Just that one time, and three or four whacks. He said something awful to my wife at the kitchen table, and I immediately whipped around and yelled, "Hey, true or not, even *I* don't get to say that."

Just kidding. We were both stunned by it, and I whispered, "I think I may have to spank him for that," and she said, "You absolutely have to." She asked if she should do it, and I said I thought it should come from me, and she agreed.

I took him into his room, closed the door, sat down on the bed and stood him in front of me, and told him what was about to happen. "Do you know what you did?" He nodded. "It was very mean to Mommy, and you will never do it again. Never. I'm going to spank you now for it. That's how bad it was. Do you understand?" He nodded again, and I put him over my knee and did it. Whap, whap, whap. His eyes filled slightly, and I said, "Now go apologize to Mommy," and he did, and then I went into my room, closed the door, and wept for an hour.

Well, not really, but you know what I mean. Our parents meant it when they said, "This is going to hurt me a lot more than it hurts you," but there's a modern version of that, too: "You'll forget about this the second you leave the room, but I'll be two inches shorter in sadness for the rest of my life."

I sometimes think teachers should go back to walloping kids, too, but only boys, and only from male teachers. Besides, let's be honest, boys are the ones who need it. It gets their attention. Most girls can probably be brought around with hushed urges and threats of checks against their names, but, as I recall, the eleven-to-fifteen-year-old boys I grew up with straightened out a lot faster from a twisted ear or a cuff on the back of the head than from a plea for civility.

To our contemporary ears I'm sure that sounds like a junior high for the SS, but I not only never minded, I even kind of dug it. It seemed to me, even then, like bear cubs rolling around and whacking each other, and was a source of pride in the lunchroom afterward.

Mr. Caruso was a track and field coach and taught metal shop, and I liked him a lot. He was a tall, powerful man with horn-rimmed glasses and a great laugh I can still hear, and he had a colorful way of putting things when he wanted you to remember something.

One day in shop he was showing us the arc welder and said, "Whatever you do, don't ever look at the blue light inside the machine when the welder starts to crackle. You'll be blind for four days. And the whole time it feels like sand being ground into your eyes with track spikes." True or not, we not only never looked at it when it was on, I don't think I ever looked at it when it was off. Come to think of it, I always crossed the room on the other side. Sand? Track spikes? Yeeesh.

He also had a thing he called the "board of education." You can probably guess what it was. To encourage staying focused on your work while operating a metal cutter, or lathe, or stamper—or anything else that might vaporize your hand—he'd wander around in his blue apron checking our techniques with a two-by-four in his right hand. It was not a small hand. If one of us forgot to turn the machine off before leaning away to say something to the next kid, he'd whack us in the backside with the wood.

Now, folks, he just used his wrist—I mean, it was always just a flick—but I'm here to tell you, that thing hurt like crazy. It stung a lot more than you'd think it possibly could, and for twenty or thirty minutes, too, the classic definition of not being able to sit down for a while.

I still remember turning around and seeing Bruce Batkin catch one that literally lifted him off his feet with a yowl. I guess today there'd be lawsuits and firings and reeducation seminars. But we never lost any hands.

Mr. Argenzio coached varsity soccer, and one day, after an away game, a handful of us got off the big yellow bus through the emergency door in back instead of filing out the front. It annoyed the driver, and Mr. Argenzio—Mr. Argenz' we called him, or Little Joe (but never to his face)—went around and made everyone who did it get back on and go out the right way and apologize to the driver. And as each one of us stepped up to the opening, he booted him so hard (side-of-the-foot kicks—it was soccer, remember) the kid shot halfway back into the bus just from the force. After seeing the first two get it, the others just stood there at the opening waiting for theirs. No big thing, and we laughed about it in the showers. Plus, if it doesn't sound too scandalous, I think he was right.

Mr. May coached football and taught health. We called him "The Bull from Indiana," which should give a rough picture of his build. Whenever one of the boys snickered too much at the mention of some body part (which hardly ever happened, since we were so mature), Mr. May picked him up by his collar, took him into the hallway, and hit him in the arm between the shoulder and elbow. It didn't tickle. Then they'd go back in and resume whatever the lesson was. (I still don't really know what an ovary is.)

Anyway, every year the Varsity Club put on a glittering evening called the Varsity Club Follies. Sophomoric would have been a compliment. It was a good-natured, though half-witted, show that was written by pinheads like, well, me, and of course all the coaches attended to see themselves imitated. (The girls came, too, perhaps hoping to chat up a pimpled wrestler afterward—as long as he wasn't in the Unlimited weight class.)

One year I borrowed an old wig my mom had in the attic to play the lead in an epic titled *Dorothy Takes a Trip*. (Don't ask.) It was wildly successful, but I didn't quite finish the script, so at one point, about forty minutes in, the thing just stopped, and all "The Players" came out onstage with cans of beer, shook them up and sprayed each other. This was the denouement. I still think it was my finest work.

The next day in class, Mr. May asked where I got the wig. I told him it was my mother's, and he got a gleam in his eye and said, "Oh? Is your mother bald?"

"Every night," I shot back.

The class roared. He marched over, picked me up, and carried me into the hall. But once we got out there he just collapsed against a locker laughing, and we both stood there laughing for a while.

Then he put his arm around my shoulder, and we walked back in as he shook his head and said, "Oh, Miller, that was a good one." There was no punch that day. I adored him.

WE HAVE A FEW RULES IN OUR HOUSE THAT I THINK ARE pretty good. No TV when they're playing with Legos or Lincoln Logs or anything. I don't like the TV on constantly as background, like Muzak. I always say, "We don't do two things at once, we do one at a time. You either watch television or play." Of course they pick television, but then I say, "No, you watch enough TV. Play." They grumble and moan, but eight seconds later they're playing happily. Another brilliant stroke from the strict but beneficent Lord of the Manor.

We don't do video games, either. I always tell them, yes, I know all your friends have them; I know you play them when you're over there. That's fine. But in our house we build things, or throw balls and hit them, or run and ride bikes. We *do* things in our family, I say over and over, not watch bad graphics of others doing them.

I have a few cartoons and shows I don't like them to watch, and they know it. Maybe I'm nuts, but I think some of the new ones just depend too much on postmodern snideness as their primary source of humor. (I don't exactly know how to explain my standards, but it's like the old definition of obscenity: "I don't know what bad cartoons are, but I know them when I see them.")

If any of this oppressive parenting sounds too much like—well, like oppressive parenting, please remember that the core principle of raising children for the last six thousand years, the wellspring technique onto which all other rules and wisdom are appended, is this: Wait till they're really enjoying themselves, and then stop it immediately. Whatever makes them happy? End it.

I know that sounds awful, but think about it, and please don't tell me that whatever children do naturally to have fun is best for them. This is colossally stupid, like the folks who cheerfully say, "A child always tells the truth!" A child never tells the truth, at least not right away. They have to be crowbarred into telling the truth, and into the habit of telling the truth, and the rightness of telling the truth. If you don't do this, the child will always lie and grow into an adult who always lies. (Perhaps you've run into one or two of these in your journeys.)

"Natural" behavior is not good.

The child doesn't "naturally" sit calmly and quietly during dinner and chew with his mouth closed. The child "naturally" wants to spit and throw the food, and scream with a full mouth. *This* is what's fun (though presumably less so when he chokes). Thus, child having fun, good parent stopping child from having fun.

The child doesn't "naturally" do homework. The child "naturally" wants to rip up the books and break all the pencils. *This* is fun. Thus again, child having fun, wise and splendid parent stopping child from having fun.

The child doesn't "naturally" want to wash himself in the bath, the child "naturally" wants to scoop up bowls of water and suds and heave them all over the walls. *This* is fun. And so, one more time: child having fun; terrific, loving, handsome parent waiting to have a drink downstairs later with Mommy stopping child from having fun. Wait, where was I? Oh, yes.

Et cetera.

TEACHING CHILDREN WELL ISN'T EFFORTLESS, BUT IT'S rewarding and important. Someone once said you're not raising children, you're raising adults. Quite so. But there's one lesson I enjoy teaching them over and over, and they enjoy learning it. In fact, they love it, and it's one of the times their perfect laughter is perfectly proper.

Watching Abbott and Costello.

I spend a lot of my time writing, acting, and performing on every screen I can get my hands on, and I think some of it's been good, and maybe some has been very good, and maybe some has even been better. But there isn't any work out there today, mine or anyone else's, that regularly, consistently, reliably and almost infallibly hits the bullseye like Abbott and Costello.

Not just them, either, and not just comedy.

I'm talking about the classics in comedy, drama, fine art, music, literature, and any other kind of entertainment, and I'm intentionally using the word "entertainment" here. It doesn't mean "frivolous," it means "moving," and it's another aspect of all art that's been thrown out with the bathwater for decades. Directors and writers and musicians today go on and on about their "vision" or their "passion," or their "need," but they all forget that the greatest creative work in history was always, first and last, entertaining. Beethoven's Fifth (and Sixth, and Seventh, and all the others) were great entertainment, as was Gainsborough's *Blue Boy*, as was *Anna Karenina*. Art that doesn't entertain is self-centered cheese.

So when I invoke "Abbott and Costello" it's a metaphor for, in this case, all the American arts from—arbitrarily—1920 to 1970. This is very rough, remember, but stay with me. Yes, of course, *The Godfather* is a great movie, and *The Sopranos* is great TV, and *Plaza Suite* and *Glengarry Glen Ross* are great plays, and *Jimmy Neutron* and *SpongeBob SquarePants* are great cartoons, and so on, and they were all made after 1970. And several lifetimes of joy are available long before 1920, from Shakespeare to Puccini. Of course. But just now I'm only talking about those fifty years, because I have a way for you to open a door for your kids bigger than you ever thought you could.

I'm talking about Americana, and I'm talking about teaching it to your children.

I can see most of you shaking your heads. "They won't watch it. I can't get them to watch anything old, or in black and white. They won't."

They will. Mine are the same as yours. Let me tell you how I did it.

Every night, even school nights, after homework and bath and Cartoon Network and story and prayers, as they're already covered up in bed, I ask if they want to watch five more minutes of TV. Of course they do, and there's always time. I make the time.

But there's a rule: I get to pick what we watch, and it has to be old.

Comedy is easiest, so start with that. Turner Classic Movies is always good, and AMC, if you get cable, but there's a more reliable method. Buy some tapes and DVDs of the old stuff. Abbott and Costello, Bing and Bob, Marx Brothers, W.C. Fields, whatever you like. They're in every store in the country or on the Internet. Hell, every car wash around here has a rack of them next to the register for, like, a buck-ninety-eight. We spend billions on boats and cars and trips and cruises, and the greatest fun available in the world is next to the pine-scented air fresheners for under two dollars.

Remember, though, and this is important: It has to be *after* brushing teeth and all their chores, the instant before lights-out. That's the key. That's why they'll grab at it desperately, like starving men, because all they know is that they're getting to stay up more. They'd watch weather maps if that's what you put on. That's your power. That's your chance. That's how you do it.

And you only need five minutes.

Because they'll laugh, and you know it. If not the first time, then the second. Or the third. But what do you care? Stay with it. If you show it, they will laugh.

They'll laugh, and they'll laugh a lot, because it's something they never see, *it's funny,* it's genuinely funny, it's finally something truly funny. Oh, they'll laugh. And once they do . . .

I TURNED THE TV OFF, AND THEY GROANED, AND I SMILED and said, remember, we said five minutes, and it's a school night. But wait a second, I said, don't get up yet.

I put the remote on top of the TV and turned to them and said, It was funny, wasn't it? And they laughed again, and screamed, *Oh, yeah!* and talked over each other about how the fat man with the mustache looked right into the camera and just shook his head, or how the funny man with the big eyebrows walked hunched over, or how the man who didn't talk honked his horn, or how the woman with the red hair and big eyes made up such a crazy story to fool her husband.

After they laughed, I said, "Okay, listen to me now. You know how when you see new movies, or watch videos with your friends, you really like them, right? But this is different, isn't it? Remember how you laughed? Okay, we'll watch more tomorrow."

And the next night, before they headed to their rooms, I said, "That was funny, too, wasn't it? Remember what we started to say last night? How it's different from the stuff you see with your friends?" Now they were listening. Closely. "In fact," I said, "the way you laughed at it was different, too, wasn't it? You and your friends love fart jokes and poop jokes, right? But the way you laughed now was different, wasn't it? The sound you made. The way you felt. Different, right? Okay. More tomorrow."

And the next night, and the next, and the next, until they were listening so closely and openly I knew I could hit them with my closer: "In fact, this isn't just different, is it? It's better, isn't it? It's funnier, isn't it? In fact, it's much better, isn't it? It's not even close, is it? They're not shocking, or weird, or gross, are they? They're just really, really funny. The actors are funnier, and the words are funnier, and the stories are funnier, aren't they? I'll never stop you from seeing the things you see with your friends, but now you know. Now you know something they don't. Now you know what's better."

And that's how you do it. It'll change your world, and theirs.

The same goes for music. If they want to listen to something on the way to school, I say, "Okay, but I get to pick the first one. One song, and then we'll put on your station, okay? Oh, this is great. That's a man called Duke Ellington. We've been on that train, you know. Wait, listen to those saxes. Listen to the rhythm. Listen . . ." And they listen.

How strange: When stacked against the Britney Spears and hip-hop of today, popular music of years past seems almost classical by comparison. R&B or the Beatles is like Schubert next to Aaron Carter. And you know what? It is.

Just a few weeks ago we were driving out of the supermarket at night, and the moon had come up and was huge on the horizon, and they said, "Look, Mommy, look, Daddy," and it was immense, and I started singing, "It's that o-o-o-old devil moon, da-da-da . . . da-da-da . . ." (another song I don't know the second line of) ". . . It's that old devil moon, in the sky . . ."

And one of the kids said, "Hey, Dad, put on the old station," and I did, and—no kidding—the instant it came on, the first sound we heard was Frank Sinatra singing "It's that old devil moon, in the sky . . ." It was so weird I pulled over, and we all looked at each other in mild shock, and one of the kids said, "Unbelievable," and the other one said, "Freaky," and my wife said, "Why don't you try that with the lottery sometime?"

Wait, I just remembered the verse from "Old Devil Moon." Hold it: "I . . . look at you and sud-den-ly . . . something in your eyes I see . . . da-da-da-da-da-da-daaaaa . . ."

Yeah, okay, forget it.

This works for poetry, too. The step from Dr. Seuss to Robert Frost isn't as great as you might think (and it wouldn't hurt you, either). It may sound like trying to turn an ocean liner with an oar, but I promise you it's not.

I don't give them great thumping doses of this stuff, and I'm not trying to change the world, just my little part of it. I don't want to remake them in my image, I just want to keep some of it alive a little longer. I just want them to know. I want them to know something's better than what they're getting.

But movies are the easiest way in. Use the movies.

Now that mine know, we watch everything. On Saturday mornings, after a couple of their regular cartoons, I'll come down and say, "Hey, how about some Abbott and Costello?" and they jump at it. We must've seen *Buck Privates* ten times, and *Buck Privates Come Home* and *The Time of Their Lives,* and *The Naughty Nineties* (the best recorded version of "Who's on First," in my opinion) and all of them, and they know the routines by heart and look forward to them, and ask for them, and they laugh out loud every time. So do I.

They love *The Road to Utopia,* and *The Road to Singapore* and all the other *Road* movies. They even think Dorothy Lamour is hot. (Oh, wait, that's me.) They love *The Court Jester* and *The Inspector General* and, of course, the Stooges and Marx Brothers and anything else. Everything else.

And not just comedy.

The other night before bed I flipped on the TV and said,

"Quick, look, watch this scene. Watch this. See, the children are talking about their mother. Well, she died, and the little girl was too small to remember, and she's asking her brother if their mom was pretty. Now watch how they tell the story. See, now the camera is outside the window and pulls back. Watch. Watch. That's her father, see, listening to them. Watch his face. He's on the porch in the swing, alone, with his arm around the space where his wife would have been. Watch his face. He's thinking about her, too. Well, he's a good man. He's a very good man. Watch. Watch." And they watched.

And a few nights later I called them in and said, "Quick, watch this scene. Those are the bad guys, and they're coming to kill the sheriff, but no one will help, and he has to do it all alone. No, the whole town won't help, and he's scared. See, he's making out his will. Okay, that's his wife. Look at her, isn't she something? Yeah, well, trust me, she is. Never mind. They just got married, but even she won't stand by him, and she's leaving on the same train the bad guy just came in on. Watch. Watch." And they watched.

And a few nights after that I said, "I know we don't see a lot of dancing, but watch how these two move together. Watch."

And a few nights after that, when we turned off the TV, my older boy turned his head from me, because he was crying and didn't want me to see. I asked why, and he said, "It's so sad. The man knew he was going to die, but he didn't want the boy to see." And I said, "Yes, but look at me. See, I'm crying, too, but isn't it a good feeling? It's great to be moved this way, isn't it? Great stories move us this way. Come on, I'll tuck you in."

LAST SATURDAY MORNING WE WERE WATCHING ABBOTT and Costello again, throwing their dice again, and the kids were howling again, and so was I. And we wound it back up to watch it one more time, and laughed as if we'd never seen it. Then we watched the wonderful Nat Pendleton get hit with the water. Again and again. We were all on the couch together, and I had an arm around each of them. There are some moments in life as good as that, a very few, but there are none better. And one of them turned to me in the middle of a particularly big laugh and said, "Lou is funny, Daddy." And I said, "You know what, he is, isn't he? Lou is funny."

That's when I knew I wanted to write this chapter, and what I wanted to say, and what I would call it. Because Lou is funny. And you can teach your children that, too, the same way I did. It'll be good for them. Do it, folks.

Teach your children that Lou is funny.

THIRTEEN

THE FIVE LEVELS OF DRINKING

YEARS AGO I WROTE A BIT CALLED "THE FIVE LEVELS OF Drinking," which was something of a signature piece for me, and a stroll through—or stumble through—a night of drinking with my friends. (Or you with yours.)

By the way, comics love the word "bit" for describing their pieces, no matter how long or short they are. Even though "The Five Levels" is about ten minutes long, it's still a "bit" to me, as in, "Hey, you going to do the drinking bit tonight?" Rodney Dangerfield, as you probably know, wrote and performed one-liners. For example: "I went to my dentist the other day and said, 'Hey, Doc, what am I gonna do about these yellow teeth?' He said, 'Wear brown ties.'" It only takes a few seconds, but it's packed with persona, a rare and potent attribute. So you could've said, "Say, Rodney, I love the yellow teeth bit," and been correct. Some of Bill Cosby's bits are hours long (and hysterical the whole way); Steven Wright's bits are wonderful flights of fancy that take only a sentence or two to play out. The world seems to begin and end with each joke, and that feels right to us. The point is, a bit is a bit is a bit; it's a question of style, not length—as it should be.

So I wrote "The Five Levels," and it's been a good bit for me. But the drinking described in it was from a very different period of my life. I was single then, and not responsible for anyone (barely myself, in fact), and my friends were single, too. Most importantly, we were all in our twenties, and nothing affected us (even the things that should have, like hurting someone's feelings). We were as strong as steel, at least outwardly, and recovered our ills quickly. More mature elements, like wisdom, barely seeped in at all. Twentysome-things, in that sense, make diamonds look porous.

But we sure could drink, couldn't we? You remember those days. We often forget the great truths of life, or never learn them, but here's one: It's not youth that's wasted on the young. It's smoking and drinking.

If we're smart (or lucky, or both), the experiences of our lives act as springboards to higher levels of understanding. If we're dumb (or unlucky, or both), those same experiences may still act as spring-boards, but not up. They can shoot you sideways into stasis, which is not good, or downward, into fear and weakness, which is not good to the tenth power. It's these most vulnerable states that can invite in the glittering world of big-ticket evil, and this is the worst of all, because if you take that step, there may be no returning. At the least, it'll be much harder.

Sometimes I think people like Timothy McVeigh have to be reincarnated a million times in a row as a roach and get stepped on every ten minutes, just so they can learn, finally and fully, that life has value. Even then they'd probably still have to come back a few times as a cow, for good measure. And I wouldn't think wriggling out of it is an option.

"But I don't want to be the cow."

"Okay," (using the eraser) "Then you'll be the lizard on a rock."

"Ooh, wait, no, I'll take the cow."

"Then you should've kept your mouth shut. Too late. Next."

"How about a woodpecker or something?"

"That does it. Now back to being a roach for a million years."

"Sorry. I'll take the lizard."

"You'll take the roach, and it's two million years and counting. You want to push it again? Get out."

"It was my childhood, you know."

"No blaming others. Three million years. Get out."

"But I—"

"You know, Tim, the last guy to argue like this wound up doing what we call *special* roach duty—crawling up the side of a latrine. He's still at it today. And every time he gets to the top, a different guy comes in and sits down. Not a skinny guy, either. The day after a trip to Vegas. And it's always August. For eternity. *And there's a free seat next to him. Am I making myself clear?*"

EVERYONE CUTS LOOSE A LITTLE IN YOUTH. THE KEY IS to be overpoweringly dumb as little as possible, and grateful afterward if you merely have a good lesson to learn.

When it comes to drinking, the bill gets higher and higher, and I don't mean because you're suddenly going to nicer places. God save us from "nice" places.

In my salad days—an ironic phrase, since it always refers to the time in our lives we almost never eat salads—the best drinking times I had were in places that would be proud to be called dives.

If I were writing some sort of perverse Zagat's Guide to Cheap Bars, I would inform adventurous young seekers that the most interesting joints are sometimes a pinky toe on the dangerous side, since these are also the places where the regulars are least likely to get a big kick out of recent college graduates out looking for "real life."

In other words, you may get your penny loafers stepped on. In still other words, you might get tagged. Hit, that is. This has happened over the years to your humble author more than one, but less than six, times, and not recently. (Hint: I had hair. Another hint: thick hair. Third hint: lots of it.)

Lest there be any confusion for the initiate in determining when the locals begin to chafe at your presence, use this infallible test: If you go to brush something off your shoulder, and it's the floor, you've just been punched.

It doesn't always end badly, you know, unless you call catching a straight right in the squash bad enough right there. But again, when you're in your twenties, who cares? In fact, once or twice in my own graduate research on the topic, the guy picked me up off the floor, clapped me on the back, leaned me against the bar, and bought me a drink.

One time I "came to" very suddenly while receiving the Bum's Rush, a time-honored invitation from the bartender to no longer be inside.

In case you're not familiar with this rite of spring, the Bum's Rush, a common enough occurrence for many generations of tipplers, was a tool administered by the experienced publican (and always dispassionately) by grabbing the back of your belt and the back of your collar, and moving you very, very quickly toward the exit. When firmly performed by a true master—and these guys are all about firmness—the offender's arms pinwheel stupidly, and his feet spin on the floor like tires on ice.

Here's a bonus tip for you first-timers: If the door isn't open, and since the bartender's hands are full—there's bound to be a good bit of confusion anyway, what with everyone shouting and the two of you steaming along so briskly at eight or nine knots—good breeding and manners always dictate that you be the one to open the door first. Whether you choose to do this with outstretched arms, or the top of your head, is your own business. I have experienced both, and find using my arms more convivial.

I was awarded the Bum's Rush (with clusters) a couple of times in those early, heady, hairy days. (I'll bet it would hurt a lot more now.) Once I had occasion to look up from a late-November sidewalk following a top-shelf heave-ho, and the guy who hoed the heave was standing above me, clapping his hands up and down in the traditional "and that's that" gesture. Then he said, "And stay out." I sat up on one elbow, shook my head like an Airedale just out of the bath, felt my blood rising, and readied myself to charge back in for another round (or another round).

Then I took a good look at the fellow and didn't move a muscle.

Not because I was hurt—I wasn't—and not because he was big and scary—he wasn't. (The toughest guys, you know, are never the biggest.) He wasn't going to see sixty again, and I was twenty-five, but he tossed me like a Hefty bag.

The reason I didn't move was that I was mesmerized, and the reason I was mesmerized was that it wasn't a man I was looking at, it was a portrait—a woodcut, an engraving, an illustration, a figure out of a past I suddenly knew the world would never see again.

What a shot: Framed in the door, legs spread, arms akimbo. Five-nine or ten. White shirt, black tie, both tucked into a tight, white apron over black pants with a razor pleat and black lace shoes. Gold tie-bar. Ruddy face, the kind that had been scraped by a straight razor every day since he needed to, and not gently. White hair with traces of black, severely parted just off center and slicked straight back with Solidified Brilliantine, or some other product not seen since the French had Vietnam. Not muscular, not the pumped-up way guys think is strong today, but *rangy*. The toughest part of him was his forearms, veterans of carrying innumerable kegs down narrow, New York basement steps. Popeye arms, which I could see as he rolled up his sleeves (in case I was feeling frisky; I wasn't).

And the accent. The accent was perfect. (See if you can guess the island nation just west of England where it originated.) I dug the whole thing so much, all I could do was stare back at him with a big smile. He looked at me for a second, hard, and then smiled too. My friends came out to see if I'd bounced (I had), and a waitress followed them, and handed our bill to the bartender, who looked at it quickly and passed it over to them. One of my friends was wearing his first-three-months, junior-bond-trader suit, with the tie down, and he started to object to something on it, but the bartender turned to them and said what I still think is the coolest thing I've ever heard: "Now, now, lads, none of that. You don't want to drink like men . . . and pay like boys."

"Yes, sir," they said in unison, and then pooled their dough and held it out. (People still used cash then, if you can believe it.) The bartender just motioned to the waitress with his head, and they handed it over, thanked her, and apologized, and she said, "You're welcome, I'm sure," with the same accent and walked inside. Dear God, folks, memory plays tricks on us all, but I swear I think she even curtsied a little.

Then he turned back to me, still on the ground, sized me up, rolled his sleeves down again, barked a laugh, and said, "Good breakfast down the block at the Greek's," before checking the sky for rain and heading back inside as well.

I don't believe I'd have traded that punch, or that lesson, or that picture in the doorway, for a million dollars. Well, maybe for a million, but you know what I mean. (And, actually, maybe not. A real lesson is worth a lot.) Of course, as he said, the breakfast down the block was great.

SPEAKING OF CLASSIC BRAWLING BAR SCENES OF THE kind you don't see much anymore, I was in a joint above Eighty-sixth Street one night we used to call the Suicide Room. That wasn't its name, just what we called it, and not because you might get into a fight (although you might), but because five minutes after you ordered a pint, someone down the bar was buying you a shot of Jameson's. Of course, you buy him and his friends a drink in return. Then they buy you another pint, and someone on the other side joins in, and so on, until by the time you leave the place you're walking like Foghorn Leghorn after The Dog has put the garbage can over his head and hit it ten times, fast, with a carnival hammer.

It was the kind of place you could never stop into for a quick one, since there was no such thing. One toe inside, and that was it. You could start saying goodnight the second you walked in and it would still take three hours to leave. "Tough joint," as Dangerfield used to say. "It was three bucks to get in, and six to get out."

That's why we called it the Suicide Room, because just walking into the place was tantamount to committing suicide. By God if we weren't right, too. They poured heavy shots, in regular rocks glasses (without the rocks), and as a Cockney pal said one dawn in the coffee shop after a long night, "They ain't doin' you no fivors, neither." (Incidentally, these places always amazed me, ethnically, because they were filled with both English guys—from England—and Irish guys—from Ireland—and there was never a cross word between them. Well, there were plenty of cross words, but at least not about that.)

So one night we were there late and a guy named Feeney was talking to the bartender, a fellow named Dunn. (I know that sounds like the start of a joke in 1880, but it's not.) Now, Tom Feeney and Mike Dunn were both from the other side, from Ireland, both bartenders (both on the same side, too, so to speak), and had known each other for years. And at one point in the discussion, Freeney chuckled softly, shook his head, took a sip, and said, "Ah, Michael, you're so Irish."

Well, that was it. I'm not Irish, and I didn't know what it meant then, or what it means now, or what it meant to them, or what was so bad about it, but that was it, and Feeney couldn't have said anything worse if he tried. Dunn looked at him for a long time, and not warmly. It was very late, after hours, and he'd been eating his supper, a stew, out of a thick wooden bowl, with one leg up on the speed rack. His chewing slowed, then stopped, and he swallowed. His eyes never left Feeney, and his look never left baleful.

He slowly put the bowl down onto the bar, the spoon next to it, and then—this fascinated me—looked at the bowl again, picked the spoon back up, placed it *inside* the bowl, wiped the spot on the bar where it had touched with his apron, *then* wiped his mouth. Then he took his foot down from the speed rack, folded the napkin neatly, and placed it next to the bowl, the way a waiter in a fancy restaurant does when the customer has gone to the bathroom.

Now, the place had been dead silent this whole time, since the instant Feeney said, "Ah, Michael, you're so Irish," and I mean silent as a tomb. It's late, remember. The jukebox was off, the front door was locked, and it was just the seven or eight of us, all bartenders from other places except me. The only sound was the faint swish of cabs outside, and the even fainter squeak of the old Chinese porter polishing the copper bar down at the end, the exact same way he always did, at the exact same time.

That porter was unshakable. Mount Rushmore changed expression more than him. He must've been eighty, or a hundred and eighty, and nothing threw him. He wouldn't have stopped polishing that bar if a pterodactyl crashed through the window and flew right at him. He worked seven days and nights a week, set the place up, did all the cooking and cleaning, the first one to open and the last one to leave—it must've been twenty hours a day—for decades, and the owners, Jimmy and Frank (not what you'd call generous men, mind you), offered him a day off a thousand times, but he'd just shake his head and walk away. I never heard him say a word except at those times, something muttered, and not in English. I don't know if he spoke English to begin with; I never knew his name—we never even nodded at each other. I don't know how they hired him or where he lived. The only thing I do know is that, somehow, the concept of even one hour of life not spent working seriously offended him.

So here's the scene, the gesture, the picture: Dunn folded that napkin, took his foot down, turned sideways facing the end of the bar, stood for a beat in the silence, and then . . .

He held his hands up, open, in front of his face, and spit into each one. Then he balled the fists up, the backs facing out, extended, like a tintype of John L. Sullivan (Himself).

Then he came around that bar like a locomotive, with a look on his face I would not like to see coming at me. It was like watching a John Ford movie. It was like *being* in a John Ford movie. It was like being *Barry Fitzgerald* in a John Ford movie.

I wasn't the only one awed. Kevin Noonan, the guy next to me, a veteran of many late nights together, also a bartender, also Irish, had also seen plenty of fights; but when he saw Mike Dunn coming around the bar that night, Kevin muttered, "Jesus," but pronounced it J-a-y: *"Jay*sus."

This time the portrait, the woodcut, the engraving went deeper and farther back than any movie. When Dunn spit into those hands and balled them up and held them out, and lowered that face, and started quick-walking down the planks behind the bar, suddenly this all went back way before photography. This was back before Parnell, before Guinness and Danny Boy, before William of Orange and the Boyne, before Cromwell, and farther still, before Elizabeth, before Reformation, before Agincourt, before all the Henrys and Phillips and Jameses, before Thomas à Becket, before the Normans. This was tenth-century stuff; all we needed now was the round drum and the shrill flute.

And farther back than that.

This was pre-Celtic—this was tribal, this was painted-faces stuff, before Patrick and the snakes, and just a few weeks after Christianity. I turned my eyes away for an instant to look into the back, half-expecting barefoot young women to shyly walk out of the kitchen with kids clutching their skirts, all waiting, mute and terrified, to see whose man got killed, all cookie-cutters of Nicole Kidman, with the blazing red hair, and the fierce blue eyes, and the white, white skin.

But it was still just the old porter polishing the bar. (He never even looked up.)

Apparently, Feeney didn't want to see that look coming at him, either, because he ran out that door as fast as any man possibly could (considering it had to be unlocked first), and I swear I thought he was going to go right through it and leave his outline like a cartoon.

Dunn stopped, lowered his hands, stood for a beat, not even breathing hard, and first went to the front door to relock it. (A good late-night bartender is like the captain of a ship: You can't just leave.) Then he strode wordlessly back around the bar, brow furrowed, jaw set, long, Liam Neeson arms swaying less than you'd think they would.

Then he picked up the bowl and the napkin, put his foot back up on the speed rack, and finished his supper.

The rest of us glanced at each other, someone whistled softly, someone else tapped a smoke out of a pack, we all sipped our drinks, and the only sound was the scrape of Dunn's spoon on the bowl, and the porter and his rag down the end of the copper bar. And a very distant round drum.

Spitting into the hands, though, and the balled up fists held straight out? I've never seen it before or since.

I'M AWFULLY GLAD I LIVED THAT WAY IN THOSE DAYS. IT'S been a long time since I've done it, for a variety of good reasons, but it was so interesting and different, and I don't think we'll ever see its like again. I won't, anyway. In a way, there was an innocence to it. A bar fight meant someone got punched, and that was the end of it. Today, I think it's far more likely one or both of the guys would go to their cars and get a gun.

This may sound odd, but sometimes I think the world would be a lot less dangerous if we all went back to punching each other in the nose.

I don't get to those bars anymore. When I go to New York at all, it's usually on a job for a specific amount of time, or maybe my wife's with me and we're bringing the kids to see my sister; and the only places we go, anyway, are the ones where the waiters fold those napkins for you. But that's okay. It's a young man's game, that big drinking.

I don't think we'll see any more honest-to-God Irish bartenders, either. Not like those. They just plain don't make them like that anymore—not the old, tough ones with the white shirts and the black ties, and the lessons to teach earnest young men from the suburbs.

I did take a look once on a trip back a few years ago, but the Suicide Room had closed, supplanted by a new, upscale place with swooping, brushed metal seats and a bar shaped like a long, thin, yellow triangle. No more dark wooden walls, no more cracked-leather stools, no more faded pictures of rugby teams or Fenians.

No more guys calling up from downtown and saying they were heading over in ten minutes, and would Brendan please start pints for them? No more, every so often, one fellow lifting his voice out of nowhere and singing a very, very old song.

And for sure, nobody spitting into his hands. Well, that's okay, too. Things change, just as they should. I was there when these places lived to see these things, and I'm the lucky one. You can't go home again, as another fellow named Tom once said.

By God, that thing with Feeney and Dunn was twenty-five years ago if it was a day, and I'll bet you a thick wooden bowl of stew they still haven't spoken.

I'll also bet you that Chinese porter is still there wiping that new, triangular bar. He probably comes with the liquor license. Hell, he's probably been wiping bars there since fire engines were pulled by horses, and he'll probably bury the next ten owners. Maybe he's some kind of immortal, guardian angel of the block.

But that distant drum? No. No, that's gone.

So. People have been nice enough to ask for recordings or transcripts of this over the years, and here it is.

•　•　•

THERE ARE FIVE LEVELS OF DRINKING. SIX IF YOU LIVE in a trailer park. But never mind that now. We will deal with five. See if these look familiar.

LEVEL ONE

Let's say it's eleven o'clock on a weeknight, and you've had a few beers. You get up to leave—because you have work the next day—when one of your friends buys another round.

One of your unemployed friends.

But here at Level One you think to yourself, "Aw, why not? After all, as long as I get seven hours' sleep . . . I'm cool."

LEVEL TWO

Midnight. Had a few more beers.

You've just spent twenty minutes arguing against artificial turf.

You get up to leave again, and now all your friends say, "Oh, come on, one more . . ." And you say, "Thank you, my good friends, and the Dear's blessings, but I must away!" And they say, "No, don't go. . . ."

But you're a responsible young man starting out in life, and hug them all and say, "We few. We happy few. Goodnight!" And you turn to leave, but . . .

Suddenly, here at Level Two, a little devil appears on your shoulder. POP! And he whispers in your ear.

And you listen. And that was your mistake.

Because once you listen to the devil, you find yourself thinking, "Hey. Wait a minute. I'm out with my *friends*. That's important to *me*. And this is a special night, too. Bobby is celebrating his . . . oh, I don't know, but it's definitely a special night, though, that's for sure.

Work. Hmmph. What am I workin' for anyway? They're trying to strangle me! *These* are the good times. Besides . . .

"As long as I get *five* hours' sleep . . . I'm cool."

LEVEL THREE

One in the morning.

You've abandoned beer . . . for tequila.

You've just spent twenty minutes arguing *for* artificial turf.

And now you're thinking, "Our waitress is the most beautiful girl I've ever seen."

See, though, at Level Three, you love the world. You feel fantastic.

On the way to the bathroom, you buy a drink for the stranger at the end of the bar . . . just because you like his face. "Hey, buddy. Cheers, man. Whoooooo!"

Back at the table, you get drinking fantasies. "Hey, fellas, if we all bought our own bar, we could live together FOREVER."

Yeah, but at Level Three, that devil . . . is a little bit bigger. And he's got his arm around your shoulder.

And he's buying.

And you're thinking, "Hey, as long as I get three hours' sleep . . . and a complete change of blood . . . I'm cool. Yeah. No problem. I'll catch up tomorrow."

LEVEL FOUR

Two in the morning.

And the devil is bartending.

He's locked the door, but he lets you stay, 'cause you're such old friends.

For last call, you order a bottle of rum . . . and a Coke.

You *are* artificial turf.

This time on your way to the bathroom, you *punch* the stranger at the end of the bar, just because . . . you don't like his face. "What're you lookin' at, man? 'Cause I'll kill you. Well, then, make your move, brother. 'Cause I'll kill you. You don't see me *runnin'*, do you? That's 'cause I'll kill you."

After he kills *you* . . . your friends sit you back up with another drink . . .

And now you're thinking, "Our waiter is the best looking man I've ever seen. . . ."

Suddenly, the whole night's not so much fun anymore, is it? In fact, it's no fun at all, you just don't know it yet. (You won't know it for years.)

You and your friends decide to leave . . . right after you get thrown out. . . .

And one of you knows an after-hours bar.

The devil says he'll call you a car, and a gypsy cab instantly squeals up the second he hangs up the phone, with flames painted on the sides (but it's not paint), and driven by a real Gypsy.

You don't even remember coming outside or getting in, but as you're roaring downtown, very fast, you look at the driver, and underneath the black hair and the hoop earring and the bandanna and the mustache and the cuffed, paisley shirt . . .

It's still the devil. Good driver, though. Fast, but good.

And here, at Level Four, you *actually think to yourself:* "Well . . . long as I'm only going to get a few hours' sleep anyway . . . I might as well . . ."

STAY UP *ALL* NIGHT.

Yeah. That'd be *good* for me. I don't mind going to that board meeting looking like Keith Richards. Sure. Few mints and nobody'll know a thing. My boss loves me in sunglasses.

Besides, as long as I get seventy-five hours' sleep tomorrow . . . I'm cool.

LEVEL FIVE

Five in the morning.

Whew.

After unsuccessfully trying to get your money back at the tattoo parlor . . . ("Yeah, but I don't *know* anyone named Ruby!")

You and your friends wind up across the state line, in a bar filled with guys who've been in prison as recently as that morning.

It's the kind of place where even the devil says, "Oh, wow, look at the time, I've got to turn in. Well, I've got to be in Hell *at* nine . . . gotta open up. This is our busy season. You know how that is . . . see ya."

Of course, they let *you* right in, and sit you all at a table in the back that smells . . . just about the way it ought to.

At this point, you're all drinking some kind of thick, blue liqueur . . . the kind they use to clean combs. "Say, what kind of wine is 'Barbisol'?" Who knows, maybe it's Aqua Velva. At least when you throw up, it'll smell like the great outdoors.

A waitress with fresh stitches in her head comes over . . . sets down a plate of finger food—made with real fingers—coughs for a *long* time, clears her nose by holding a nostril shut . . .

And you're thinking, "Someday I'm going to marry that girl."

This time, on your way to the bathroom, the stranger at the end of the bar punches *you* . . . and then returns to making out with his identical twin.

The bathroom has rats, but that's okay, because that's what the snakes are for.

(In a rare moment of wisdom, you decide to hold it in.)

Back at the table, one of your friends suddenly stands up and screams, "We're driving to Florida!"

And bursts into flames.

You ever make one of those trips? Far away, late at night, with six friends? In a Fiat? I'll tell you one thing. That ride back . . . is mighty quiet. ("Tell the girls we're *Kennedys*?")

Back at the Bucket of Blood—its real name—you decide it's time to leave when a coffin opens, and Dracula sits up and yells "Last call." You check your watch and notice both hands are running backwards.

You ease off the chair—which follows you—and head to the front door, which keeps getting farther and farther away the closer you get. You finally crawl outside . . . and hit the worst part of Level Five:

The sun.

Ooh. You weren't expecting that, were you? You never do. You walk out of a bar in daylight, and people are on their way to work . . . or jogging . . .

And they look at you . . . and they know.

And they say, "Who's Ruby?"

Look, folks, let's be honest. If you're nineteen, and you stay up all night, it's a victory, it's like you beat the night.

But if you're over thirty—or forty—or fifty—that sun is like God's flashlight.

And it doesn't miss much.

And we all say the same prayer then. Say it with me now:

"I swear. I will never do this again. As long . . . as I . . . live."

And some of us have that little addition: *"And this time . . . I mean it."*

FOURTEEN

THE POETRY NOT YET WRITTEN

THERE IS A GIANT RACE PROBLEM IN OUR COUNTRY. IT has not healed, it is still bubbling like a volcano, and both the Left and the Right need to look at it and think hard. All Americans of goodwill must look at it and see it fully, perhaps for the first time.

When I say race, by the way, you know the word encompasses three main categories and many subsets, all with stories to tell. There is the Asian race, with its dozens of different cultures and a history in America of, to pick one, nineteenth-century Chinese who were not exactly welcomed as regular dinner guests at the homes of the Stanfords, the Chandlers, or the Mulhollands. (Neither was anyone else who didn't own a steamship line, but you know what I mean.)

Japanese immigrants might not have been greeted with hugs, either, but their place in both Asia and America has changed dramatically over the years as well. How many of us remember when the phrase "Made in Japan" was a joke? (I wonder if the folks at General Motors are still cackling quite so much over that one.)

But we all grow with the passage of time (or should). Asian-

American patches have altered the American quilt powerfully since *South Pacific* and *Sayonara* days (great movies, and reflective of a culture that looks at the world—and itself—and changes as it goes). A glance at the engineering departments of the fifty best colleges in the United States probably has the founders of most of these schools doing the Electric Boogaloo in their graves, but there you are. Sorry, fellas, and thanks for the dough.

Remember, though, all people—even the bad ones—are remarkably alike: For the last five hundred years Europeans were no more welcome in Asia than Asians were in Europe.

But Americans of Asian descent aren't the race problem that needs so urgently to be addressed.

HISPANIC AMERICA, OR SPANISH AMERICA, OR LATIN America, or Chicano, Latino, or Mexi-Texi-Nica-Guate-Costa-Pera-Para-Uru-Brazi-Puerto-Iberian America is not the problem we'll be focused on, either. (That last sentence itself is a problem, but it's already written, so what the heck.)

I know that Spanish-descended peoples are not a race, strictly, but there are so many cultural and political questions in contemporary American life concerning them that the size of the word "race" is sometimes useful. It's dangerous to lump people together by language, though. After all, Argentina is as different from Costa Rica as France is from Russia.

Of course there is, just lately, something of a focus on Mexico in particular—perhaps you've noticed—which officially started when Gringos began registering that the folks who had just trimmed their hedges weren't exactly leaping back across the border. Anglo mouths dropped even further when it struck home that most of these folks had ideas about building and cleaning houses for themselves, too.

On the other hand, only an idiot would not acknowledge that the nation of Mexico is (a) thrilled—giddy, in fact—to get rid of millions of people a year it can't, won't, and plainly has no interest in feeding, (b) orgasmically raking in hundreds of millions of dollars mailed to families back home monthly into the bargain to prop up the peso, a currency which, at the best of times, gets the vapors, (c) so shatteringly corrupt it makes Chicago in the twenties look like Thomas More's *Utopia,* and (d) planning all along to retake the Southwest anyway. How nice it will finally be when California and Arizona look like Chiapas and Sonora.

But Americans of Spanish descent aren't the race problem I'm talking about, either.

INDIANS, OR NATIVE AMERICANS (REAL ONES—NOT THE approved football mascots of the NCAA or Ward Churchill) are similarly not technically a distinct race, but their history as Americans, and a good deal before that, and a good deal since, has at least several more generations of addressing intractable problems before every one of us can look around in brotherhood and goodwill for the first time and finally agree that Gordon Lightfoot needs to stop singing. Custer might have been a man of his times, but his times were flawed.

Of course, gambling casinos on tribal land have helped Native Americans, at least with money, and at least a few of them. I don't know how many silver dollars they've legally lifted from slightly lard-butted palefaces, but it's enough to add a meaty new clause to the definition of the word "comeuppance," don't you think?

By the way, is it just me, or are all the casinos on Indian land from tribes no one's ever heard of? Have you noticed this? I'm sure they're legitimate, but why aren't any of the better-known ones cash-ing in at the trough? How come there are no Apache casinos, or Sioux, or Navaho, or Comanche? Is there an unwritten rule that no one who ever rode around in circles in a John Wayne movie can ever deal blackjack?

You've heard these come-ons for casinos that can't help sounding the littlest bit ersatz: "Come bury the hatchet with us at the Undunda-Pekoo-Fuhfuhfuh Lodge and Gaming Village, on our ancestral burial grounds just off the Yale campus. And bring the kids, or just lose them."

Geronimo would've had trouble finding these folks.

A cynic might suggest that the reason only these lesser-known groups are running the dice tables is that almost anyone could find the name of an obscure tribe in the public library (or just make one up), call himself the long-lost chief, gather together a few cousins who have as much Indian blood between them as Kirsten Dunst, and start playing keno. All they need is the initial funding, a go-ahead letter from some bespectacled desk jockey at the state capitol, and a little enthusiastic, but firm, guidance from someone with experience in the, ahem, gaming and related-entertainments business. "The Chair recognizes our dear friend, blood-brother, beloved ethnic cousin, member of the tribal council, co-chief, and trusted adviser—Paulie Walnuts."

Well, Lord knows the people Columbus first called "Indians" (because he made a slight mistake and thought he had sailed all the way to India) have been shafted often and deeply enough to be cut a little slack in the matter. I just hope some of the folks who are finally making a few bucks on this are the actual Indians who've been living in squalor for so long, not just the ones with good enough acting skills and prominent cheekbones to make commercials with tears running down their faces.

Of course, money does strange things to people, and a lot of money does a lot of strange things, and it wouldn't be the first time in ethnic politics of all stripes that the starving ones with the flies buzzing around their heads were kicked aside once the photos of them were taken for the brochure.

BUT AMERICANS OF INDIAN DESCENT AREN'T THE PROBlem I'm talking about, either.

Neither are Ukrainians, Armenians, Indonesians, Filipinos, Hindus, Arabs, Jews, or anyone else who spent their first generation here driving cabs.

No, there is only one horrible (and horribly unsolved) race problem in America, and you all know what it is, because you've known it since the first sentence of this chapter—the one that was there at the beginning, the keystone, the wound that keeps reopening and surprising us all, the one that hurts more, and more often, than any other, the fractious past and present that keeps playing on some nightmarish loop, that has changed somewhat but never been fully addressed, but will, someday, and enable us to finally leave it all behind and move forward together into a greater future than our country has yet known. I believe we're getting there. Not so soon, though. Not soon.

It's the relationship that's as simple as black and white, because, of course, that's what it is: Black America and White America.

This has been bouncing around my head and heart for years now, a sense that we're not past anything, we're not even in the middle, we're still right at the beginning. A hundred and fifty years (roughly the time since the Emancipation Proclamation) is the merest blink in the scope of history. It's yesterday, this morning, a couple of hours ago. It's right now. And no matter whether your ancestors came to America on the *Mayflower* or last week, we're all caught up in it. We need to reflect honestly together and apply Abraham Lincoln's timeless words: "Honey, these are great seats."

Just wanted to see if you were still listening.

The hurricane in New Orleans brought this up again—and don't get all riled here, but it did, it raised it again and you know it, not because anyone in Washington is greedier or more corrupt than anyone in Louisiana—that would be very difficult—but because sometimes in life perception does matter. It doesn't do anyone any good to say, "Oh, come on, it's a majority black city, so of course the majority of the victims were black," or "But so many white Americans sent money and volunteered to help," or "The overwhelming bulk of White America bears nothing but goodwill toward Black America." All that is true, but sometimes it just . . . all . . . comes . . . up . . . again, and stuns us, everyone, black and white, because it's still right there. And we at least have to see it.

Folks, there's a reason any news story with white men and black women, or black men and white women, bounces onto the news and stays there, no matter who did what or didn't do what.

Black America is having a discussion with itself that began with Harriet Tubman and Frederick Douglass during slavery, and continued with George Washington Carver and W. E. B. Dubois as the last century shot forward, and is going on vibrantly today. Perhaps, in the end, the most that white Americans of goodwill can add is to say, "We will help when needed, and watch when not needed, and be there with you the whole way."

It's like a marriage: "I won't leave. I won't let you go. I won't run away. I won't be this mad in ten minutes. Okay, I wish you hadn't said that."

•   •   •

I'M A STORYTELLER SO MY CONTRIBUTION WILL BE TO tell you a story. We all have them. Here's one of mine.

This happened about fifteen years ago, and since my wife is going to be proofreading this, let me begin by saying it was before we were married, all right? Or even engaged. So there's no big deal. Maybe we were going out, but only a little. Okay, I think we were going out, but it was definitely, like, at the beginning. Maybe not the *very* beginning, but way, way before we had that discussion at your place, remember? The first time you asked where our relationship was going, and I pretended not to hear you? The one where you brought it up again a week later? And then every couple of months until one of us finally blinked and realized this truck was rolling downhill and couldn't be stopped anyway, and he's not even driving, so he might as well jump on and enjoy the ride? Or just not get run over by it?

Where was I? Oh, yes. Race.

I was on the road, and I don't want to name the city—seriously— because it could have been anywhere, the middle of Montana, or the middle of Brooklyn; the South, the North, the East, the West. And until this happened, it was the best road week of my life.

By the way, any comic I know will talk about the best cities he's worked, and on the surface he's telling you about the club, or the theater, or the ads, or the local TV; and the audiences, and the money, and the new stuff he wrote. But if you ask him directly, and he answers honestly, he's really talking about the women.

I have a bunch of friends who are great female comics, and per- haps they, too, put part of their off-time to recreational use, but it's just not the same thing at all as what my guy friends tried to pull.

If you ever hear a comic saying something like, "Oh, Seattle was my best town. Great club, always packed, rang like a bell. Wrote all the stuff for my next Letterman, too. Great city," try quickly saying something in return like . . .

"How many women did you date?"*

"Oh, man, it was nuts. Like the Russians were around the corner. They were throwing it at me. It was berserk. I had to go to a monastery for a year just to heal up."

So the place I'm talking about was a brand new club, opening week, and there was a pretty fair to-do locally. It was beautifully built, and money was no object (another phrase I've never understood). The new place was designed, built, and owned by two guys in their late thirties, lifelong friends since birth, and two of the most enormously appealing guys you could ever meet, with the laughs and confidence and carriage of ex-athletes. We hit it off so well, it was as if I were a lifelong friend, too. We drove to all the radio and TV spots, walked around together, had lunch, everything. They showed me the sights, and I really, really liked them. More than I'd ever experienced in that kind of situation.

They also owned the most popular disco in town, right next door to their new comedy club, so these guys were doing very well, and every night after the show the three of us would walk through the connecting hallway together into the music and the lights and the dancing, and drink till we felt like stopping. We laughed a lot and were inseparable.

I was so instantly comfortable and accepted, I'd just walk behind the bar at the disco—a huge place with three long, oval bars and two bartenders at each one, in a giant room of hundreds of people—and serve drinks, and stand there talking with my foot up on the speed

---

* We all know I'm talking about a verb other than "date" here, but why ruin a nice clean book?

rack, and grab one whenever I wanted, and I had the best time night after night. Oh yeah, and the shows were terrific.

And in the matter of women (Honey, you can skip this part. The publisher has proofread it, and it's fine. Go back to the chapter about Little League, because, frankly, I could use your thoughts on the end. Or the one where I brought you all those gifts from the Peninsula. Remember how happy you were that day? And the kids got all those hits? Yeah, that was great, wasn't it? Okay, I'll be up in a minute.)

Is she gone?

Okay, so in the matter of women, I guess that in addition to being their new best friend, these guys wanted to ensure that I'd send a good report back to the other comics who might work there, because they made every effort (and it didn't take an awful lot) to introduce me to the prettiest women, most of whom didn't need a ton of aggressive nudging to find their way over anyway (bless their hearts), and all of whom seemed delighted to cement, as it were, their no-cover-charge-for-you-darlin' relationship with the club by setting up shop on Convivial Lane.

It was all fine with the owners, Bob and Tony (not their real names), and fine with the women, and it can't come as a great shock that it was fine with me too. By God, folks, once or twice along the way, a cheer actually went up when I reentered for a few more drinks with whoever had just taken me to park by the river and watch the barge races. It was positively Roman.

By the fourth or fifth night I was seriously considering moving to this place and opening a potpourri shop, and on Saturday night we did three packed shows and then went next door for the usual revels; and after a couple or three behind the bar, and a few handshakes with the regulars, I swaggered over to the front door to hang with the guys. It was a small alcove, and they had a pretty employee sitting behind a table taking ten-dollar cover charges from the steady stream of customers entering. There had to be at least five hundred people in the joint, so this, plus drinks, was a solid chunk of dough they had coming in, and Bob and Tony smiled when I came over. And why not? (This reminds me of the time my dad met one of the Rockefellers, and when he came home from work, I said, "Was he a nice guy?" and my dad said, "Why wouldn't he be?")

The guys and I sat down on boxes behind the table, and someone else pretty brought us fresh drinks, and we picked up our yakking and laughing as usual. They even periodically lateralled me large, wrapped hunks of money to spike like footballs into the cash box I was resting my leg on.

It was all pretty great, and I felt like an owner, and I looked like an owner, and I liked the feeling. Plus, I really began to believe something I'd always suspected: that I was the coolest guy in America.

Then Tony glanced over to the door and muttered, "Uh-oh." I asked what was up, and he nodded at three black guys in their twenties who had just entered and approached the table. I didn't immediately get the point, and I guess it showed in my face. "Can't let 'em in, pal. Scares the women off." He winked and smiled, and clapped me on the back, and stood up to move to the table. "Sorry, fellas, no jeans inside." He was still smiling.

Suddenly, it seemed the music and laughter and talking all vanished, like someone had pushed the mute button on the whole thing. Bob and Tony were saying something to them, and I watched for a second, puzzled, still not getting it (or getting it just fine but not wanting to), and then thought of something, and turned around to look back into the club, and saw for the first time . . .

They were all white. Dancing, laughing, pouring, drinking. They were all white. Mingling, eyeing, venturing, asking. They were all white.

And I hadn't noticed.

Then I turned back to the table, the mute button still on, and looked closely at the young men. All three were focused on Bob and Tony, and two were saying something, angry, pointing, but the third (the youngest, I thought) was just looking across the table steadily, a small shake of his head, and I caught that look like the wind from a giant door closing very quickly. It was hurt. That look was hurt. A knowing, seasoned hurt. And maybe my mouth fell a little, and maybe I took a breath in quickly, but I stood up and squeezed my way around the table to head for the door, because I needed some air.

ALL THE SOUND STARTED AGAIN WHEN I STOOD, LOUDER, it seemed, and as I pushed around the table, I heard one of the three say, "Aw, man, this is b———," and then Bob said, "Now, come on, you got your places and we got ours, and you know it. Let's not have any trouble." And then the second one said, "Trouble? You lookin' for trouble? Well, come get some trouble."

I was just at the door, opening it, and I sensed movement behind me as I stepped outside. Someone back inside—someone white—shouted, "Fight! Fight! Fight!" and in an instant five more humans piled outside right behind me—Bob and Tony and the three guys. There was going to be a fightafightafight, and in the tiniest fraction I realized, in horror: I was sitting there laughing like the cock of the walk when they came in; I looked liked one of the owners; I hadn't preceded anyone outside at all, it looked like I *led* them outside; and now there were six men on the sidewalk, and I was one of them.

There was going to be a fight between them and us, *and that was it, do you see, there was a "them," and an "us," and they thought I was part of the "us."*

No. No. I was lying to myself: I *was* part of the "us."

As fast as I had the thought, two squared off against two, and one squared off against me, and I looked up to see, of course, it was the youngest, the one who'd been so hurt. Oh, no, not him, just not him. He raised his fists, and I saw his face, so close now, not angry, trying to be, but not, still just hurt, and I thought, Oh, God, what now? Not because I was afraid of getting hit (I'm not tough, but I've been hit before), but I felt so wretchedly incapable of saying something, doing something, stopping something, stop this, stop it, no time, too fast, what could I say, wait, don't, I don't . . . I'm not . . .

What do I do? Do I defend myself? But if I do, doesn't that make me even more officially part of "us," a card-carrying, dues-paying member of Us, Inc.? Or when someone raises his fists does all that vanish into Me, Inc.?

And now I, too, was suddenly filled with sadness, sadder by far than when I had stood up to come outside. Not afraid, just sad, and I couldn't decide whether to raise my hands, turn and run, or just take a punch. Maybe that's it? Look him in the eye, try to apologize with a nod (permission? assent? sacrifice?), and take a punch. Then what? Punch him back? Block the next? Take another? Scream at the idiocy of it all? How much is any one of us capable of apologizing for? And to whom, and for what? Something yesterday? Today? Tomorrow? Forever? This was all happening *now*, right *now*, any second *now*, pick something *now*, here it comes *now*—

And then in that flutter, maybe the same kind that held the first thought, the first word, the roaring, rushing, screeching, accelerating decision to create, something did happen.

A pause too small to measure, and something turned in one of us, or was turned in one of us, or all of us, or none of us, and just like that one of the angry "them" dropped his hands and said, "F—these guys, man. Come on." And the second dropped his hands and backed off, too, but my guy didn't move until the first one said, "Tim. Hey. Come on. He ain't worth it."

And suddenly they were gone. I don't know where. I don't think I was even seeing, or at least I wasn't registering. Maybe they walked down the block or got in a car. All I knew, all I could think was, "No, you're wrong. I am. I am worth it."

But it wasn't quite over. This omelette needed a sprig of parsley before it was ready to serve. Bob and Tony nodded at each other, a job well done (and not the first time, I'm guessing; they didn't have bouncers), and as Bob opened the door, Tony put his hands on my shoulders, squeezed, and said, "Thanks, buddy." Then he smiled that great smile, and Bob laughed and mimed a flurry of quick punches, pointed at me, and they both went inside.

Oh, no. Oh, no, no, no. They thought I had stood with them, in fact had led the charge, facing the enemy together, shoulder to shoulder and backs to the wall, hands at the mast, the final French square at Waterloo. Dear God, if I went back inside I would be walking in to another cheer, bigger than the others.

A big, white cheer.

Well, on the good side, if you're looking for ways to get sober fast, try that one.

I stood on the sidewalk for a minute, alone on the warm night, then looked around pointlessly (since I didn't know where I was or which way the hotel was). I looked down at my feet, then up at the sky, then straight ahead, then breathed out and walked inside.

There was no cheer. Perhaps worse, everything was right back to normal. One or two people smiled at me in respect (Home the Conquering Hero), and some guy across the room gave me a thumbs-up.

I went to the bar, but not behind it, and asked for a Coke. When the bartender set it down I handed him a couple of bucks for a tip, but he just shook his head and knocked on the bar twice, and left to fill a waitress's order.

I had been introduced to a pretty girl earlier, and she came over and told me that the guys had asked her to drive me back to the hotel whenever I was ready. I was ready.

We pulled up in front, and she looked around nervously for a spot and said, "So, you want me to come up?" And I looked at her, for the first time, really, and asked what her name was, and she told me, and I asked where she was from, and she told me, and she was pretty, really pretty, and didn't belong there. On the other hand, who did? And I said, "You know what, I think I'll just go up alone if that's okay," and she said the strangest thing in return, just "Thanks," and smiled, and I looked at her again and said, "Safe home," and went inside.

The next night was the last show, and it was fine and filled, and the club was off to a good start, and the guys paid me in the office, and we all shook hands and smiled, and they asked if I wanted to come next door for a drink, and I said, "No, I think I've had enough for the week" (which was certainly true).

Of course they knew something was wrong, and they knew exactly what it was. They knew I hadn't led the way outside that night, and they knew I was shocked. There was no awkwardness from them, though, no toe turning or ear lobe pulling, or rocking from one foot to the other, or "You see, Larry, uh, well, that is, the way we see it . . ."

No, that kind of embarrassed, parenthetical throat clearing was made for people like me, who get to push the meanness of life away and skip around the country whistling, with a pocketful of jokes and the borderless opportunity to pretend everyone you meet is a perfect part of a perfect world. To pretend *we're* perfect. And drink and play the role of new best friend for a week.

There was no need to speak, anyway, because their expressions were five thousand–word essays. Not superior, or solemn, or combative, or anything, really, but in-depth and final all the same: "Look, this is our dream and our business. We scratched for it and built it with our own hands, and we're going to do anything—*anything*—by our lights that makes it a success and keeps it going, and if you don't like it, well, I guess you'll just have to learn to live with that, won't you?" You have your places, and we have ours.

They drove me to the airport the next day, and we shook hands and smiled, and hugged, too, those quick, male, backslapping hugs, and I swear, I didn't know what else to do. I still don't. They said, "Hey, you've got to come back again soon," and I said, "Oh, absolutely." And I stared out the window a lot that flight, my unread airport book face down on the tray at page three, the same thought going through my head again and again, the one I've gone back to so often since, always prodded by a different sadness (but the same), always putting another book or something else down to look out another window wherever I am.

I never did go back. I'm not even sure I know why. Nothing heroic. But I didn't go back. Should I have asked before I went in the first place? Asked what? How? Shall I pass out questionnaires in the future to all prospective employers? "Please describe in a paragraph of not less than twenty-five or more than five hundred words your personal attitudes about your business and city as concerns the past, present, and future of race relations. For Section B, indicate bar graphs of the ethnic backgrounds of your audience and how they trend. (Show your work.) In a related question, What, if anything, do you feel you can do to help?"

Idiotic. Offensive, really. It's horrible enough when governments do it, but individuals?

I'm an actor, a comic, and a writer, and wherever the car stops, I get out and perform the best I can, and somehow that has value. When the lights go down, I have something to give to that room, and for that hour, they're no longer whatever they were when they walked in, but nine-year-olds in striped polo shirts with toothy grins. And if I'm any good, it'll be time well spent. After that? We're all on our own. But I guess a lot of those grins aren't quite as toothy the next day, are they?

A few days later, back in my apartment, the girl who drove me to the hotel that night called. She'd gotten my number from them, and she asked if we could get together sometime, and I said sure, and she said she worked in a clothing store but could take some time off, and I flew her out the following weekend. She wasn't feeling well, once-a-month not well, and she said, "Wait, let me," and I took her hand and held it, and maybe for the first time stopped being perfectly stupid with women, and said, "No hang on, I'll get you a soda from the fridge," and we drove around the next day talking, and I took her to the airport on Sunday. She had a daughter back home. When she was really young, I guess. We didn't speak after that, but she called a year later to tell me she had met someone and they were getting married, and I congratulated her, and after a little awkwardness asked why she had called, and she said she just wanted to thank me, and I asked what for, and she said just for being nice. Oh, that's me. After hanging up I stood very still, and then turned and looked out the window again with that thought. That old thought.

• • •

IN THE MOVIE *GLORY,* ABOUT THE FIRST BLACK REGI-ment in the Civil War, Matthew Broderick, Shaw, has been speaking honestly with Denzel Washington, Trip, and after a quiet beat, Shaw says:

"I suppose it stinks, doesn't it?"

And Trip says, "Oh, yeah. And we all covered up in it, too. Ain't nobody clean. Be nice to get clean, though."

And Shaw says, "How do we do that?"

And Trip says, "Ante up and pitch in."

The Left is right and wrong on race: Sure, more programs and money, and more apologies, and more help. Fine. Except that it hasn't helped, has it, and it won't help, will it, and it can't help, can it?

And the Right is right and wrong on race: "Come on in, the water's fine! It's the greatest pool in the world, you know, and everyone's welcome. What do you mean, you can't swim? Well, you better learn. 'Bye!"

The Left needs to stop saying, "Everything's rotten, and always was." It's not.

The Right needs to stop saying, "Everything's fine, and always was." It's not.

MY WEEK AT THAT CLUB WAS SIX GREAT DAYS . . . AND then something happened. Maybe that's a metaphor for our country: All sorts of terrific stuff . . . and then something happens. But does that say more about the thing that happens or what's been bubbling beneath the terrific stuff all along? Who's responsible? Me? Hey, I'm just in the pool kicking.

Since then, since that hurly-burly week, every time something happens—every time a man is dragged behind a truck, or a senator has a long-lost daughter surface, or someone says something stupid in public, or someone awful plays the race card, or a billionaire star is refused entry into a posh store in Paris, or a stunned black face looks out from a magazine cover—I wonder what, and when, and how long, and I try to think of something more than money and goodwill. But I never can.

So I do the only thing that comes to mind, the only thing that seems to make sense, the only thing at hand, the only thing I'm certain of, the thing I did on that flight home, and when I hung up with that girl, and so many times since.

I put down the book, or turn from the computer, or click off the TV, and look out the window and think, "Tim. Tim. His name was Tim."

FIFTEEN

DRINKING II: THE SLOWENING

(THAT'S RIGHT, *THE SLOWENING*. NO, IT'S NOT THE SAME thing at all, just a tiny play on . . . the other one. You know which one. Yes, you do. It starts with "Q," and rhymes with *The Quickening*.)

At any rate . . .

I can't drink anymore, but it hasn't stopped me.

If I ever go past Level Two again—okay, maybe Level Three—I'm seriously terrified of what might happen that night; and, worse, the following day.

When you're in your twenties, you can drink all night and bungee jump off a bridge the next day. If I drank all night, I'd want to go off that bridge without the cord.

Some of my friends have stopped completely. Some of them had to stop. Some were politely asked by their families and a judge to stop. Some have. Some have not.

Colin Quinn told me he knew it was time to stop years ago

when "Degenerate alcoholics with no standards whatsoever would come up to me in bars and say, 'Son, you really have a problem.'"

It's not only the body that changes, is it? The soul changes, too. (At least it ought to). In college the concept of a limit was just another day you missed in calculus and had nothing to do with drinking. But now? As my friend, Hunter, says, "Why do you only recognize your limit an hour after you pass it?"

Here's one of my rules: You know you've had way too much when you take a sip of whatever you're drinking and think, "Say, I didn't know how much I *liked* the taste of bourbon. This is delicious!" If straight liquor ever tastes like candy, take a last look around and have a seat, because you're dead, and you just don't know it.

Here's a story about grown-up drinking. Perhaps it will sound familiar.

SATURDAY EVENING, SIX-THIRTY. I AM OPENING THE front door and saying hello to the baby-sitter, and my wife is entering her seventh hour of hair and makeup, because we are going out. All wives prepare themselves for going out as if they were nominated for an Oscar, because most parents go out just about as often as, well, they get nominated for an Oscar.

Anyone bothered by female prep-time is an idiot. It's part of the pleasure a wife has in going out, and what's wrong with that? Of course you don't understand it. You don't have to understand it. You just have to understand that *they* understand it. Besides, Quiz Kid, in case you haven't fully perceived this over the years, the lovelier a woman feels getting made up, the better your chances are later to see the parts of her that don't *need* makeup. So wise up, lather up, strop up, and shave close. Check your nose for that one, white, incredibly long hair that always seems to have grown, mushroomlike, just that morning—along with its annoying cousin on your ear—and put on a suit. Boots and Saddles, my son, Boots and Saddles, and stop crabbing because you have to go out in the first place. It's good for both of you.

And now she's ready, and looks lovely, and I'm ready, and look lovely, and we're going to do the town, or at least have dinner with our friends the Engels, who, I have it on good authority, also look lovely.

We show the sitter where the refrigerator is, as if she couldn't have guessed, because maybe we're the only ones from Nome to Key Largo who ever thought to put it in the kitchen. With one of us on each side like models on a game show, we gracefully extend our hands up and down to point out the laminated, magnetized 8½ x 11 printout (underneath the mesh rack of takeout menus, and just to the left of the flier of a car service we haven't called in seven years) of the dozens of emergency numbers, cell phones, doctors' offices, friends' houses, restaurants, agents, publicists, and any other place we not only *might* be, but have ever gone. Antietam was conducted with less planning than the average couple on a night out. (Actually, it was, and with tragic results.)

One of us kisses and hugs the kids while the other stands in the door to the garage saying, "Okay, okay, if we're going, let's go" (see if you can guess which one), and we warn them against doing what they will certainly do the second we leave anyway. Thence: *Avanti!* And as we stepped into the gorgeous early spring evening light, I remember thinking, "Boy, those three drinks really hit me. I guess not eating all day before a big meal sends it right to your head."

HOLD IT. I CAN HEAR BRAKES SQUEALING ALL ACROSS America. "Three drinks? When did you have three drinks?"

It was one, actually, but supersized, and I had it while my wife was still sequestered in the tile sanctum with her spray guns and belt-sanders. See, I was already duded up, myself, smooth, fancy-smelling and idle-handed, and going around the house doing what I always do—turning out lights—when . . .

LIKE EVERY FATHER SINCE EDISON WENT AND RUINED everything, I spend at least 40 percent of my time at home turning off lights. My wife leaves everything on, the kids leave everything on, and I have a suspicion that even the dog has learned to flip the switches up, and then *he* leaves everything on. (He pretends not to understand when I confront him with this, but I've got my eye on him, the cur.)

No one turns out lights except me. My nephew stayed with us last year for a few weeks, and he's a great kid. Graduated from Cornell with honors, All-American in crew, editor of the school paper, and five or six other immense things I never did in college, although I'll bet I threw up more than he did. Then he went to Michigan Law and made the Law Review. I think he gets two hundred job offers a day, and he's popular, fun, and handsome.

And the whole time he was with us, he never turned off a single light. Not one. The place always looked like a night game. At first I tried sarcasm, then earnestness, then bluntness. Finally, I called his mother, my sister, and she said, "Oh, didn't I tell you? He's an idiot. Can't remember anything." Some genius.

So there I am, turning off lights, and the kids are downstairs watching a James Bond movie. It was one of those "Thirty Hours of Bond" weekends (which increasingly feels like every weekend, doesn't it?), and they're still at the age when, "Oh, James . . ." doesn't mean a lot, but "No, Mr. Bond, I expect you to die" does.

I was standing behind the couch watching it with them and thinking, "Hey. Connery's wearing a suit and tie, just like me. Lace shoes, too, just like me. I'll bet he turns all the lights in the house off, too, just like me. He's even bald, at least now. And he drinks all day long! They have one waiting for him when he checks into the hotel, and they bring him another one in the room, and give him one wherever he goes. I'm not asking to wrestle Pussy Galore in a hayloft, so why not have a drink while I'm waiting?"

This is how men think, you know: A plus B equals C. Very linear. Pathetic, but linear.

I was already walking into our bar off the den to make one. A martini, too. (Or is it a martooni, tee? It is if you have enough of them.) I brought out the olives and the fancy shaker, and even took down one of the nice glasses. Why not? Do it up right, eh? Welcome back, Commander Bond. May I show you to your suite? My name is Huge Creamy Breasts.

Then I looked at all the stuff I had just put on the counter and thought, "Oh, why get everything dirty?" and put it all back, grabbing a red, sixteen-ounce, plastic stadium cup from underneath instead, and pouring a wee dram of gin into it. Right before the juniper hit the fan, though, I glanced into the mirror over the bar and caught the elegant picture of myself pouring warm liquor into a red soda cup alone in a basement with the lights out. Lovely. Rather than Sean Connery in a dinner jacket at the chemin de fer table in Monte Carlo, I had mistakenly channeled Telly Savalas for the Players Club in Atlantic City.

This slight ripple to the ego is what caused my pouring arm to lock, and turned a wee dram into three big blasts.

When I finally came to and stopped pouring, I couldn't put it back through the plastic top (Yeah, it was a half-gallon. So what? Want to make something out of it?), so I shrugged, capped it, and reached into the ice maker. It was frozen like a rock on Pluto, so I shrugged again (I'm a good shrugger) and drank: Mmmm, a nice, big sip of eighty-two degree gin from a soft, candy-apple red cup. Who loves ya, baby?

More good news. The cup was dusty, stunk, and had a bug in it. Telly Savalas? That was reaching too high. Try Pigpen from the Dead. (Surprised? I'm a giant Deadhead. Always have been, always will be. Been a long time, but, yes, there is nothing in the world like a Grateful Dead concert.)

Anyway, a bon vivant of my caliber doesn't panic, so I took the bug out. It wasn't alive, and might not have even been a bug in the first place, just a paint chip (or so I kept telling myself). Euchhh. At least throw the rest out, right? Nope. Why waste it?

What would Ace do?

The second sip included a second bug. *Quel bonheur!* That's when the doorbell rang.

I gagged for a bit, and yelled for the kids to answer it, but there was never a chance of that happening, was there? "Fellas. (Gaaaaackkk.) Could you get the door, please? (Ptooey. Ptoo. Ptoo.) Guys? (Acch. Ucch. Yerg.) *HEY!*"

But the only thing coming from the den was the voice of a young actress with only two more scenes to live: "You could have run me off the road. And those were new tires! Please take me to a *ga*-rahge."

The bell rang again on my way up the stairs, and this somehow knit everything together into a good enough reason to chug the rest including—naturally—a third bug. Three sips, three shots, three bugs. Nice. That cup was probably a summer home for them, and I drank the whole family.

I was still coughing, gagging, red-faced, and dribbling warm gin onto my suit when I opened the door for the sitter, who actually recoiled. Very sophisticated.

Miller. Larry Miller.

And that's how I had three drinks before leaving.

LET'S JUMP AHEAD NOW TO SEVEN-THIRTY. MY WIFE AND I and the Engels are on our second martini at the restaurant, or at least I am. The other three are still nursing a first, single glass of wine.

The good news is that I've had my appetizer as well, and I'm talking about my appetizer in the restaurant, not the bugs in the house. As long as you eat while you drink, you're okay, or, as my friend J.J. Wall says, "You don't want to send all that down there unsupervised."

The bad news is that my appetizer was the arugula salad, the kind of weightless nonfood that takes a lot of chasing and chewing, but fills you up just slightly less than when you walked in.

Why do restaurants sadistically put these goofy things on the menu when they know people are going to be drinking? Or why don't they at least have a section labeled, "For Drinkers"? Most menus have kids' sections, and asterisks and hearts and chili peppers to indicate spicy and fat-free and low-salt things. Why not add a little tilted glass with bubbles coming out of it next to items that might actually soak up a little liquor? "I'll have the fried bread with cream sauce, please? And a chocolate milkshake. And some fish sticks. And a wheel of Brie. You have defibrillators in the back, don't you?"

But my appetizer didn't soak up anything. I had had nothing to eat since breakfast but a world of gin, and that's rarely the keystone of a successful evening. My wife surreptitiously moved a water glass my way, but on the whole she was thrilled with things: It's a beautiful place, she's out with her friends, and she certainly loved *her* first course, the nutmeg soup du jour with the vegetable garnish in the shape of the chef's face.

IN FACT, YOU KNOW, IT'S ACTUALLY BEEN A LOT MORE gin than you think. The martinis in fancy restaurants now come in glasses as big as the neon ones outside. This is so they can charge twenty-seven dollars for them without laughing right in your face. Not only is each martini a punch bowl of gin, but they leave the rest of the shaker on the table with twice as much more, lest, God forbid, you run out.

Remember the martinis people used to drink in old movies? Nick and Nora Charles, Barrymore, Bogart? Tiny glasses, right? Delicate. Almost sherry glasses, really. *And they were drunks*. But today? Immense glasses. Surreal. Cartoonish. Like a nineteenth-century drawing of the Irish in *Punch*. "Oh, look at this fellow, Binky. A bright green suit, and he's drinking right out of the barrel! They all do, you know."

Two official martinis and that buggy blast at home? God only knows how much was already in my blood. I didn't have another and didn't want one, and I'd ordered steak and mashed potatoes for the main course, but like the police in the first ten minutes of a kidnapping movie, they were never going to get there in time. I was now playing catch-up for the rest of the night, and knew it. I also knew the exact moment I left the building and wouldn't be returning. It was coming right in the front door.

One of those four-foot-nine women with a bucket of flowers and a perilously tilted beret walked up to our table, held one out to me, and had such an expression of sorrow I was actually stunned when she didn't say, *"Flores por los muertes?"*

Now, for whatever it's worth, I give money to everyone. I don't care if the guy's going right out for drugs or booze, I give him whatever's in my pocket, and hand out tens and twenties like sample packs of cigarettes. I don't think that makes me a great guy, and maybe it's guilt, and maybe it doesn't help, but I figure I'm making money, and anyone who buttonholes me can have some of it. That's all. And I always buy the roses in the restaurant, or whatever someone's selling. Not because I want the thing, but because maybe it gets them home earlier that night. I always buy.

That night, however, for some reason, I turned to the woman and politely said, "I'm sorry, but no, we don't need any flowers. Thanks, anyway." I know there's nothing wrong with that. I don't have to try to support everyone I meet, and don't have to feel bad if I don't. I just didn't happen to buy one that night. No big deal, and I'm fine with it. No reason to overthink every little moment in our lives.

Oh, but it was a big mistake. I'm not saying she put the whammy on me; all she did was nod solemnly and move on. It was a mistake, though, all right, and I should have kept my mouth shut and bought the flower. Hell, I should have bought all of them.

You see, when I opened my mouth to speak to her, I slurred my words.

It's so odd when you slur your words, because it always happens out of nowhere. The sentence starts out okay, and you're cruising along just fine. Then suddenly you hit a patch of ice and shoot through the guardrail into oblivion.

It's unmistakable, too. Slurred words can't be anything other than slurred words, and no matter how noisy the restaurant is, everyone at the table knows it. The waiter knows it, the woman with the flowers knows it, the maitre d' knows it, and if the dishwasher stuck his head out the kitchen door, you'd see that he knew it, too. You slurred your words, and you can't take it back or pretend it didn't happen, and there's no other possible explanation. Well, there's one, but you'd better have just had a stroke, because if you didn't, it was slurred words.

The first part of the sentence was fine: "Sorry, we don't need any flowers . . ." and I should have stopped there. Of course, you never know it at the time. So when I added, "Thanks, anyway," it came out "Thangs, eddywade." What's more, as soon as it's out of your mouth, you realize without looking . . . that your eyelids have shut a little (just a little), and your smile is only going up one side, and your whole body is down by the bow and listing to port.

And I remember having one thought with perfect clarity: "I can't believe I just wasted my last sober sentence of the night on the flower woman." It was so obvious, and the table was so silent, I tried to make a joke out of it, like Dudley Moore in *Arthur,* and turned to my wife, saying, "You're a hooker? I just thought I was doing incredibly well with you." On the whole, it was a lot cuter in the movie.

Well, be grateful for small things. That's when our main courses came.

You know how they do steaks in these places. Sizzling, crackling, snapping platters coming across the room supporting ten thousand–degree, fourteen-pound, cadmium-rod-bone-in, telephone-book-thick pieces of slathered animal carried by teams of strained, frightened servers. You know what that crackling sound is? The molecules of the plate, about to explode.

Why do they sell steaks that big? You can't eat them. And I didn't even get the Diamond Jim Brady Cut. You know how they always have one on the menu that's twice as big as the regular? So big it gets its own nickname? The John Wayne, the Henry VIII, the Linebacker, the Big Chew, the Mutton Glutton, the New Set of

Veins. You ever seen someone actually order one of these? They're kind of creepy. The people, too, but I'm talking about the steaks. They're so unsettling and large, for a second you think it might actually *be* Diamond Jim Brady. I'm not a vegetarian, and have no problem eating animals and sitting on leather, but when they set that much meat in front of you it's like you're on Pitcairn Island in 1780, and the chief says, "Mmm, Captain Cook good. Always bring gift. Now *him* gift."

I think the only reason restaurants offer the Diamond Jim Brady Cut in the first place is that people like John Madden have a problem ordering anything with the word "Milady" in it.

THIS IS WHY THE WORLD HATES US, YOU KNOW. THE WAY we eat. It has nothing to do with oil or Israel, it's us—it's the size of the portions we order, and the volume of what we ram down our gullets. We drive around in a glucose daze from one restaurant to another in our rolling warehouses, belted into optional, premiere-package, captain's chair Barca-seats, with the music and the air-conditioning blasting, faces and shirts stained with sauces, red from breathing, just waiting to digest enough to pull over again. "You ready for a Chicago dog, Bets'?"

Thank God they've never shown us eating on Al Jazeera—that would be the end of it.

We're gluttons. All of us, and I don't mean white, suburban "us": this is everyone, and you know it. Black, white, rich, poor, urban, rural, north, south, east, west. All of us, and the fattest kids are often the poorest.

Yes, I said fat. Please, folks, we're not helping anyone by using kindler, gentler words. Fat people are not "big" or "husky," or "morbidly obese," whatever that means. As Alan King used to say, "My wife says her family isn't fat, they're just 'big-boned.' Yes, and every big bone is covered with the biggest fat you'd ever want to see."

We eat like pigs, except that that would be an insult to pigs. Pigs may eat their own feces, but every once in a great while they *stop*.

I can prove it with a taste we all share: Chinese restaurants. They're the worst. They're the best, but the worst: the best for taste, the worst for gluttony. You know what I mean.

You ever go to a Chinese restaurant and order twelve dishes for four people? Of course you have, because that's what we do.

Chinese people are the thinnest, fittest people in the world. There hasn't been a fat person in China since Buddha. What are *they* eating? Not what they're selling, I'll tell you that. It's not their fault, though, it's ours. It's always, "We'll have the Kung Pao everything, please. That's right, everything. Beef, chicken, duck, scallops, shrimp, everything. Take whatever's back there, and Kung Pao it. In fact, go next door to the pizza place, get one of those, and Kung Pao *that*. Now, we like extra spicy, but our friends don't, so bring two of each dish. And some egg rolls, fried rice, and those dumpling things. Dim sum, yeah. Steamed or fried? Both. In fact, microwave a third batch, and bring those, too. Fantastic. And the lo mein, and the chow mein, and the water main, and Remember the Maine."

No one feels guilty about ordering that much, because someone always says, "We'll all share, and have a little taste, and just take home whatever we don't eat."

This is a noble sentiment, but you know what's really, really frightening? When it's time to pack up, there's never a lot left, is there? Some, but not nearly as much as you thought. Very little, actually. In fact, almost nothing. The only reason you even go through the motions of wrapping it up is because you're too mortified to walk out without carrying something, and admit you ate it all.

No, we just keep shoveling, and with Chinese food it's hard to stop. It's so good you want to keep going. "Oh, God, I'm stuffed. I'll never eat again. I'm sick. You gonna finish that? No, no, forget it. I can't move. I'm going to explode. I'm nauseous. Are you going to eat that one? Only if you don't want it."

You ever open Chinese food the next day in the refrigerator? Not much there, really. It's always just a couple of orange slices and those weird, dark green vegetables. Some baby corn. (Which has freaked me out since I was a kid. I don't know about you, but big or small, I need a cob). Come to think of it, all Chinese vegetables are strange, aren't they? Those long, leafy, bulby things? They're like *Star Trek* vegetables. ("Welcome to Rajal 12, Kirk. Have you tried our salads? They *sing* to you!")

The point is . . . never any ribs left the next day, are there? (This is actually lucky, you know, since refrigerated, day-old ribs turn into horrifying, white fat speckled with infrequent gristle. On a stick.)

Well, that's us. Plenty of magazine covers of actresses when they lose too much weight, but never any shots of the average American walking through Magic Mountain from behind. There's a reason for that. Everyone might think it was *him* in the picture.

THERE'S ONLY ONE TIME AMERICANS EAT TINY PORTIONS. When we drink. The one time you actually need food is also the one time you get very dainty, just take a bite or two and think, "I guess I wasn't as hungry as I thought. No sense making a pig out of myself. They say four or five almonds has all the protein a man needs."

Lance Armstrong, all of a sudden.

Once you're a little loaded, even if you don't say a word for the rest of the night, everything else you do is just as revealing. You lean in too far, or listen too closely, or laugh too much, or too little, and when you finally do speak, you sound even worse, because you overenunciate everything. "I couldn't . . . agree more about . . . the décor."

I don't know about you, but I also become the Shell Answer Man of Alcohol. "They say red wine helps digest the steak." Yeah, but only if you *eat* the steak. Otherwise, it's like throwing gas on a fire. But there's no end to your digestive wisdom, is there? "Brandy helps settle the stomach." Not an empty stomach, it doesn't. "Sambuca in the coffee dissolves heavy sauces." Well, at that point, you'll say anything. "Crème de menthe is good for the breath, and Bailey's is good for the dailies, and port is good if you're short." It's all just very, very good for you.

My friend's wife is from Ireland, and after she had her first kid we were at their house and she said, "You know, back home, all the new mothers have a pint of Guinness a day, because it's good for the breast milk."

I laughed and said, "Yeah, one, not five."

She looked at me evenly and said, "Seriously. It's good for the babies."

And I said, "Hey, I'm sure it is, and who doesn't love a pint of Guinness? Look, if you want a drink, have one. Lord knows you went nine months without it—you did, didn't you?—well, a few weeks, anyway. The point is, if we do these things, let's just do them, and not say it's for the kids. Our mothers drank and smoked all day, and we're okay."

Her expression hardened. "It's a fact. It's good for them." I felt my wife's hand on my arm, but the Count of Monte Sarcasm was already out of his cell and off the island.

"Hey, you get no argument here. Whiskey's good, too, you know. Helps their teeth come in. Have you heard that one? Plus, it knocks the newborns out cold. They nap, you nap, it's a win-win. Hey, wait a minute! Why not give it straight to the kids in their bottles? If it's good for them, let's go for it. No doubles till they're nine or ten, of course, and always with a chaser—and just a splash for the toddlers, naturally—but for the infants? Don't strain it through the milk. Let's give it to them straight, skip the middle man, and put that breast where it might do some good."

It often amazes me I never went into the State Department.

BACK AT THE RESTAURANT I PICKED UP THE CHECK AND tipped like a guy who'd just won the lottery, the way you always do when you're shined up like a new penny.

We said we'd meet the Engels back at their place for coffee, and Eileen and I took a stroll first, and the air felt good. She wasn't mad, and confined her comments to taking my hand and saying, "Well, you're just getting smarter every day, aren't you?" before cracking up. She'll do. I had my uneaten meal swinging from the other hand, three big cartons in a bag with a handle. (A heavy bag, for once.)

We passed a liquor store, and I saw someone come out with a pack of cigarettes and light one, and I felt that little tug and shook it off. Crazy habit. It's not youth that's wasted on the young, re-member?

Eileen drove us over, and we all had a nice time, and a hot cup of coffee really hit the spot. So did the can of ginger ale and the two bottles of water that followed it. I felt so good, in fact, that I excused myself to the kitchen and gnawed on my steak bone a little over the sink, eating mashed potatoes and creamed spinach with my fingers like poi. Is there any better meal in the world than food eaten over the sink? (Thanksgiving night's the best. Eleven-thirty, everyone gone and everything clean, leaning into the refrigerator in your underwear, light spilling into dark kitchen, tin foil bent back on pie plate, dog waiting, watching.)

GOODBYE TO THE ENGELS. THEN HOME WITH THE WINDOWS down. Sky, lights, signs; quiet, blinker, garage. Huh. *"Ga-rahge."* A hundred years ago. I pay the sitter and walk her out, and my wife decides to jump in the shower, and I decide to jump in with her.

And why not? No one was mad at anyone, it was a nice night, and now it's even nicer. You get into bed with flannels and socks and turn on the TV, and hold hands and drift off. Mmmm. Goodnight, moon.

This perfect rest lasts for two hours, which is when the late shift in your body shows up for work and punches in to start cleaning the alcohol out of your blood. And it shakes you awake to do it. Oh, your liver still works, and it'll get the job done, but now it's like an old vacuum that runs loud but doesn't pick up a lot. And that's all the REM cycle you're going to see tonight. You could snooze through it in your twenties. A marching band could walk through, and you'd barely stir. But those days are gone, too, aren't they? Getting up for water and going right back to sleep for eight, ten, twelve hours? Not in this life, my friend. Not anymore.

So let's add that to our list of things that are wasted on the young: smoking, drinking . . . and sleeping.

You are *up,* buddy, so put on your robe, go downstairs, pour some milk, grab the remote, and be grateful it's only the twenty-fifth hour of Bond, and there's still five to go. Yup. There it is.

Oh, great. Start the night drinking with Sean Connery, and end it sleepless with Roger Moore.

Don't tell me God doesn't have a sense of humor.

SIXTEEN

JERRY ALLEN

I STARTED OUT IN SHOW BUSINESS AT THE COMIC STRIP in New York.

Someone once asked in an interview in the eighties if it was a great time to be a comic, because so many comedy clubs and television shows had sprung up, and I said, "No, it's a great time to be a comic, because I'm alive now."

His eyes glazed a little, but I filled the gap by saying, "Think about it: Fifty years ago, or fifty years from now, it would've been a great time for me to be a comic, too, because that's when I would've been alive. The rest doesn't matter. More clubs, fewer clubs, vaudeville, television, any era in history, forward or backward; Greek theater, commedia dell'arte, traveling troupes in Britain, a performer will always find places to work. That's the goal and the burden. Whenever the book is open on a person's life, that's the perfect time for him to be alive, no matter what he does. Unless, of course, you want to be an astronaut, and it's the Bronze Age—but you see what I mean, don't you?"

He didn't, so I pressed on. "Okay, look. There are a lot of interview shows on TV these days, right? But that's not why this is the perfect time for you to be alive."

"Yes, it is," he said, getting nervous. "Television is perfect for me."

"Of course it is," I said, "Take it easy. Breathe in, breathe out. You're exactly right. It's perfect, but not *because* of television, per se. This, right now, is the perfect time for you to be alive, because, well, here you are. But you could've, and would've, found work in entertainment a thousand years ago."

"There was no television a thousand years ago," he said with a *"Duh* . . . " edge.

And that's where we left it, by mutual consent. Come to think of it, I don't believe that portion of the piece made it onto the air. Ah, well. Best to keep things simple for the New Breed, eh? Splendid chap, though. Sharp clothes.

Anyway, there were three main showcase clubs in those days in New York: the Improv, Catch a Rising Star, and the Comic Strip. The Comic Strip was our place, although you eventually wanted to work in all of them, and get the best spots in all of them, and be known as an "A" act in all of them, and go on every night in all of them, and receive the coveted ". . . works *all* the major showcase clubs in town . . ." introduction in all of them.

I eventually got the introduction, but for the first couple of years my home was the Strip, and I was there every night. That's every night, as in every night.

That's how you did it. You passed the audition and started hanging out. You got there early, and they'd put you on late, like one or two in the morning. Or three. Or later, since bars are open in New York till four. (If Prohibition ever comes back, that'll be why.) For a while at the Strip, on Fridays and Saturdays, as the waitresses were counting up, and getting chatted up, the shows even went to five. This was especially commonplace during prom season, which was good business for the comedy clubs. Whip-and-chair shows, but good business.

Richie Tienkin, one of the owners (who went on to great success as a talent manager), always pulled a very sharp move every prom season. He gave free coffee and food to all the limo drivers. No place else did; just the Comic Strip. Now, if you were a limo driver, and a bunch of kids asked you for suggestions about fun places to go, where would you take them? As I said, a very sharp move.

Lord, but those proms were a roomful and a handful and a snootful. If I close my eyes even now and turn away from the window very quickly, I still have the retina burn of three hundred lime-green tuxedos and dusky-pink gowns; and the same of lime-green faces (from drinking) and dusky-pink acne. I don't know about you, but on my prom night I had both. If you throw in long, stupid side-burns, I was three for three.

I don't mean any of this to sound tough or hard knocks-y, because we all loved it in those clubs. I saw every show, every comic, every joke, every night, seven nights a week, six, seven hours a night, for four years, and it was the best education in the world, if that's what you wanted to learn. I couldn't do it again now, but I sure could then.

They didn't pay the comics, but they fed us every night for free, and that's one of the two things young comics wanted most anyway. (If you're wondering what the other one was, take a second and think: What's the other one *you* wanted?) My friends and I ate so many free hamburgers at the Comic Strip we used to say the minimum amount of chopped meat a good comic needed to be funny was twenty-eight pounds a month. If chopped meat turns out to be good for you, I'll probably make it to a hundred and fifty. If it's not, and my lower intestine looks like the floor of a packing house in *The Jungle,* this may be my only book. I hope you enjoy it, and thanks for the use of the hall.

They let you drink for free at the Strip, too, and all these places.

No kidding. Isn't that cool? For your date, too, if you had one. And we all drank a lot. Not everyone, but most of us. Well, many. Well, some. Well, I did.

Plus, they gave you T-shirts with the club name that everyone wore constantly, onstage and off, and jackets if you were an MC. Every family photograph of me in those days at home on a holiday clearly shows a bright red, green, or blue Comic Strip T-shirt jarringly visible underneath a button-down shirt and tie, like the Superman outfit under Clark Kent's suit. That's what they were for us: our uniforms.

It was no small thing, those comedy club clothes. I was as proud of those T-shirts and jackets as a marine with a Semper Fi tattoo, and wore them everywhere. The jackets were flimsy nylon shells with dryer-lint lining, but I wore each one till it fell apart, on the hottest summer days or the dead of winter (with ten layers). But I never took it off. I never took that jacket off.

Most important, money or no money, I got onstage every night. A lot of times there were just two or three drunks left in the audience, but we always went up. We performed for two or three people many times, and sometimes just one. When it got that small we called it an "audient." In fact, if word got around that there were two drunks at the Strip, other comics would come over. The MC's job after each act was to say to whoever was left, "Please stay, folks, come on, there're just a couple more comics, and it means a lot to them to get on. Please? Come on. One more guy, how about that? One more guy." I guess I ran into a few mean drinkers over the years in audiences on the road, but never at the Comic Strip. The drunks always stayed, and the comics always got on.

I played drums there, too, backing up singers and playing the comics on and off on Fridays and Saturdays. The comedy spots were free, but the drumming paid twenty-five dollars a night. That's when the chance to make money bartending came up.

John McGowan, another one of the owners (Bob Wachs was the third), came up to me one night and said he knew I worked days at Amtrak in Penn Station, and would I like to add a couple of shifts bartending? Each shift was twenty-five dollars, plus tips, and together with the drumming it might be enough for me to quit and concentrate on show business. I was thrilled and grateful (and still am), and of course said yes, and thank you, thank you, thank you. I just knew I could be a great bartender, too, and I was—a natural, if I do say so myself. I was friendly, a good talker, good listener, honest, took pride in the cleanliness and order of the bar, and never broke a glass. There was just one tiny problem.

I didn't know how to make drinks.

Seriously. I couldn't make drinks. (I can drink them okay, just not make them.)

I know this sounds stupid. Why would anyone who couldn't make drinks be a bartender? Additionally, who in his right mind would hire a bartender who couldn't make drinks? Let's take the second part first: Lots of stupid people who can't do their jobs get hired, don't they? You probably know some at work. In fact—be honest, now—you may be one of them.

I wasn't lying to John, I just thought somehow the drink-making part would take care of itself, and I could concentrate on the cool part: holding the *Daily News* open with my leg up on the speed rack when someone came in (not even reading it, just holding it open); answering the phone with that above-it-all, New York-y "Yeah, Comic Strip. Two shows, eight and ten. How many?" tone; tossing napkins in front of people when they sat down, and saying, "Hiya, pal. What's your pleasure?" or just raising both eyebrows and chin slightly without saying a word; wiping down the bar and the ash trays, filling the peanut bowls (first rule of bar owning: peanuts make people thirsty, give 'em all they want); washing glasses under the bar on those stiff, soapy, vertical brushes and rinsing them in the sink next to it while never taking your eyes off the customer telling a sad story; taking bottles down to wipe the mirrored shelves; signing for deliveries on clipboards while winking hello to the jukebox guy; nodding to regulars.

I knew I could do all those things, and that's the part I was interested in anyway. It was a role, and I knew I'd be great. Of course, as you probably know, in any bar, and especially in the middle of a huge city, someone will eventually come in and order a drink. That's what happened, and that's when things got bad—and fast.

Some drinks I figured I could do. I mean, how hard is a scotch and soda? You put ice in a glass, then the scotch, then the soda, right? So what if I was impossibly slow and always misplacing the ice scoop? And used the wrong glasses, and put bottles back in different places and couldn't find them again, and was constantly forgetting what I had walked down the end of the bar to get, and poured amounts that were . . . inconsistent.

Once I actually lined up five glasses touching each other and filled them with whiskey by moving the bottle back and forth, like in the movies. (You spill quite a bit, in case you were wondering.) No one had asked for those drinks, by the way. I just always wanted to do it.

As I said, though, anyone can make a scotch and soda, right? A Martian could make a scotch and soda. It was the other seven hundred drinks in the mixology that were a mystery. Additionally, old-fashioned mixed drinks were pretty much unheard of in the New York dating scene of the comedy clubs. No one had ordered a scotch and soda since the Algonquin Round Table.

I was a couple of hours into my second night of bartending, and the show was cooking along. The showroom was separated from the bar and bathrooms in front by two sets of swinging doors and a hallway, creating a very effective sound trap, which was a good idea. (By the way, if you think about it, it's actually hysterical to realize that I made it through one night of bartending and into another, isn't it? I mean, really. *I can't make drinks.*)

One of the waitresses, Joanie, who knew me only as a comic, came up to the ordering area and said, "Oh, hi, Larry. What are you doing back there? Two grasshoppers; two slow, comfortable screws; and two white Russians."

"Hi, Joanie. Yeah, I just started, isn't that great? Last night was my first night," I said, smiling, and opened six bottles of Budweiser and put them on her tray. She looked down and said, "They didn't order beer, Larry," and I said, "Yeah, but I can't make those other things. Take these." We looked at each other, and she said, "What if they don't want beer?" And I said, "I don't know. Tell them it's free." She shrugged and took them inside, and everyone seemed happy. I know I was.

This, of course, is how I made it through the first night and half of the second. Anything I didn't know how to make—which was everything—became a Budweiser. And when someone said, "But I don't want a Budweiser," I'd say, "Just take it, it's free," and they always did.

Of course even perfect stupidity can't go on forever. I knew that eventually, and probably very soon, Richie and John, who were the exact opposite of wimps, would notice a huge space in the cooler in the shape of a canoe, and nothing in the till. I was ready with plenty of good cheer and sound reasons, which was lucky since just a minute or two later John came in for the night (the proud and successful owner of a great New York nightclub, King of His World, calmly ready to survey his smooth operation). Someone took his coat, someone else said hello, and he nodded graciously to all and sundry as he strolled the length of the bar, looking very much like a new pope coming out for that first wave. He got to the waitress station in the back, began leafing through mail and receipts, and tossed a "Hiya, girls. How's it going with Larry?" over his shoulder.

J.C. and Michelle were the nearest ones, and they exchanged a glance before Michelle said, "Larry? Uh, well, John, everyone likes Larry, you know" and J.C. nodded and said, "Yeah. Everyone likes Larry. You know."

John chuckled and shook his head while doubling a rubber band around a stack of checks and said, "Yeah, yeah, we're all nuts about him. I mean the bartending. Everything okay?" The girls looked at each other again, then down at the floor, and finally Michelle said, "He doesn't know how to make drinks." And John said, "I beg your pardon?" and J.C. nodded again vigorously and said, "Yeah. He doesn't know how to, you know, make drinks. You know."

He wasn't chuckling now. Suddenly, he looked like a man who'd hidden lots of cash in a secret spot in the desert and went all the way out there only to find it was gone. He whipped around to say something to me that would, no doubt, put paid to the matter, but when he turned he saw something he couldn't comprehend: I wasn't there. No one was there. The bar was empty, leaderless and rudderless, and six other waitresses were wandering about like flawed androids, making small circles, or bumping again and again into a wall.

In case you didn't know it, a bartender leaving his bar is like a soldier falling asleep on guard duty: They're both capital crimes. The only difference is that the bartender gets yelled at first, then slapped silly, then skinned alive, and *then* shot.

As the faint whistle of the tea kettle in John's head grew louder and louder, and his head began to jerk left and right searching for his bartender (while he considered whether to start on me with knives or clubs), Michelle tapped him on the shoulder and said, "If you're looking for Larry, he's inside watching the show. Paul Reiser came in for a spot, and said he was going to do a new bit, and would Larry watch it? And Larry said, Oh, yeah, definitely." And J.C. nodded again and added, "Yeah. Paul asked him to watch. And Larry said,

Oh, yeah, definitely. Then Ronnie Shakes went up, too, and Larry and Paul stayed to watch him, 'cause they like him. You know."

I really wish I had a Polaroid of John's expression right then, but I don't. I saw it soon enough, though, since he plowed through the first set of doors into the showroom to find me. (Find me, tear me limb from limb, whatever.) I think "homicidal" would adequately describe his mindset. Naturally, that was the same instant I entered the hallway from the other side.

PERHAPS YOU'VE NOTICED THIS OVER THE YEARS OF your own life, but sometimes it pays to be an idiot. This was certainly one of those times for me. I smiled like the mental nine-year-old I was, and said, "Oh, hi, John, I was looking for you all night. Where you been? Anyway, listen, I put forty dollars in the register tonight but didn't ring it up, because I've been giving out beer the last two nights, and thought I should tell you. I don't know how many, but I think two cases would cover it. I probably should have kept count, huh? I'll get three to make sure. Some Tuborg and Schaefer, but I'll make it all Bud. What is it, fifteen, twenty a case? I'll just put the rest in when I get paid tonight. Should I go to Gristede's tomorrow and check? Ooh, wait a second, I almost forgot, some friends of mine from school came in before, and I gave them a bunch of shots on the house, so I owe you a bottle of Murphy's, too. Or was it Paddy's? Isn't that funny, I can't remember. Hold on, I know it wasn't Jameson's or Bushmill's . . . oh, well. They didn't drink all of it, there's still some left, but I think I should still buy a full bottle. Then they can finish off the old one, right? You know what, by the way? Maybe you could hire another bartender to work with me who can carry more of the drink-making load, because, frankly, I can't keep handing out beers and putting in my own money. I can do scotch and sodas, but nobody orders them. Anyway, back to the ol' salt mine, eh? Don't want to leave the bar for too long. See you out front. Oh, and guess what? Reiser's got a new bit, and it killed. Ooh! Tullamore Dew! It was Tullamore Dew!"

And that was the end of my career as a bartender.

But you know what? He didn't yell, and he didn't kill me. He didn't even fire me. He just stood there with his mouth open for ten straight minutes after I clapped him on the shoulder, finally shook his head clear, walked out front, motioned me over, and quietly suggested I might be better off switching to days. There was no day trade at the Strip, and it was just for deliveries and reservations, so he wouldn't have to hire a second bartender to make the drinks. This was fine with me, since I was too stupid to notice that his shaking hands were held out stiffly in front of him in the shape of a neck.

So I switched to days, and, sure enough, no one came in except for deliveries (or to add Christmas records to the jukebox in December and take them out again in January). So I took reservations on the phone, and wiped things down, and stood there behind the bar. And since they had no TV, I mean it: I just stood there.

On St. Patrick's Day, John came in early specifically to show me how to double-bolt the door and tell me to keep it locked. I asked how come; after all, he was certainly the experienced bar owner here, no dispute there, but I had to take exception in this case and tell him that I thought he was missing out on a lot of good business. After all, it was St. Patrick's Day, and that meant a lot of people would be drinking, or didn't he know that? "Really?" he asked, and I said, "Oh, yes, absolutely, in fact many people drink quite a bit, often to excess." The parade ended just a few blocks up on Eighty-sixth Street, I pointed out, and a lot of the police and firemen who were marching in it would probably wander down Second Avenue looking for places to stop in. And here was an idea! Even if they didn't, I could always call some of my friends from school again, and *they* could come by. Prime the pump, as it were.

He looked at me evenly across the bar and said (in a tone I've used many times since with my children), "Larry, I'm only going to say this once. Lock that door when I leave, and keep it locked. Do you hear me?" I spent the afternoon writing jokes and looking out the window from time to time to watch all the laughing, singing, uniformed police and firemen carrying each other down the block from bar to bar, stopping at the Comic Strip, trying the locked door, peering in, and moving on.

Years later John and I were having a drink, and he said, "Do you know why I never fired you that night?" I didn't, and he said, "Everything you said in that hallway was the worst thing you could ever say to a bar owner. The worst. Each one was a gold medal winner, a death offense. You left the bar, you're watching the show, you're giving away booze, taking money out of my pocket. Any regular guy? Never mind fire him, I'd have to kill him." I asked why he hadn't, and he thought for a second and said, "I don't know. You weren't trying to lie or hide anything. You didn't think you'd done anything wrong. That was it. You didn't think you'd done anything. You thought everything was great. It was the way you said it, though. I'd never take that from someone who worked for me. Like you were glad to see me. Like we were equals, or friends, or something."

I said, "I thought we were," and he took a sip and motioned for another round, and said, "Not then, we weren't. I guess it threw me enough so I just put you on days instead of taking you out to Jersey."

He didn't live in New Jersey.

MY LATE-NIGHT BUDDY IN THOSE DAYS WAS A COMIC named Jerry Allen. "Late-night buddy" was my phrase for it, as in "swimming buddy," or "Don't go swimming without a buddy." In the comedy clubs it meant the guy you came up with. We were both starting out and moving up at the same time. He would go on before me one night, and I would go on before him the next, and we both moved up at the same speed from three o'clock to two, to one, to midnight, then opening, then prime time. There was no tension about it between us, because we were late-nighters together, huddled in the same foxhole, and lucky enough to know somewhere deep down that the only real competition in life is with yourself.

I lived at Seventy-eighth and Amsterdam on the Upper West Side of Manhattan, which used to be cheap and loaded with actors and writers and comics. (It isn't anymore, because it isn't anymore, and vice versa.) Jerry Allen lived in New Jersey, which, no matter how you slice it, was a pretty big haul. And he wasn't Jewish, either. I don't know why I feel like saying that, but I do. Maybe because so many comics are. I don't know what he was. Protestant or Catholic, I guess. Regular.

I didn't know where he was from, or where he lived, or whether or not Jerry Allen was his real name. "Don't you ever ask people anything?" my parents said constantly when I was growing up. I always shrugged and said I guess not. I still guess not. Just living in whatever moment in life I'm in always seemed like the important thing, anyway.

So Jerry came in every night from somewhere across the George Washington Bridge, in a light brown '65 Pontiac Tempest convertible. He always parked three or four long avenue blocks away on Park or Madison to save the expense of putting it in a lot. The Comic Strip is on Second Avenue, between Eighty-first and Eighty-second Streets, and he usually found a spot below Eighty-sixth Street. Usually.

That may not sound very far, but at three-thirty in the morning in the middle of winter, four avenue blocks across and five blocks up is a very long, cold walk. Shivering cold. Crazy cold. The globe may be getting warmer, but I don't think they've told Manhattan yet.

Whenever Jerry Allen and I left the club at the same time, which was just about always, he'd offer me a lift back to the West Side on his way to the bridge, which was nice of him, and we'd walk to wherever he'd found his spot. We never said a word, just buried our heads as low as they would go, and jammed our hands, and walked and walked. If there's a demon of the wind, he doesn't like comics, because every night, no matter which way we turned, or which block we took, the wind turned with us and cut right back into our faces.

However cold it was on the way to that Pontiac, it was far, far colder once we got inside. As soon as we hit those leatherette seats, the shivering doubled, and, as you may remember, the heaters in cars from the sixties never got warm till just after you got where you were going. Arctic or not, though, he had to turn on the defroster and blow it on high, since the windshield was opaque with ice, and the only other choice was to drive with your head out the window like a basset hound. Either way, this put us at about the same level of comfort as a French private strolling back from Moscow in 1815. At least *we* had sneakers.

Actually, he didn't. Jerry Allen, that is. I did, because all the rest of us wore sneakers, and that was the uniform: Comic Strip T-shirt under a button-down shirt, under a sweater-vest from the Gap, over Levi's black 501s, over sneakers. This was before Americans discovered wearing running shoes (if that's what they're still even called) with their clothes, and my sneaker of choice in those days was either Pro-Keds or high, white Chucks. But mostly Pro-Keds. I liked that brand an awful lot.

But Jerry Allen wore shoes. Lace-up shoes. Not wing-tips or

cap-toes, just . . . lace-up shoes. Brown ones. He wore slacks with thin belts, and shirts with straight collars, and his coat had buttons. If you wrote all those things down in a column and put a line under them and added them up, it would come to just about . . . a '65 Pontiac Tempest.

He was married, too, and had a baby, a son. This was something none of us could even picture at that point in our lives. Married? Babies? We were all still drooling over waitresses and girls from Queens. A wife and kids was like an ant trying to imagine the Eiffel Tower.

But not for Jerry Allen. He had a family. And a job. I don't know what it was, but he had one. A day job. And he still drove in every night to stand there with the rest of us and wait to get on. And drove back home every night to get up and go to work. And drove back in again next night. And home again. We were all committed and energetic, and we all wanted to be comics, but when I think of Jerry Allen—the same age as us, mind you—I shake my head in wonder. (See? I even said "us" there. The same as "us." It was all different for Jerry Allen.)

JERRY ALLEN AND I DID OUR FIRST BIG ROAD JOB together. Oh, it wasn't so big, I guess, but it was to us. Comedy clubs were just starting to open up here and there, and one of the best known and most successful was the Laff Stop in Newport Beach, California. (That's right, Laff Stop. L-a-f-f, *laff*. It's not the ballet, here, folks.) They were casting their net and hiring New York acts. Not everyone, just some, which made getting booked even neater. Flights were pretty cheap in those days, $99, $89, even $69. They paid us $150 each for the week, and fed us at the club for free after the shows. (Guess what we ate. Go on, guess. Come on, give it a try.

No, idiot, *hamburgers*. What kind of guess is blackened tuna?) Jerry Allen and I even took turns going onstage first there, too.

They put the comics up in what came to be known around the country in subsequent years as a "comedy condo." It was a two-bedroom apartment that was cleaned once a week when the three comics who'd just been working there left, and before the next three came in.

Look, it was nice of them to try to clean the thing, but hiring a maid for these places was the very definition of the phrase "token gesture." Comics were overwhelmingly single men in their twenties, who—well, that's enough right there, isn't it? Use your imagination. (Actually, don't.) Unless you were among the first three to stay there opening week, you can forget about it. The maids surely tried, the way a glass of water "tries" against a forest fire, but, come on, three guys a week, month after month, year after year; same apartment, same plates, same glasses, same sheets, same beds, same towels—you get the idea.

Don't get me wrong, I loved it. I worked all over the United States and Canada for quite a while, and the first five or six years exclusively involved comedy condos. Not only was nobody twisting my arm, but at the time I thought they were gorgeous, and why wouldn't I? I was a working comic, I was on the road, I was a kid, and what else could possibly matter? Certainly not beige, beaverboard walls; beige, damp curtains; hard, beige carpeting; cottage cheese ceilings; and bent forks. If the place had rats, I would've thought they were angels. (Well, that's not quite true. I had a suburban upbringing, and the first rat I ever saw on the road froze me faster than Lot's wife.)

But I did love those places, I surely did, or at least I didn't know any better. Of course, we all change, don't we? The second I graduated to hotel rooms and left those dumps behind, I looked back on the memories and promptly threw up.

Like most of you, I don't consider myself spoiled and prissy, even though, like most of you, that's exactly what I am, but those condos were so disgusting, that unless the world explodes some day, and we're all reduced to hugging for heat in caves and snarling at each other for possession of water holes, I would sooner duct-tape a UT lineman's underpants over my face after a week of two-a-days (without changing) during an unusually humid August, than sleep on a comedy condo bed again.

I very clearly remember, and not because I want to, putting my head down on a way-too-soft pillow, on a way-too-thin mattress, on a way-too-rusty box spring that dipped and groaned in the middle, in a comedy condo in Atlanta, and instantly noticing the pilled nubs across sheets so worn, there used to be a pattern, but I couldn't tell what it was. I looked over the side and quickly dismissed the possibility of sleeping on the floor, balled myself up . . . and still got twelve fabulous hours of sleep. Ah, youth. (Can you imagine how bad the carpeting was to make that bed the better option?)

Additionally in all these places, and worse—far worse—they had a smell. Not the same, but certainly the same phylum. It wasn't that it was a bad smell, or even awful. It was, but that wasn't it. That would've been too easy. It was worse than awful: deep, complex, cloying, unafraid, almost a caress. It was horrible.

But that first time at the Laff Stop in Newport Beach? Jerry Allen and I were in hog heaven the second we walked in.

With one tiny exception.

WE FLEW IN AT NIGHT, THE FIRST TRIP TO CALIFORNIA (or anywhere) for both of us, and got picked up by the pimpled though cheerful assistant manager and driven to the condo, hanging out the windows the whole way like happy spaniels. We walked in and put our bags down in, took the key and said thanks, looked at each other with kid-grins, and set about to settle who would take the bedroom on the left, and who the one on the right. Looking back, I suppose it was just dumb luck that the first one we picked was still occupied. Very occupied. Actively occupied.

About as active as four humans can get, I think, although perhaps I've led a sheltered life. That's right, m' friends, I said four, not one, not two, not three, but four, count 'em, four people in the same room. Step right up, folks, and don't be shy. (Go 'way, son, you bother me.) Pick a room, any room, any room a'tall. . . . You sure that's the one you want? Final choice? Okay, here we go, just turn that corner, walk right in, and . . . Whoa-ho, look at their faces! Two beds, two men, two women—two of everything!—and how they maintained those positions long enough for our contestants to come all the way from New York just in time to walk in on them is beyond me. What a mystery is life! How wonderful in reason!

And how curious that out of all four, exactly zero of them were comedians.

It was a Monday night, you see, and normally that's a comedy club's day off and they're closed, but the Laff Stop's enterprising owner decided to see if he couldn't do something else with the place that would succeed. He could, and he did, and it was.

Male strippers. Remember how the eighties saw a rise in—that is, increase in—male strip shows like Chippendale's? The Laff Stop had tapped into this vein (oh, fine), and their Monday Night Ladies Only Extravaganza was rolling like a big wheel.

Now, club owners are there to make money, and there's nothing wrong with that, and male strip shows were very popular with women, and there's nothing wrong with that, either. And as I noted earlier, this isn't the ballet.

For years I've said that the difference between men and women is never clearer than in a strip show. It's like the difference between shooting a bullet and throwing it. Have you ever seen women at a strip show? They laugh and scream and cheer and clap, and elbow each other and whoop. It's a party just being out together.

It's not quite the same with men, is it? You ever seen men at a strip show? You ever seen lions watching a herd of elk? You ever seen a hawk on a branch watching a mouse cross the field? You ever seen a crocodile gliding toward a guy with a camera? Not a lot of noise, is there? (It alerts the herd.)

For the most part, I think, when women go to a strip club they're celebrating friendship, sisterhood, and personal power. Men aren't celebrating anything; they're not fooling around, either. If the entire music system ever suddenly died someplace where naked women were dancing, you could hear a pin drop. It's actually frightening.

In any event, two of the women in that night's audience were apparently celebrating so much friendship and power that they decided to seal it with a kiss, or several, and accompanied the guys back to where they were staying; and you already know where that was.

Jerry Allen and I absorbed this historical tableau for the billionth of a second it needed to tattoo itself eternally onto our cortexes, before tiptoeing in extreme fast motion back across the living room and into the second bedroom. There actually *was* something historical to it: Remember that painting of Washington crossing the Delaware? One of the fellas was standing very much like that. That's where the similarities ended—so far as we can know—although both had strong profiles.

Anyway, the other bedroom was empty, and we closed the door gently, but quickly enough to make the air hum. We sat down on the only piece of furniture, another bed, and there we stayed, knees together, hands clasped in front, petrified, averting our gazes, not daring to saying a word, like an expensive caterer changing planes in Tehran.

It was puzzling: We didn't hear anything. I mean nothing. You'd have to go to public housing in Burma to find walls as cheap as these, and the mixed doubles in the other room weren't exactly showing forbearance. But there wasn't a sound. (It occurs to me now that if the four of them ever decided to start a sketch comedy group, they could do far worse for a name than "The Mixed Doubles." I'm pretty sure they didn't; our loss, I suppose.)

Anyway, there we sat, Jerry Allen and I, listening for a clue, a sign, anything. Why was there no sound? Had they (pick one): Finished? Left? Stuffed socks in their mouths? Seen us, too, and run screaming through the other wall leaving only their outlines? After several minutes of silence, Jerry Allen leaned over to me and whispered, "You don't think they used *this* room, too, do you?" which caused us both to vault back up making a few sounds of our own. (Ironic—they probably heard us more than we heard them.) After just a little blithering and nausea, I collected myself and said, "Nah, no way," and he said, "Yeah, no way," and we sat back down. But we didn't open that door for the rest of the night; not even when we remembered our bags were still in the kitchen.

The strippers and their guests were gone the next morning and didn't return, and when the Haz-Mat team from housekeeping came in to give the place its weekly *China Syndrome* scrub, we took a stroll to the market to give them plenty of elbow room. But we didn't cross that living room again the whole time we were there, Jerry Allen and I. We stayed together in the other room like shy campers, which is really what we were, and my own daydreams about meeting a California girl and spending part of the trip doing exactly what we'd caught the other folks doing stayed daydreams.

I'll tell you what I remember most about that trip. All Jerry Allen bought and ate was peanut butter. It was cheap, and he was sending every penny back home.

The night we closed, the headliner, the wonderful George Wallace, said he was going to drive to Las Vegas, and did we want to come along? We had one night left and said sure, and Wallace drove us all the way in his Rose Quartz Lincoln Mark IV. Jerry Allen sat in the back. I don't think we flipped for it, he just got in the back. Then Wallace paid for the room, too, which was really nice of him. It had two double beds and a cot they brought in, and Jerry Allen took the cot, too, and I don't think we flipped for that, either. Wallace and I went downstairs to gamble a little, and we asked him to come with us, but he said, "No, thanks," and I said, "Oh, come on, this is our first time in Vegas, you gotta come down," and he said, "No, thanks, go ahead." He didn't want to risk the money. He sat on the cot and watched TV, and we drove to L.A. the next day and flew back to New York.

MOST OF THE EAST COAST COMICS I KNEW MOVED OUT to Los Angeles in the eighties to start looking for agents and television shows and movies; even the big traffic in comedy clubs was booked out of L.A. But not Jerry Allen. He had the family, I guess, and maybe he just wasn't the type anyway. He was doing really well, though, and I heard things about him from time to time, and they were all good. He was finding lots of work as a comic along the East Coast, and starting to do TV, and finally quit his day job. I guess he and his wife were happy where they were. Whenever people over the years passed on tidbits about him, they'd say, "You knew him in New York, right?" and I always smiled and said, "Knew him? He was my late-night buddy." Every comic knew what that meant.

A year or two later, somewhere around '85, outside the Improv in L.A. a few of us were standing around talking about who got Carson, and who didn't, and how pretty so-and-so was. And then somebody said, "Hey, did you hear? Jerry Allen died." I stood there, rooted, as someone said, "What?" and someone else said, "How?" An aneurysm, they said, one of those things that's with you from birth and just explodes one day, the kind you never know about till it happens. Sometimes it never happens, and you live to be a hundred. Like turning over a table in your living room after years of books and vases sitting on it, and seeing the legs were rotted away the whole time and just holding on for no good reason at all. Jerry Allen had one, but it didn't wait till he was a hundred.

I never found out anything else, whether that was long after the funeral or just before it. I thought about sending a note, but didn't. I never even knew where he lived. I never knew his son's name. I knew his: Jerry Allen. He held the mike at the bottom. Not around the middle, like most of us, but at the bottom, where the cord went in. Not tightly. Just a few fingers, resting there. He held it at the bottom.

You think life should be fair? I don't even know what the word means anymore. Maybe I never did. Maybe no one does. I know it's good to be alive, so good, and that the chance to care about someone, to work, to strive, to look up, to heal the world, big and small, to laugh, are all great things. I know life is wonderful.

But it's not fair. Oh, no, it was never fair. Not for Jerry Allen. We Americans have more food, and toys, and dreams, and vacation plans than any other people in the world, and we think it should all be fair, but it's not, is it? He worked so hard, so long, so well, so quietly, and he never whined, and he sent every penny home, and we all wanted it, but I think maybe Jerry Allen wanted it just a little bit more. And he finally got to a place where he could let a breath out and smile a little, and break through the clouds and enjoy the sunlight, and follow it till it went down slowly. Then one day his head hurt, and he went to the doctor, and keeled over in the waiting room. And that was that.

There may be a word to describe all that, but it's certainly not fair.

You may have noticed I use his whole name each time I mention him: Jerry Allen. Jerry Allen did this, and Jerry Allen did that, and Jerry Allen drove me home, and Jerry Allen and I flew to California. It just sounded right that way, a writer's thing: the rhythm, the flow, the feel.

But there's another reason, a better one. Maybe if he had lived you would have heard his name on your own. Maybe you would have heard it a lot. Maybe he would have made comedy specials, or hosted a talk show, or worked in radio or movies or television. Or had another kid. Or written a book.

We can all go in a second, folks. It's not just a blessing to wake up in the morning, it's an astonishing blessing, and if you don't know that, you really should, and if you do, you ought to say thank you every so often. You ought to say it a lot. You ought to say it every day.

Ask Jerry Allen. I'm not a very weepy guy. I never cried when my parents died, and still haven't, and God knows how much I loved them and still do, and always will.

But I did the night I heard Jerry Allen died. I do whenever I think of him. I am now.

His son would be twenty-five or thirty, I guess. Maybe the wife remarried. Jerry Allen. Jar of peanut butter next to a mattress on a floor in Newport Beach. Jerry Allen. Lace shoes lined up under a cot in Las Vegas. Jerry Allen. You think I should send the money home, or just hold onto it till I get there? We'll be home soon, why mail it? You sure you don't want to come downstairs? No, thanks. Have a good time. Jerry Allen. Knit gloves at ten and two in a Tempest.

So now you know. Jerry Allen.

It's the least I could do.

After all, he was my late-night buddy.

SEVENTEEN

THE QUICKENING II: THE QUICKENING

THE QUICKENING.

The quickening, the quickening, the quickening the quickening, the quickening the quickening the quickening, the quickening. The quickening. The quickening. The quickening the quickening the quickening the quickening.

The quickening? The quickening. The quickening the quickening the quickening the quickening the quickening the quickening the quickening the quickening the quickening the quickening the quickening the quickening the quickening, the quickening.

The . . . quickening . . . The quickening. The quickening. The quickening (the quickening the quickening the quickening),

the quickening the quickening the quickening. The quickening—
heh, heh, heh—the quickening the quickening the quickening.

The quickening. The quickening the quickening.

The quickening the quickening, the quickening the quickening,
the quickening, the quickening: *The quickening, the quickening, the
quickening, the quickening.*

THE QUICKENING! THE QUICKENING, THE QUICKENING,
the quickening the quickening the quickening.

THEQUICKENINGTHEQUICKENINGTHEQUICK-
ENING

Okay, I think it's out of my system.

ACKNOWLEDGMENTS, AND A GOOD JOKE EVERY TWO PARAGRAPHS

That's right, you read that correctly, that's what this final section is: Acknowledgments, and a good joke every two paragraphs.

Look, let's be honest, thanking everyone who should be thanked in the making of a book is a very important thing to do, but no sane reader has ever had the strength to plow through them. I defy any of you to make it through a book's thank-yous without someone holding a gun to your head. Unless, of course, you're one of the people being thanked. Even then it's a tough slog.

A bunch of my friends have written books, and I support them all, and buy a lot, and give them as gifts, and talk them up whenever it's appropriate. But I draw the line at reading the acknowledgments. It's just not possible.

The only person who's interested at all to read more about the newest Rumanian translation by Prof. Yehuda Buchsbaum, of

Nippleslick College, is Prof. Yehuda Buchsbaum of Nippleslick College. Most likely, he doesn't really care that much himself. Even his mother will probably say, "Oh, let's be honest, Yehuda, you have a boring job. Did you like the kasha I sent? Good. I'm sure the skinny shiksa loved it, too. I know her name is Mary. Margaret, whatever. I'm not yelling. This is how people talk."

Anyway, a lot of people deserve a lot of thanks here, but to keep your attention I'm going to sprinkle in a good joke every two paragraphs. Ready? Here we go.

In chronological order of how this thing got made: I've written and sold a bunch of scripts, but after 9/11 I asked my publicist (and one of the six people not married to me who really know how crazy I am), Michael Hansen, to see if someone wanted to buy columns from me. He found Jonathan Last and Victor Matus at the *Daily Standard* and *Weekly Standard*, who said okay, and then asked their boss, Bill Kristol, who said okay, too. They're all friends now, but Jonathan became a real phone pal for a long time, and still is, and helped make me a better writer. Andrew Stuart, a book agent in New York (or so he says), spotted the columns and called me. I was napping, but I took the call. Andrew said he thought he could get a book deal for us if I thought I could write one. I did, and he did, with the great folks at Regan, which is part of HarperCollins. If this book sells well, I'm going to insist they put the space back in their name.

The wonderful Judith Regan and all her folks have been great, like Matt Harper and Rachel Berk, but *primus inter pares* is Cal Morgan. It's not possible to have had a better editor, colleague, and guide than Cal was with me. We both love words, he immersed himself completely, and, I think, has an astonishingly good sense of humor for an old-line Protestant. (I wrote that just because I know it'll make him laugh.) They brought in one of their great publicists, Suzanne Wickham, who worked with Hansen and my wonderful manager of many years, Arthur Spivak, who, considering he's such a prominent and successful Jew in show business, has no sense of humor at all.

So a guy walks out of the house one morning and notices there's a gorilla on his roof. He gets out the Yellow Pages and finds an ad for gorilla removal and calls the place. A truck pulls up, and the driver gets out, opens up the back, and pulls out a ladder, a baseball bat, a net, a pit bull, and a shotgun. And the owner of the house says, "What's all this for?" And the guy says, "Well, I lean the ladder up against the house and climb up to the roof. Then I hit the gorilla with the baseball bat, he slides off the roof, the dog runs up and clamps his jaws onto his crotch, while I climb down and throw the net over him." And the owner says, "What's the shotgun for?" And the guy says, "Well, sometimes the gorilla hits me first, and I slide off the roof instead. If that happens, you shoot the dog."

Tom Shadyac is a great director and friend who has not only given me some of the best parts I've ever had, but hired me as a writer several times, too (in addition to teaching me a great lesson about philanthropy). It is his company at Universal, Shadyacres, where I've been lucky enough to hang my shingle. I wrote most of this book there, and am more grateful for that space than I can say. I'm something of a complete idiot with computers and faxes and such, and his executive assistant, Jordan Wolfe, helped me out over and over again, with the same procedures, literally hundreds of times, up to and including things such as not having it plugged in. Seriously. She and I laughed so hard together, so often, about how I could never remember how to perform even the simplest tasks around an office. This laughter continued right up until it stopped being funny to her. That's when Dina Delkhah, a couple of doors down the hall, started helping me. After similarly interrupting her work for several months to ask the same stupid questions, she began to look at me very, very angrily, which is when I moved one more office over to bother Jennifer Howell. Ditto her, and Ginnie Durkin, and Andy Hopkins. I finally ran through everyone at Shadyacres, and began calling in Joe Rudio, who takes care of every computer and program and system at Universal, and could probably run the NSA if they asked him to. He had a lot of difficulty believing I was as stupid as I am, but was a big help, especially once he learned to speak very loudly and slowly to me, the way you would talk to someone who'd just been hit in the head with an omelet pan.

Bruce Breslau is one of my oldest friends from childhood, and, so far as I know, the only gay Jewish flight instructor in history. He was my go-to guy on all sorts of things, like spelling "Koechel number," or the difference between Beulah Bondi and Mildred Natwick. Admittedly, that didn't come up a lot. Rabbi Aaron Benson is the rabbi at our temple, and my wife and I just love him, and, perhaps not surprisingly, he helped out with facts on the Torah. (He was no help at all on Beulah Bondi and Mildred Natwick, but fantastic on anything to do with Laird Cregar.) I remember calling him up to ask something about Moses and saying, "Thanks again, Rabbi. You just got yourself into the acknowledgments." To be honest, he didn't seem that thrilled, but a promise is a promise.

A groom is with his new bride on their wedding night, and he's very nervous. And they're next to each other under the sheets, not doing anything, and she says, "Darling, why are you so afraid?" And he says, "My mother always told me women have teeth down there, and I'm scared." And she says, "Oh, that's silly. Why don't you slide under the sheet and have a look?" He does, and when he comes back up, she says with a smile, "Now, did you see any teeth?" And he says, "No, and frankly, with a set of gums like that, I'm not surprised."

I blackmai—that is, asked some very good friends to take the time to read The Creature and write overgenerous blurbs to help sell it, and you already know who they are from the back cover.

I've teased my wife an awful lot for two hundred and seventy some-odd pages (and some of them were pretty odd), but she's been a great sport about it.

No, she hasn't.

Just kidding. Yes, she has, and without her, there wouldn't be a book.

I can never remember any "priest, a rabbi, and a minister"-type jokes (which is pathetic considering I'm a comic), and the regular jokes in this acknowledgment were provided by Paul Reiser, Norby Walters . . . and this last one by Eddie Driscoll:

A bar in New York catches fire and burns down, and the firemen carry out an elderly Irishman named Murphy and say, "Mr. Murphy, can you tell us when the fire started?" And Murphy says, "How the hell should I know? It was on fire when I went in."

Cheers, folks.